Tibor Eckhardt: His American Years 1941–1972

Katalin Kádár Lynn

with a Foreword by Dr. Otto von Habsburg

2007
East European Monographs, Boulder
Distributed by Columbia University Press, New York

East European Monographs, No. DCCIX

ISBN: 978-0-88033-548-5
Library of Congress Control Number: 2007927324

Printed in the United States of America

Contents

Preface

Although Tibor Eckhardt's name has now been almost forgotten, he was an important and in many ways a pivotal figure in the political life of the Hungarian nation from the 1920s to the 1940s; and after his post-1941 involuntary exile in the United States during World War II, he remained a strong influence within the Hungarian émigré community and with the political decision-makers in his homeland. A well-educated and highly principled man, Tibor Eckhardt was both celebrated and vilified—prior to and after his death, in Hungary and abroad. Born in Makó, Hungary, in 1888, Eckhardt became a major figure in the political life of Hungary during the inter-war period, heading the Smallholders Party and leading the opposition in Hungary's Parliament. He also represented Hungary as its Chief Delegate to the League of Nations in 1933–1934.

This work focuses primarily on Tibor Eckhardt's American years, which began with his final trip to the United States in 1941 on a mission for his government, and on the concatenation of world events that prevented him from returning to his homeland. He died in New York City in 1972, after thirty-one years in the United States.

For the past six years it has been my privilege to research the life of Dr. Tibor Eckhardt, the topic of my doctoral dissertation at Eötvös Loránd University in Budapest. I found the subject compelling, for my initial research into the historical accounts of Eckhardt's American years showed them to be extremely fragmentary and based primarily on secondary information and anecdotal evidence. No clear picture was available of Eckhardt's motives and political activities after going to America.

I discovered primary source documents that contradicted much of what had previously been written about Eckhardt's American years and made it clear that a great deal of disinformation was part of the historical scholarship on Eckhardt and his activities in both Hungary and in the United States. Much of the erroneous or distorted information was a result of an active, decades-long campaign of slander directed at Dr. Eckhardt as a result of his anti-Communist stance and his activities during the period of the Hungarian Bolshevik Revolution of 1919 and during World War II and the Cold War. There was also substantial material labeling him as pro-Nazi, fascist and anti-Semitic—recurring themes that have roiled through scholarship since the inter-war period. The objective of my research then became to attempt to clarify the history of Eckhardt's American years by sifting through the disinformation and attempting to validate what actually transpired, using documents available in various repositories and in private hands.

While this book does not intend to rehabilitate Tibor Eckhardt, it does attempt to clarify his story and present it as accurately as possible, using a body of comprehensive archival material that has been overlooked by previous scholars—a portion which has been unavailable until recently. This book also speaks to the power of change and of how Eckhardt's views developed as his travels in the United States and the time he spent outside of Hungary increasingly influenced him to move to the center politically. In pursuing my research, I often found missing facts or new information that threw a different light on Eckhardt's life story, so although the focus in this work is on his American years, I have also updated and modified his biographical information and provided a brief history of his inter-war activities based on my findings. In no way is this an attempt to cover the inter-war period comprehensively but only to bring to light recently discovered archival material relating to the topic. Tibor Eckhardt Jr.'s cooperation with my work, as well the cooperation of the European members of the Eckhardt family, contributed greatly to my ability to present a more complete picture of the man.

This book also presents, in brief, a history of Hungarian émigré political movements and their workings in the United States, both during and after World War II. The larger story in this recounting of Eckhardt's American years is that of the changes American policy went through during the war and subsequent Cold War with respect to the countries of Central- and East Europe that became Soviet satellites. Eckhardt's success and failure and the success and failure of the various émigré political movements were directly affected by American foreign policy changes, particularly the shift from a pro-Soviet to an anti-Soviet stance during the war and its aftermath. After the Hungarian edition of this book was published, I discovered valuable new information specific to this topic, most notably at the National Archives of the United Kingdom but also elsewhere. The additional information from these sources is included here, most prominently in Chapter 2.

I have attempted to demonstrate how Eckhardt and other émigré political leaders tried to work with and around the policy changes. I propose that Eckhardt's significance and the legacy of his work are to be found in investigating the role model that he presents today. He was a politician, but more than that he was a statesman who stayed true to his values and his moral code, a man who spent a lifetime working for the benefit of his countrymen and his country of origin. He did not compromise his relationship with his adopted country in these efforts, in fact his highly principled and selfless work was much admired and was supported by many officials in the United States up to the highest level, including U.S. presidents. After Eckhardt's death, President Richard Nixon sent Tibor Eckhardt Jr. a telegram (see Appendix) lauding his father and his contributions. This not only amply illustrates Eckhardt's importance but also effectively debunks the often-repeated view, especially in Hungarian scholarship, that Eckhardt was not a respected or meaningful figure in the U.S. political world.

While there is a strong emphasis on the views of Dr. Otto von Habsburg in this work, it is not because Eckhardt was a legitimist. Rather, Dr. von Habsburg and Eckhardt had a day in, day out, working relationship during three critical years of World War II, and they maintained an ongoing collaboration thereafter. Thus, Dr. von Habsburg's remembrances of Eckhardt, which remain fresh and full of interesting detail, are those of a close collaborator and a principal participant in twentieth century European affairs. They are exceedingly valuable for their first-person aspect and for the observer's immense political sophistication and knowledge.

Acknowledgements

I very much appreciate the personal time that Dr. Otto von Habsburg, president of the Pan-European Union and former representative to the European Parliament, took to cooperate with me in my work. He not only provided his generous assistance in my research and contributed his personal memories of Tibor Eckhardt but was also kind enough to write this book's Foreword on the significance of Dr. Tibor Eckhardt and his place in twentieth century Hungarian history.

I would also like to express my appreciation to the many other individuals whose cooperation and support have been instrumental in making this book possible:

My thanks to Tibor Eckhardt Jr., who has given his full and enthusiastic cooperation since I began my research. He has provided me with invaluable insight, family documents and personal memories of his father. Thanks to his help, this book presents a much fuller portrait of his father than would otherwise have been possible. I also thank Mr. Eckhardt for his permission to edit his father's final work and publish it under the title *Tibor Eckhardt in His Own Words*.

Dr. Stephen Fischer-Galati, Distinguished Professor Emeritus at the University of Colorado and editor of East European Monographs and the *East European Quarterly*, has served as my advisor and mentor since my days as an undergraduate. I am grateful for his encouragement and support over the past three decades. To Nancy Tyler of East European Monographs and *East European Quarterly* I extend my thanks for her assistance and encouragement. My thanks also go to Jill Hannum for editing this work and polishing it for publication and to Johanna Cummings for the design, layout and indexing of the final text.

I also wish to thank the board of the American Hungarian Library and Historical Society in New York City, particularly President of the Board Dr. Ottó Hámos, for allowing me unlimited access to their archives and for their cooperation in providing me with Dr. Eckhardt's memoirs, which were in the library's possession in manuscript form. Dr. Hámos was also kind enough to write the Introduction to *Tibor Eckhardt in His Own Words*, Tibor Eckhardt's memoirs. I would also like to thank Miss Gabriella Mauthner, who is the heart and soul of the American Hungarian Library and Historical Society in New York City, for her generous and kind assistance in working with the library's archival material and for her continuing assistance to me in my work. Miss Mauthner also provided me with a great deal of first hand information on Tibor Eckhardt and many other prominent Hungarians, among them Francis Chorin, Victor Bator and Manfréd Weiss, the noted Hungarian industrialist and Miss Mauthner's grandfather.

In Hungary, I received enormous assistance and guidance from distinguished historian Dr. Tibor Frank, my dissertation advisor and Professor of History at ELTE, and from Dr. Jenő Gergely, chairman of the Department of Twentieth Century Hungarian History of the History Faculty at ELTE. As a scholar from abroad, unschooled in the ways of European academic institutions, my progress was aided immensely by Mrs. Alice Csoba, director of the Ph.D. program at ELTE, and Mrs. Ildikó Horváth, the administrative assistant in the history department. I would also like to thank for their support all the faculty members with whom I had the opportunity to work, as well the members of my oral examination committee and those who participated in my dissertation defense.

Péter Strausz did an excellent job of translating this work from English into Hungarian for publication in 2006 by L'Harmattan Press, Budapest and Paris. I am also most grateful to prominent historian Dr. Károly Szerencsés of ELTE for his oversight of that work.

My archival research began in my own back yard in California, at the Hoover Institution Archives at Stanford University, which house an important portion of the papers not only of Tibor Eckhardt but also of other Hungarian émigré political figures and are an irreplaceable scholarly resource. I would like particularly to thank Head Archivist Dr. Elena S. Danielson, now retired, and Assistant Archivist Carol Leadenham for their assistance with my efforts. Tanya Chebotarev, curator at the Bakhmeteff Archives at Columbia University in New York City, also provided invaluable help to me. Many other libraries and archives were also part of my research, and all of them provided me with generous assistance. There is not room in these introductory pages to name each of the individuals who assisted me, but I am grateful to all who took the time to help further my work.

In addition to Tibor Eckhardt Jr., I would like to thank those descendents of Tibor Eckhardt whom I was able to locate through my research. They have been helpful and generous with their memories of family history and have provided me with rare photographs for use in this book. Significant among them are Mr. Sándor Betégh, grandnephew of Tibor Eckhardt, and his wife Mrs. Annemarie Betégh of Budapest and Mr. Andor Hertelendy and his wife Mrs. Maria Hertelendy, great niece of Tibor Eckhardt.

In Budapest, Márta Berényi and Katalin Laki were extremely helpful to me at the Hungarian National Archives. In Makó, Hungary, Eckhardt's birthplace, the director of the Makó Museum, Dr. Pál Halmágyi, was helpful in providing material on the Eckhardt family.

Finally, I'd like to thank my family—first and foremost, my husband, Douglas G. Lynn, who did not think it quixotic that I would desire to pursue a doctorate in history late in life and provided his wholehearted and generous support. My thanks also to my husband's sons, Timothy and Gregory Lynn, and to Timothy's partner, Gary Sullivan, for their encouragement and unflagging support; and to my recently deceased mother, Ilona Kádár, and the countless friends who lent their support and encouraged me during the times when my health prevented me from working to the fullest.

This book is dedicated to the memory of my father, István borosjenői Kádár, whose intellectual curiosity I like to think I inherited. His opening salvo of "óriási tévedés" in our political and historical discussions always got them off to a vibrant and often heated start.

Foreword

Hungary is historically speaking a rather unique country. The Magyars started as an Asiatic invasion in Europe, when a number of nations from the Far East entered the Old World after the collapse of the Roman Empire. All these nations soon disappeared, amongst them big and powerful hordes like the Huns or the Avars. Only the smallest group has survived for over a thousand years. It suffered one of the greatest historical defeats, the battle of the Lech, and this turned out to be the start of a European, soon to be Christian kingdom, because the Magyars listened to the wise advice of a great saint and statesman, King St. Stephen. Hungary was occupied for two centuries by the Turks and lost nearly all of its inhabitants to be re-settled by Germans and Slavs, who without compulsion or pressure became Magyars. In our days the Magyars lost by the Trianon dictate at the end of the First World War almost two thirds of their national territory by borders, making Hungary the nation with the largest number of minorities beyond their border in Central Europe. The Trianon dictate was established under the slogan of the self-determination of nations, a goal which was proclaimed and never carried out.

If Hungary has survived all the storms of history, this is due not only to the resilience of the Hungarian community, last but not least to its great cultural capability, producing famous artists, poets, musicians, but equally scientists—witness the number of its Nobel Prize winners—and an equally impressive number of great statesmen. They became well known in foreign policy, but equally in domestic and social affairs, as shown by Francis Deak, Count Szechenyi, and closer to us Albert Apponyi, Alexander Weckerle, Kristoffy and last, not least, Tibor Eckhardt. They all were partly successful, partly they only showed the way to a better future.

In Eckhardt's stormy political life, one of the most important phases was the action of Eckhardt during the Second World War. In this historical period he fought the Hitlerite power, first as the leader of the opposition in the Hungarian Parliament, later as an emigrant in the United States. As a fighter for human rights and democracy, he saw in an early stage the dangers for his country of all forms of totalitarianism, of Stalin just as much as Hitler. He realized long before many leaders in the West the danger of totalitarian policies, whether red or brown. This led to the violent campaigns against him by the powerful Russian propaganda machine and its allies, especially in Central Europe, where Czecho-Slovak president in exile Edward Beneš became one of the most active supporters of Russian ambitions. Backed by strong financial reserves, the campaign against Eckhardt unfortunately had a strong impact in Washington and hence gained control of influential sectors of the European emigration in Great Britain and the United States. Eckhardt soon became one of the main targets of a concerted campaign, which got the support of powerful American politicians, who believed in the peaceful goals of Stalin. Even after the war, Eckhardt was prevented from returning to his homeland; this ban was only ended when the Communists had firmly established their rule. Thus Eckhardt died far from Hungary, which he could have served well with his great vision and his political knowledge.

His tragic death was widely ignored, and the silence was so much supported by all those who have good reasons to try to avoid the mentioning of his name, because they have no interest in a discussion concerning the free world's road to Yalta and to its consequences. To this came the action of certain persons, whose interest it was that the activities of Eckhardt should not be known, since they feared that this would lead to a revision of the distorted historical picture of Hungary's wartime policy.

Fortunately history cannot be eternally falsified. There are historians, like the author of this book, who have not had personal experiences of the critical times. They started investigations without prejudice, which now are revealing the real facts. It is thus that young Americans, who were educated in a falsified history, are now finding the path to truth. Fortunately this takes place when some of the personal witnesses of the events are still alive and can help them with their testimony. Hence the book, which in its quest for reality is both non-partisan and honestly interested to find that truth, which is indispensable if one wants to give a firm base to the knowledge of what really happened. One must be grateful to them, since objective history is a firm base for a constructive policy.

Otto von Habsburg

Pöcking, Germany

Introduction

TIBOR ECKHARDT:
The Significance of His American Years

The prominent Hungarian politician Tibor Eckhardt made his fourth and final trip to the United States in 1941. Since then, historians have speculated about but shed little light upon what actually prompted an individual of Eckhardt's stature to leave his homeland at that particular time to travel to the United States and what event(s) subsequently forced him to stay in America. Eckhardt left Hungary at the peak of his influence and power for what was intended to be a mission to help bring his country over to the Allied side in World War II. He and his mission became the victims of the dynamics among the Allied powers, dynamics that changed rapidly after Hitler attacked the USSR and again when the USSR entered the war on the side of the Allies. These events occurred while Eckhardt was on his six-month journey from Hungary to the United States. Though his mission was clear, it was ultimately made impossible by the set of demands for the USSR's participation in the war that Stalin presented to the Western Alliance.

Tibor Eckhardt's fascinating life is worth revisiting from today's perspective, especially because greater access to historical and archival sources, including newly discovered Eckhardt memoirs, has lately become available. Recently published under the title *Tibor Eckhardt in His Own Words*[1] (also referred to throughout this work as Eckhardt's memoirs), it gives a detailed account of his life and career, with a focus on World War II, shedding new light on the subject and correcting some glaring errors that have become part of the scholarship related to him. Eckhardt's memoirs were written in approximately the last three years of his life, and what he had written had not been completely transcribed by the time of his death in 1972. The manuscript itself had not been completed; he passed away before he had the opportunity to write the full history of his collaboration with American intelligence during and after the war. He specifically intended the memoirs to be published by the American Hungarian Library and Historical Society (Amerikai-Magyar Könyvtár és Történelmi Társulat), which had also published his earlier work, *Recollections of Tibor Eckhardt: Regicide at Marseille*.[2] After his death, Eckhardt's devoted long-time secretary, Dr. Magda Barany, transcribed the final four chapters of the memoirs, and the first rough draft was turned over to the leadership of the American Hungarian Library and Historical Society for publication.[3] Although a solicitation went out for money to underwrite the publication of the work, the correspondence of the day shows that it was not successful, and the transcript lay largely forgotten in the library's archives for thirty years.[4] The American Hungarian Library and Historical Society lost contact with Tibor Eckhardt Jr., Dr. Eckhardt's only surviving heir, shortly after 1972, and nothing was done with the manuscript over the years. In the early 1990s, however, the library sent a photocopy of the manuscript to the Széchenyi Library archives, fulfilling that library's request for it and many other papers and documents from the Eckhardt Collection and that of Hungarian National Council (Magyar Nemzeti Bizottmány).[5]

In the fall of 2003, I went to the American Hungarian Library and Historical Society in New York City knowing that it housed some of Tibor Eckhardt's papers. I was also aware that there was no finding aid or index to the materials. I was astonished to discover the manuscript of his memoirs among the Eckhardt papers there. I harbored a slim hope that I might find the manuscript at some point in my archival research, but Tibor Eckhardt Jr. had told me that he thought the manuscript had been stolen from his father's apartment shortly after his death, and I had not counted on locating it. I have a close working relationship with Tibor Eckhardt Jr., with whom the library had long-since lost touch, and I immediately contacted him to inform him of the find. The papers I found were in the form of rough first drafts and photocopies, but it is evident that they are original, for the first fifteen chapters, which were written in English, contain many notations and corrections in Eckhardt's own hand. After his death, his secretary,

Dr. Barany, also made notes on the chapters she transcribed, organized, and where necessary translated from Hungarian into English.

Eckhardt used his personal diaries, which he faithfully kept from at least 1920 onward, as the basis for many of the specific quotations and references to dates, events and individuals that he wrote about in the manuscript. Tibor Eckhardt Jr. remembers his father's diaries, but says that they had disappeared by the time of his death. Whether they were spirited away by the American intelligence service, with which Eckhardt had been cooperating for several decades, remains a matter for speculation. There is also speculation that Eckhardt personally destroyed them in order to prevent their falling into the wrong hands. That he was still actively cooperating with American intelligence at the time of his death has been verified by Tibor Eckhardt Jr., who told me that when he went to his father's apartment the day of his death, the manuscript of the memoirs and the diaries were both gone. According to Tibor Eckhardt Jr., workmen in the apartment at the time were removing wires that ran from it to the apartment below, and the comment was made, "We have to monitor what he has to say, after all he is an old man."[6] Eckhardt never made his son privy to the details of his secret work, and although the latter suspected his father was working with an arm of the American intelligence community, he knew little of the association.

I was able to obtain gracious permission from the American Hungarian Library and Historical Society, New York City and from Tibor Eckhardt Jr. to have the manuscript of the memoirs published. Written by Eckhardt in English, the work shows his fluency and high level of mastery of that language. However, there is no question that these were the thoughts of an elderly man going through the process of validation and vindication of his life's work. The work is in part riveting, in part historically interesting, and in part rambling and repetitive, particularly in its insistent references to those who worked against Hungary's best interests, as defined by Eckhardt. The memoirs' value is in the detailed explanation and clarification of his and others' work on behalf of Hungarian interests during World War II and in the Cold War period immediately thereafter, as well as for some of Eckhardt's inter-war reminiscences, which were previously unknown. There is no question that Eckhardt had scores to settle and self-vindication in mind when he wrote this final book. There is also no question that it represents a search to ascribe meaning to his life's contribution. Nonetheless, it is a reliable memoir by a man who was an intimate participant in Hungarian politics for three decades, through some of the most turbulent times in the nation's history.

Many latter-day historians, using previously published sources and material unfavorable to Eckhardt, have accepted an unflattering portrayal of him as fact. Some of the inaccuracies recently swirling through scholarly circles include statements that Eckhardt led the White Terror of the immediate post World War I period and statements that flatly brand him as an anti-Semite. Both issues will be carefully examined in this work and the charges found to be without substantive proof. An example of such accusations surfaced in a recently published journal article, which not only labels Eckhardt as an anti-Semite but also states that he served as president of the Hungarian National Council, which is not true.[7] This book is an attempt to clarify who Tibor Eckhardt was and what he stood for, and it will strive to peel away the layers of disinformation that have been part of Eckhardt scholarship for over six decades.

In many ways, Eckhardt's life story is that of a man's metamorphosis, and it illustrates the power of change. Born under the Austro-Hungarian monarchy and having survived the chaos of the breakdown of the old order in Europe at the end of the World War I, Eckhardt took part in the political life of his nation during the emergence of modern Europe's new nation states and throughout the inter-war years. He was increasingly influenced by his exposure to the democracies of the West, particularly the United States. Having spent the first thirty-two years of his life under the Austro-Hungarian monarchy, he initially reflected the values, views and prejudices ingrained in his class and his homeland's culture. As he matured, and after his post-doctoral education abroad and other extensive travel outside of Hungary, he embraced a more humanistic tradition.

Eckhardt was a man whose early political career and ideology can be accurately described as having a "far right" point of view, particularly during the period of World War I and the tumultuous years that immediately followed it. It must be noted that while labeling someone "far right" during the inter-war period would today imply that they held racist, insular and nationalistic views, Eckhardt can only be accurately accused of the latter. He originally was and always remained a Hungarian patriot, and he did all he could for his country of origin during some of the most trying times in her history.

There is no proof of the charge that Eckhardt had been a leader of the post World War I White Terror. Contemporary accounts of the period from objective sources—including various British reports such as those of British admiral Sir Ernest T. Troubridge, chairman of the Inter-Allied Danube River Commission and the British High Commissioner in Hungary, and Mr. (later Sir) Thomas Hohler, as well as the May 1920 Report of the British Joint Labour Delegation—do not even mention Eckhardt's name in that connection. Neither do the memoirs of Brigadier General Harry Hill Bandholtz, the American representative to the four-power Inter-Allied Military Mission that governed post World War I Hungary. A book on the White Terror in Hungary by former member of the Béla Kun government Joseph Pogány (published in Vienna in 1920 in both a German and a Hungarian edition) describes the atrocities from the Bolshevik point of view and lists all perpetrators directly responsible, naming many individuals but *not* Eckhardt.[8] None of the other contemporary books on the White Terror written by authors with both centrist and leftist bents mentions Eckhardt by name. These include Béla Szántó's book, *A magyaroszági proletariátus osztályharca és diktatúrája*, published in Vienna in 1920, and Ladislas Fényes's book, *Le peuple hongrois accuse!* (written in French).[9]

Another of Eckhardt's associations, which has continued to stir controversy, was his membership in the 1920s in the anti-Semitic Fajvédő Party, officially named Magyar Nemzeti Függetlenségi Párt (Hungarian National Independence Party), as well as the Ébredő Magyarok Egyesülete (ÉME, Union of Awakening Magyars). Eckhardt's two-year association with ÉME is taken by some scholars as proof of his supposedly life-long anti-Semitism. Others of his contemporaries who were members of the same organization are treated much more kindly by some of the same pundits. They do not, for example, project as evidence of life-long anti-Semitism Endre Bajcsy-Zsilinszky's membership in the ÉME and the Fajvédő Part during the same period as Eckhardt.

Applying twenty-first century standards of political correctness to that turbulent period of twentieth century history is misleading when evaluating the circumstances of that time. That the sentiments expressed by the ÉME were not limited to countries such as Hungary is highlighted by an article entitled "Harvard Klan" from the *New York Herald Tribune* of 23 October 1923. It reads in full:

> Cambridge, Mass. – The Harvard student body is in the grip of the Ku Klux Klan. This much was admitted editorially today by the "Harvard Crimson," the undergraduate daily campus paper, which forecasts a Klan membership drive and announces that the Klan has existed at the university for two years. It is stated in the same article that the hooded empire is now gaining great popularity, especially with fraternity men. Less than a year ago Harvard was sorely split over the Semitic question, many students urging that a limit be set on the number of Jewish students who could enroll in any year.[10]

The article makes clear that the organizational purpose of and support given to the Klan by the educational elite at Harvard were rather analogous to the circumstances surrounding the mission of the ÉME in Hungary at the same period of time. While critics of Hungary and Eckhardt use the ÉME to illustrate what they say was the racist bent of the Hungarian leaders, further research demonstrates that these viewpoints were not unique to Hungary, and if history is to pillory Hungarians for their views, they should not be made to stand alone in the stocks.

In *Hungary Between Wilson and Lenin*, well-respected Hungarian American historian Peter Pastor offers the provocative opinion that some of the anti-Semitism projected in Hungary during the 1919–20 period was a result of the Hungarians' desire to please the Western powers and that the deep-seated anti-Semitism that was supposedly a part of Hungarian society was not nearly as strong as it is considered to have been from the present day perspective.

> The fact that in March 1919 the Magyars accepted an almost wholly Jewish leadership may indicate that Hungarian public opinion had no specific objection to Jews in power so long as they were doing what was expected of them. There is no indication that Kunfi as Commissar of Education (who was himself Jewish and had expressed concern about the preponderance of Jews in the government) in the Béla Kun cabinet ever protested against its Jewish majority. It is more likely, therefore, that discrimination against Jewish Magyar leaders occurred primarily to please the Allies. It was in line with the basic objective of Hungarian foreign policy—to project the image of Hungary that would be most pleasing to the West. The repeated humiliation of Hungarians of Jewish background by Allied officials was proof that Kunfi's cares were not unfounded.
>
> Anti-Semitism was on the upsurge in 1918–1919 in the West, where it often identified with anti-Bolshevism. Though it was not voiced as openly and in such justifiable fashion as anti-Bolshevism, anti-Semitism was embraced by many Allied officials. Even such a prominent statesman as Winston Churchill could later speak of a Jewish-Bolshevik conspiracy. At the time of the Polish-Russian crisis he accused the Bolsheviks of bringing about an 'international of Russian and Polish Jews.' White Russian refugees in the West, with a tradition of anti-Semitism, helped to perpetuate this fear of an international Jewish and Communist conspiracy. Well-publicized witch-hunts, such as the Overman Judiciary Subcommittee hearing of the United States Senate, helped give substance to that fear even in America. In February 1919, witnesses testified to the subcommittee that the Russian revolution had been directed by East-Side Jews.[11]

Unlike the anti-Semites or those who were political opportunists, Eckhardt's membership and leadership during the later years of the ÉME were not a result of his belief as a Fajvédő, a racial supremacist. Rather, they stemmed from his desire to protect the Hungarians, the people, the nation (nemzetvédelem), and to strengthen and ensure their survival. Throughout his life, regardless of his personal idiosyncrasies and his shortcomings, Eckhardt's efforts were always oriented toward preserving the Magyar nation and its homeland. This cannot be disputed, despite whatever criticism may be leveled at him.

Eckhardt spent the second chapter of his life in Hungary during the highly-charged inter-war period from 1920 until 1941. This was a different phase for him. The monarchy had been dissolved, and though he was absorbed with many Hungarian interests and obligations, he also spent a great deal of time abroad in America, Germany, France and Great Britain and was regularly exposed to life in those countries. Eckhardt was fluent in German, French and English and was able to function at the highest levels of political life without using a translator. These linguistic skills afforded him career opportunities with the Horthy regime and also later in America, where he worked closely with the Department of the Army Military Intelligence Service (MIS).

While Eckhardt certainly held to a conservative ideology throughout his life, he became a great deal more centrist and developed a broader worldview as he entered the midpoint of his career in the late 1920s and the 1930s. Journalist and political writer Paul Nadanyi presents this view of Eckhardt's development: "No doubt his visits to America, his acquaintance with American free institutions and the true democratic spirit greatly influenced his mind, and the Eckhardt who returned to Hungary was a different Eckhardt than the young politician of the turbulent anti-revolutionary period."[12]

Tibor Eckhardt had a cordial working relationship with many of the twentieth century's great figures, and a number of them, both inside Hungary and in the international political arena, respected him and held him in high regard. A close examination of Eckhardt's life reveals that he stayed true to his own values and maintained his independence, remaining beholden to none and fiercely loyal to the cause of Hungarian nationalism and independence to the end of his life.

His development as an individual and the contributions he made at each level of his career in public service are both worth revisiting. As Dr. Otto von Habsburg, the heir to the Austro-Hungarian throne, aptly put it in a personal interview with this author, "Tibor Eckhardt became a greater man in emigration ... contrary to what happened to many other émigré politicians." Dr. von Habsburg explained that in his view Eckhardt "did great work on behalf of the Hungarians, tirelessly and with little support. He dedicated his entire life to the nation. You see, the whole term of his life was in the ascendancy. He started as an ébredő magyar and became one of the great statesmen of his country."[13]

On initial examination, Eckhardt's career appears to have peaked during the years just prior to World War II, a period when the party he led had the country's greatest number of registered voters, his was one of the most prominent names in Hungary and he wielded both power and influence. It is the third of Eckhardt's life-phases, however, the years he spent in self-imposed and then involuntary exile in America, for which he deserves the greatest credit. For three decades after leaving Hungarian soil, he served Hungary with dedication, with little or no hope for political gain, worked under great adversity and lived in hugely reduced circumstances. Such circumstances, too, make his life and career worthy of reevaluation.

It is worth emphasizing that as a multilingual, internationally-connected and respected figure, Eckhardt was unlike most other members of the Hungarian emigration, who not only lost their status when they emigrated but also lost their direction in life. This was particularly true of members of the 1945 wave of immigration. It is merely speculative to ponder the various options that were open to Eckhardt in the United States, but he had the skills and connections to have been able to set himself up there in any number of prestigious and lucrative private sector positions. Instead of utilizing his diverse portfolio of skills for personal gain, he opted for work that kept his finances unstable for the balance of his life, staying out of the international spotlight to labor tirelessly and often futilely for the cause of Hungarian independence. An avowed enemy of Soviet Communism, Eckhardt also endured decades of vilification and criticism by the communists and the Left in an extensive program of character assassination that was part of a much wider all-out propaganda war.[14]

This campaign against Eckhardt and his post 1941 activities on behalf of Hungary had its successes. It had an impact on shutting down the Eckhardt-backed Movement for Independent Hungary (Független Magyarországért Mozgalom) and an effect on Eckhardt's work, particularly during the critical period of 1941–1946. This is confirmed in Nandor F. Dreisziger's article "Horthy Regime's Reinsurance Policies in 1941", published in *War and Society* in 1989.[15] As noted earlier, the effects of the anti-Eckhardt campaign still linger in the work of present day historians and journalists, for the amount of disinformation generated about him was voluminous. On the other hand, very little is known of his full-time dedication to the cause of Hungarian freedom and independence during World War II.

Revisiting with fresh eyes the war years critical to United States–Hungarian relations and to Hungary's post-war fate also allows us to examine more closely Eckhardt's initial (1941) attempt to rally Hungarian American and American public sentiment behind the Movement for Independent Hungary. Speaking of this organization to U.S. Assistant Secretary of State A. A. Berle in 1941, Archduke Otto von Habsburg is quoted as saying, "90% of the Hungarian colonies in the U.S. are solidly back of Eckhardt".[16]

It is clear in retrospect that the communists saw the first organization with which Eckhardt became involved after his arrival in the United States in 1941 as posing a real danger, mainly because of the level of support it received, which was unprecedented in Hungarian America and has never been equaled. Eckhardt's papers at the Hoover Institution at Stanford University provide a great deal of information clarifying the events surrounding this short-lived organization. Eckhardt's personal papers, his posthumously published memoirs, additional papers located in the American Hungarian Library and Historical Society in New York, and papers of other prominent Hungarian émigrés also provide ample evidence that the Movement for Independent Hungary did not fail because it was a mission without merit but because the mission *had* merit. Therefore, it was a threat to those whose plans for post World War II Hungary were to fold it into the Soviet Union's sphere of influence.

The Movement for Independent Hungary was unique in the annals of émigré political activities within the Hungarian community in the United States. During its brief life the diverse Hungarian American community rallied behind one person, one set of values and one set of goals for the first and perhaps the only time. Such overwhelming support would have been impossible without the backing of the powerful American Hungarian Federation and all of its leadership.[17] The Movement for Independent Hungary failed because of external pressures placed upon it. In contrast, it is clear today that its successors—such as the Hungarian National Council, the Assembly of Captive European Nations and others that were heavily funded by the U.S. State Department—failed because they could never create internal unity and did not have broad-based support in the émigré communities in the United States or the rest of the free world.[18]

It would be impossible to write about Tibor Eckhardt without exploring in some detail the characteristics and political dynamics of the various Hungarian immigrant groups. The background of émigré politics has to be outlined if the reader is to understand the massive conflicts and cross currents that existed in Hungarian America, indeed, in the entire Hungarian emigration. It is also important for an understanding of how and why Eckhardt functioned in collaboration with some groups and in conflict with others and why it is so difficult for outsiders to comprehend the Hungarian émigré community's constant self-destructive infighting and back stabbing. Indeed, the entire history of the political activities of Hungarian immigrants has been colored by historians' acceptance of the fact that such self-destructive behavior was a result of the Hungarian immigrants' inability to get along with one another and unify behind the common cause of support for Hungary.

This simplistic view takes into account only the overt causes of such internal dissent. The underlying cause is more complex, murky and unsavory and has slowly been revealed in recent scholarship. Since the end of World War II, and particularly since the end of the Cold War, secret documents and archival materials have been uncovered that make it clear that the Soviet propaganda machine and security apparatus reached beyond the countries in its immediate sphere of influence to individuals within the foreign offices and security agencies of the major and secondary powers. Thus, regardless of the internal issues facing the immigrant groups, the outside pressures working against their success were enough to ensure their destabilization, if not their failure. The tentacles of the Soviet propaganda machine reached far and wide to discredit those who opposed communism and communist expansion. In describing the work of the KGB and the Comintern in the West, Robert L. Benson, who wrote *The Venona Story* for the

U.S. National Security Agency website,[19] states that the classic Comintern methodology abroad could best be described as "subversion rather than espionage".

The Soviets had a plan. Their security apparatus preyed on the immigrants' naiveté, their lack of languages, their egos and their fears. The tactics included disinformation, sowing seeds of dissent and doubt, funding two different factions and pitting them against each other in order to neutralize them. The Soviet machine engaged in these tactics relentlessly, either directly or in support of its designated agents. While the émigré Hungarians were often their own worst enemies, it can also be argued that the powerful destabilization program intended to neutralize and discredit their leadership was an equally destructive influence. Sadly, the most damning charge that can be levied against most of the émigré leaders is that they did not recognize that they were being manipulated to destroy their cause from within.

Eckhardt's early and accurate pinpointing of the Soviet campaign against the free world made him less than popular in circles that had been convinced, largely as a result of the Soviet battle against Hitler, of Soviet Communism's benevolent nature. During and immediately after the war, many considered Eckhardt's fervent anti-communism to be excessive, and his attitude was often described as paranoid. Throughout the war, the American media emphasized the positive nature of the Allies' association with the Soviet Union. Eleanor Roosevelt went so far as to call Stalin a "true democrat". There was no question that the United States was grateful for the alliance and the burden that the Soviet Union had borne in the fight against the Germans. The gratitude was backed up by the billions of dollars and the materiel that the United States was willing to "lend" the Soviet Union in order to build up its infrastructure for the war effort, none of which was ever paid back by the USSR. Eckhardt was not alone in his views, however. It is important to note that as early as 21 August 1944, Lord Moran, Churchill's personal physician, wrote in his diary: "Winston never talks about Hitler these days; he is always harping on the dangers of Communism. He dreams of the Red Army spreading like a cancer from one country to another. It has become an obsession and he seems to think of little else."[20]

While Churchill was uncomfortable with the post-war intentions of the Soviet Union, key figures within both the United States and the United Kingdom had mistrusted the Soviet leadership throughout the war. A prime example was that neither country informed Stalin about intelligence breakthroughs such as the ULTRA program, which decrypted German ciphers. President Truman—hardly pro-Soviet, as his rather candid notes from the Potsdam Conference attest[21]—chose not to inform Stalin of the United States' decision to use the atomic bomb on Japan. In his personal notes written in Potsdam on 17 July 1945, Truman notes, "I shall inform Stalin about it at an opportune time".[22] Within days after the end of the Potsdam Conference of 17 July–2 August 1945, the atomic attacks on Hiroshima and Nagasaki took place (6 and 9 August 1945). The Soviets viewed Truman's failure to inform them prior to deployment as a major diplomatic affront, even though they had been aware of the Manhattan Project as early as 1944 through their elaborate spy networks, as the VENONA Archives attest.[23]

Eckhardt's views and Churchill's fears were shared by other informed political figures of the time, including State Department professionals such as William C. Bullitt, the first United States ambassador posted to the Soviet Union (in 1933). George F. Kennan, a key State Department policy maker, viewed the Soviet Union's expansionist intentions in Europe with alarm throughout the war years. Fluent in Russian, Kennan was a diplomat and a leading expert on Russia who served on the staff of the U.S. embassy in Moscow in the 1930s. He authored the two documents that gave rise to the Truman Doctrine and the U.S. foreign policy of containment—a "long telegram" to Secretary of State Byrnes sent from Moscow on 22 February 1946 and a subsequent anonymous article, "The Sources of Soviet Conduct", written under the pseudonym "X" and appearing in the July 1947 issue of *Foreign Affairs*. In them he argued that the Soviet regime was inherently expansionist and that its influence had to be "contained" in areas of strategic importance to the United States. Kennan's writings on the Soviet Union formed the ideological basis for the Cold War and for the Truman administration's anti-Soviet policies, although, as noted, Truman's distrust of the Soviets was already in place at Potsdam.[24]

As early as 29 January 1943 and several more times in that year, Ambassador Bullitt wrote to President Roosevelt warning of the consequences of the alliance with the Soviet Union. Bullitt's anti-Soviet opinions were public knowledge by 1936, when he returned to the United States from his ambassadorial post. He was a friend of several Hungarian politicians and diplomats who were in exile in the United States and was knowledgeable about Central Europe, having served the U.S. State Department as chief of the Bureau of Central European Information beginning in 1917. Bullitt's candid opinions about the progress of World War II and the threat of the USSR were expressed in a conversation with former Hungarian Minister John Pelényi, which will be addressed in detail later in this work.[25]

At war's end, the European continent lay in physical and economic ruin, and England was close to bankruptcy, the wartime Labour government having been voted out of office in 1945 due to dissatisfaction with its wartime policies. With the exception of the United States, which was slow to make a policy turnaround despite its apprehension about Soviet intentions, none of the Allies was in a position to challenge any moves the Soviet Union chose to make. It was a pity that the obsession about the Soviet plans that Eckhardt shared with a few key individuals was not more prevalent in Western diplomatic and political circles. However, even among those leaders who were apprehensive, there was the realization that not much could be done to reverse the tide of Soviet expansion. It would take a few more painful years before the full extent of the Soviet threat become clear. It was in March 1947 that U.S. President Harry Truman responded to their expansionist policy with a speech proposing the foreign policy changes that would become known as the "Truman Doctrine". Congress and other U.S. policy makers were spurred into action, establishing and funding the programs to rebuild war-torn Europe and counter the Soviet threat worldwide.

In addition to Eckhardt's efforts during World War II on behalf of a democratic Hungary and his warnings about the intent of the Soviet Union, a third issue deserves reexamination—the causes of the failure of his and several other key wartime organizations that promoted the noble goal of Hungarian freedom. The failure of these organizations had a great deal to do with the world's chaotic political situation during World War II and the Cold War period, which figured significantly in the inability of the various Hungarian émigré organizations to find their place and contribute to the welfare and future of the Hungarian immigrants. It was difficult for all of these organizations accurately to assess the political situation from their respective countries of exile. Either there was no clear Allied policy regarding Hungary during the war years or if there was a policy it was not made known to the emigrant groups or made clear to the participants. This is amply evident from the futility of the work of the Movement for Independent Hungary and the Barcza-Pelényi "Committee of Ministers" and from the frustration those groups' leaders encountered simply in trying to work with the American administration and the State Department.

Such efforts were hampered by the fact that Hungary was not an important factor in the European scene; and as a German ally, even though a reluctant one, the concerns of its émigré leaders were not at the top of the Allied priority list. A review of confidential documents assessing the Hungarian wartime situation, produced in 1944 by the Office of Strategic Services, reveals the prevailing State Department sentiment about Hungary as Germany's ally. Regardless of the high regard in which some Hungarian leaders were held by the U.S. government, the documents focused on Hungary's "opportunistic policy of maintaining its own political position without either entering into irrevocable commitments to Germany or breaking away enough to provoke German reprisals".[26] Quite simply, the view was that Hungary was in the German camp.

After the war years, the turmoil on the continent, the need to move huge refugee populations, and the clash of superpowers in what became the Cold War certainly did not bode well for the success of any immigrant organization. These organizations had longevity and some semblance of influence only after the United States, having made the policy change to turn against Soviet expansion, decided it was necessary to support pro-democratic exile groups from the Soviet Satellites. At that point, the United States solicited the formation of and provided funding for post-war groups such as the Hungarian National Council and the Assembly of Captive European Nations.[27]

While the United States was willing to provide such support, according to historian Stanley Max, the British were reluctant to institute "a policy of anti-Soviet bravado, over a non-crucial region, [which] was not only impractical; it was unjustifiably hazardous. Britain wanted to avoid yet another war in Europe, and it certainly did not want to get involved in one over Eastern Europe."[28] The British, absorbed with their post-war domestic problems, allowed the United States to take the lead in conducting and funding the Cold War, despite the fact that Churchill had been one of the first prominent statesmen to speak out about the Soviet occupation of Central- and East Europe.

Endnotes

1. Tibor Eckhardt, *Tibor Eckhardt in His Own Words: An Autobiography*, ed. Katalin Kádár Lynn (Boulder: East European Monographs, distributed by Columbia University Press, 2005). Eckhardt wrote this over a number of years prior to his death in 1972.
2. Tibor Eckhardt, *Recollections of Tibor Eckhardt: Regicide at Marseille* (New York: The American Hungarian Library and Historical Society, 1964).
3. Tibor Eckhardt to Tibor Eckhardt Jr., 19 August 1969 (epistolary will), Tibor Eckhardt Papers, Box 2, Library Correspondence Folder, American Hungarian Library and Historical Society, New York. In this letter donating his personal papers and books to the library after his death, Eckhardt gives the library permission to publish his manuscript and gives permission to Sándor Szent-Iványi and László Acsay to handle its publication. Eckhardt refers to the papers and books as his only assets—"egyetlen vagyonom".
4. László Acsay and Sándor Szent-Iványi to multiple recipients, undated, Tibor Eckhardt Papers, Box 2, Library Correspondence Folder, American Hungarian Library and Historical Society, New York. This undated letter was written after Eckhardt's letter of donation of 19 August 1969, but it is unclear whether it was written before or after his death in 1972. The letter solicits funds for the publication of the manuscript, eventually published in 2005 as *Tibor Eckhardt in His Own Words*.
5. Láczay Ervinné (Mrs. Ervin Láczay) to István Vida at the MTA Történettudományi Intézet, 16 December 1991, Tibor Eckhardt Papers, Box 2, OSZK Library Correspondence Folder, American Hungarian Library and Historical Society, New York. This letter confirms the loan of the Eckhardt manuscript to the Országos Széchenyi Könyvtár (OSZK), as arranged by Somogyi Pálné (Mrs. Pál Somogyi) of the OSZK.
6. Tibor Eckhardt Jr., interview by author, Florida, 9–10 April 2002.
7. Judith Fai-Podlipnik, "A Decade of Bedlam: Hungarian-American Émigrés vs. the Muscovites, 1945–1955", *East European Quarterly*, September 2003, p. 320.
8. József Pogány, *A fehér terror Magyarországon* (Vienna: Arbeiter Buchhandlung, 1920).

9. Paul Nadanyi, untitled article on Tibor Eckhardt, *Amerikai Magyar Népszava*, 27 July 1942. See also: Harry Hill Bandholtz, *An Undiplomatic Diary*, ed., Fritz-Konrad Kruger (New York: Columbia University Press, 1933); Henry James Papers, Box 1 (United States Representative to the Inter-Allied Danube River Commission 1919), Hoover Institution Archives, Stanford University; Béla Szántó, *A magyarországi proletariátus osztályharca és diktatúrája* (Vienna: A Kommunisták németausztriai pártja, 1920); Ladislas Fényes, *Le peuple hongrois accuse! Marseilles et le système de la dictature hongroise* (Paris: Les éditions Rieder, 1934).

   At the defense of my dissertation on this topic in March 2005, Dr. István Vida, a well known Hungarian historian and authority on the period who served on the ELTE defense committee, acknowledged that while all the circumstances regarding the White Terror are still not known, there is no evidence to date that implicates Eckhardt in any of the atrocities associated with it. Dr. Vida does feel that Eckhardt was an anti-Semite, as his association and activities with various anti-Semitic organizations during the inter-war period would indicate. However, in dealing with his writings and correspondence during and after the war, I found no evidence that would substantiate that claim. C.A. McCartney in his book *October Fifteenth* also states that Eckhardt was an anti-Semite, but he offers no archival proof in his otherwise heavily annotated history of Hungary.
10. "Harvard Klan", *New York Herald Tribune*, 23 October 1923.
11. Peter Pastor, *Hungary Between Wilson and Lenin* (Boulder and New York: East European Monographs, distributed by Columbia University Press, 1973), pp. 45–46.
12. Paul Nadanyi, *The "Free Hungary" Movement* (New York: Amerikai Magyar Népszava, 1942), p. 24.
13. Otto von Habsburg, interview by author, Pöcking, Germany, 28 October 2003.
14. *Harc!*, 25 December 1941 to 3 February 1945, Hoover Institution Library, Stanford, California. Demokratikus Magyarok Amerikai Szövetsége (The American Federation of Democratic Hungarians), the Rusztem Vámbéry-led political group, began publication of *Harc!* (Fight!) in December 1941. From the first issue to the last, Eckhardt was vilified in various ways. In the December 1941 issue he was even accused of being funded by Jewish industrialists at the same time that the Vámbéry faction was branding him as an anti-Semite.
15. "Bridges to the West; The Horthy Regime's Reinsurance Policies in 1941", *War and Society*, Vol. 7, No. 1 (May 1989), pp. 1–23.
16. A.A. Berle, Department of State Dispatch 863.01/656, 16 October 1941, United States National Archives (hereafter NARA, National Archives and Records Administration), College Park, Maryland.
17. The powerful umbrella organization, the American Hungarian Federation, was established on 27 February 1906. It is still a force in Hungarian America today, representing most of the Hungarian organizations in the United States.
18. Steven Béla Vardy, *The Hungarian-Americans* (Boston: Twayne Publishers, 1985), p. 111.
19. Robert L. Benson, "The Venona Story", www.nsa.gov/venona. The VENONA Archives originated with the U.S. Army's Signal Intelligence Service, the precursor to the National Security Agency, which began a secret program in February 1943 that was later code named VENONA. This small program's mission was to examine and exploit Soviet diplomatic communications, but after the program began, the message traffic included espionage efforts as well. It took American cryptologists

almost two years to break the KGB encryption. Thereafter, the information gained provided the U.S. leadership with insight into Soviet intentions and treasonous activities by U.S. government employees until the program was cancelled on 1 October 1980. (The VENONA Archives are usually referred to in capital letters, representing the code name for the files; in book and article titles, "Venona" generally appears in lowercase letters.)

20. Lord Moran, *Churchill: Taken from the Diaries of Lord Moran, The Struggle for Survival 1940–1965* (Boston: Houghton Mifflin Company and Cambridge: The Riverside Press, 1966), p. 185.
21. Harry S. Truman, notes on the Potsdam Conference, 16–17 July 1946, President's Secretary's File, Truman Papers, Truman Presidential Library, Independence, Missouri, www.trumanlibrary.org.
22. Ibid.
23. www.nsa.gov/venona
24. In President Truman's speech to a joint session of the U.S. Congress on 12 March 1947, he stressed the duty of the United States to combat totalitarian regimes worldwide and emphasized the Wilsonian principle of the right to self-determination of nations and the Atlantic Charter. "We shall not realize our objectives, however," he stressed, "unless we are willing to help free peoples maintain their free institutions and their national integrity against aggressive movements that seek to impose upon them totalitarian regimes." Address of the President of the United States: Recommendation for Assistance to Greece and Turkey, 12 March 1947, Truman Doctrine Documents, www.trumanlibrary.org.
25. "Energetic Diplomat, William C. Bullitt, First U.S. Envoy to Soviet Dies", *New York Times*, 16 February 1967, pp. 1, 44. It is worth noting that after the World War I Armistice, President Woodrow Wilson took Bullitt to Europe as part of the delegation. Bullitt served as chief of the Division of Current Intelligence Summaries, a position from which he resigned to protest the terms of the Treaty of Versailles, about which he famously stated that he saw "at least eleven wars in it".
26. "Political Hesitation in Hungary", Document #2513S 22, September 1944, Office of Strategic Services: Research and Analysis Branch, United States Government, Confidential, www.archives.gov. The author accessed this OSS document at the NARA website before 2001. In 2007 it was no longer accessible there, and the author could not locate at any other site. It may have been re-classified.
27. It should be noted that it was not just the Hungarian groups that were fraught with infighting. The extensive papers of Stefan Osusky (Minister of State of the Czechoslovakian Government in Exile and long time Czechoslovak delegate to the League of Nations) at the Hoover Institution Archives at Stanford University detail more than just his early opposition to Eduard Beneš's pro-Russian policies. The biographical file also includes legal documents "which demonstrate, among other things, the lack of ability of the Czechoslovak émigré community to stop engaging in bitter personal fights and start to unify and coordinate the activities of the Czechoslovak exiles." Blanka Pasternak, "Scope and Content Note: Stefan Osusky, A register of his papers in the Hoover Institution Archives", Hoover Institution Archives, Stanford University, 1999.
28. Stanley M. Max, *The United States, Great Britain, and the Sovietization of Hungary 1945–1948* (Boulder and New York: East European Monographs, distributed by Columbia University Press, 1985), p. 143.

CHAPTER 1

Tibor Eckhardt's Family History and Early Political Career

Born in Makó, Hungary (Csanád County), on 26 October 1888 to a family strongly rooted in the Hungarian gentry,[1] Tibor Eckhardt, whose full name was Tibor József Ákos Eckhardt de Posonyi, was the son of Róza Ugron and Oszkár Eckhardt. His father's family originally immigrated to Hungary from Bavaria. His great-grandfather, János Eckhardt, owned paper mills in the Austrian province of Bukovina.[2] His grandfather Vilmos (Wilhelm) Eckhardt (néhai Eckhardt Vilmos, százados) was a "Riding Master First Class"[3] in the Austro-Hungarian Army and held the rank of captain in an Austrian cavalry regiment.[4] Eckhardt's paternal grandmother was néhai pozsonyi Jozefa Eckhardt. On 26 February 1882, Emperor Franz Joseph I gave permission to the mayor of Makó to grant the honor of Hungarian nobility to the family. Eckhardt's father, Oszkár Eckhardt, born in 1853 and a landowner in Makó, selected posonyi as the "előnév", and thereafter it was used by the family.[5] He died in 1902 at the age of forty-eight.

Tibor Eckhardt was descended on his mother's side from the Ugrons, a Transylvanian family that traces its lineage back to the Hungarian conquest in the ninth century A.D. They settled on an estate in Szombatfalva, Udvarhely County, and lived there until the Soviet Army drove them off their land in 1945.

Tibor Eckhardt's godparents were Ákos Ábrafalvi Ugron, a member of Parliament (országgyűlési képviselő), and Sarolta Felsőbükki Nagy. Notable members of the Ugron family have included senators, archbishops and leaders of armies.[6] His father and his mother's older brother Gábor Ugron (the great Hungarian nationalist politician who advocated Hungarian separation from its Austrian "partner" and the Dual Monarchy), were both strong early influences in fostering Tibor Eckhardt's political interests. Gábor Ugron appears to have served as a role model for young Tibor's early political ambitions, even though he passed away when his nephew was just seventeen years of age.[7]

Eckhardt recounts in his memoirs, *Tibor Eckhardt in His Own Words*, that his father was a successful and affluent landowner and farmer in the Makó region, farming land that had been in his family for generations and shipping their famous Makó onions all over the world. Oszkár attended high school in Szeged and Pozsony and received his university diploma in Pozsony. Beyond his agricultural interests, Oszkár Eckhardt was very involved in political life and served as a member of the county governing body and the Makó city government. Eckhardt's father was also president of the local Independence and 1848 Party, "Függetlenségi és 48-as Párt". In addition to business and politics, he was heavily involved with horse breeding and served as president of the horse breeders' association as well as head of the governing body of the földeáki Roman Catholic Church.[8]

Tibor Eckhardt was first exposed to international travel during his childhood, as his family usually spent summers in Italy and sometimes on the French Riviera. He writes in his memoirs that his grandmother and mother often traveled to Paris and Berlin to attend the opera or other cultural events. From the time Eckhardt was a small child, he was comfortable functioning in societies and situations outside of his homeland and his multi-cultural exposure had steeped him in languages. He spoke German and French fluently and later became proficient in English.[9]

There were four children in the Eckhardt family. Tibor's older sister Marika (Mariska) was born in 1887, followed by Tibor in 1888 and Vilmos in 1889. Another sister, Ilona, was born in 1892. Marika married Sándor Betégh, a marriage that produced three children, two of whom, Sándor (named for his father) and Rozalina, lived to adulthood. Marika passed away in 1972 and is buried in Szengyel, the small Romanian town where she lived (located between Kolosvár and Marosvásárhely). Vilmos lost the family fortune during the world wide Depression. He never married and died during the inter-war period, as did Ilona, who also did not marry.[10]

Tibor Eckhardt's Family Life

Tibor Eckhardt was married three times. His first marriage, to Erzsébet Vásárhelyi of Budapest, is confirmed in a book published in 1913 on noble families in Csanád County.[11] Eckhardt's son, Tibor Eckhardt Jr., told me that although this early marriage to an "actress" had been mentioned in the family, his father never discussed it with him. During our interviews, Tibor Eckhardt Jr. indicated that he did not have any details confirming that the marriage actually had taken place.[12] For some unknown reason, Eckhardt's first marriage seems to have been dropped from his personal history. However, the author's recent personal interviews with Eckhardt descendants living in Hungary have revealed details of this marriage and subsequent divorce. According to family accounts, Erzsébet Vásárhelyi Eckhardt apparently could not have children, which was one of the reasons for the breakup of their marriage. The most important reason, however, was that Tibor Eckhardt was very absorbed with his career and neglected his wife. She was often thrown into the company of Eckhardt's secretary, Géza Weckerle, and they began an affair. A scandal ensued, she and Eckhardt were divorced, and she subsequently married Weckerle. After his death, she moved to be with her mother in Nyáregyház.[13]

Eckhardt's second marriage was to Baroness Ellen Podmaniczky, a union that produced first a daughter, Ilona, born 10 August 1926, and then a son, Tibor Jr., born 3 March 1928. Baroness Podmaniczky had previously been married to an Englishman, Colonel H.M. Graham, and she had two sons by him. The elder son from that union, Robert, went to live with his father after the divorce, and Tibor Eckhardt raised the younger son, Douglas John, as his stepson.[14]

Although he and his family led a life of privilege, neither Eckhardt nor his wife was more than well to do financially. They appear to have lived on Eckhardt's earnings and to have had no great family wealth. They lived in a portion of Eckhardt's cousin's home, and though they employed household staff, including a cook, their financial situation was such that Ellen Eckhardt was not above asking influential friends for items that were difficult or expensive to obtain in Hungary. More than once she wrote to John Montgomery, the American minister to Hungary who along with his wife had become close family friends, to request favors. In one instance, she asked for the tea and coffee from the Montgomery's pantry when they were returning to the United States, saying in her note, "my supplies are running low and we cannot afford the price of these articles as sold in the stores."[15]

Ilona, Tibor Eckhardt Jr. and Douglas Graham were all three fated to spend the years of World War II in Hungary with their mother, while Eckhardt was in the United States. Eckhardt left Hungary for the United States in 1941, having been assigned by Admiral Horthy and Prime Minister Count Pál Teleki to try to establish a beachhead for a Free Hungarian movement among the million or so American Hungarians then living in the United States. In addition, Eckhardt was to attempt to move Hungary over to the Allied side, a task that still seemed minimally possible when he set forth, though when he arrived in America six months later the window of opportunity had closed. The Hungarian leadership was aware of Eckhardt's strong personal relationships with influential Americans, among them John Flournoy Montgomery and his predecessor as U.S. minister to Hungary, Nicholas Roosevelt.[16]

Eckhardt was roundly chastised by many in Hungary for abandoning his family and emigrating during the war, but it is clear from his son's recollections that that was not the case. Eckhardt's trip was planned as an extensive mission abroad for the Hungarian government, with no intention of emigrating. Eckhardt was well aware that he might be away for several years on this assignment, but his son remembers him leaving that day as if he were departing on a normal business trip. There were no special good-byes or a great deal of ceremony, nor did he take a lot of luggage or personal items.[17]

Tibor Eckhardt recounts in *Regicide at Marseille* that the Nazis made it difficult for him to depart from Budapest, but at that point in time he did not realize that he was leaving his homeland for good.[18] Eckhardt was not able to return to Hungary, and at the end of 1941, after he formed the Movement for Independent Hungary, he was stripped of his Hungarian citizenship. The Hungarian government felt compelled to do this in response to the Movement's anti-fascist stance. During the war, Eckhardt was often reviled in Hungary for having deserted the country and taken the easy way out by moving to the United States. In fact, he had gone abroad on what proved to be an impossible assignment from the Hungarian government and then was stranded outside of his homeland.

Prior to Eckhardt's 1941 departure from Hungary, he made arrangements for his wife to purchase a share in an exclusive women's fashion house in Budapest. Her management position in the store provided the family with an income during the war years; although after 1941 the Smallholders Party (which Eckhardt had headed before his departure) also continued to look after them, even after it became clear that Eckhardt would not soon be returning. Tibor Eckhardt Jr. recalls that his mother communicated with his father through an army military attaché at the United States legation in Budapest, a Colonel Kovacs, with whom she met on a weekly basis. In this way she was able both to provide intelligence to the U.S. government and maintain contact with her husband.[19] Eckhardt also had extremely close ties with the Polish underground, and throughout the war he communicated with his family and his diplomatic contacts around the world with the assistance of their courier network, which he describes in extensive detail in his memoirs, and for which he was exceedingly grateful.[20]

During his war years in Budapest, Tibor Jr. began his studies at the Piarista Gimnázium and attended other secondary schools in Miskolc and Budapest as well. However, the war and the need to keep him in hiding severely fragmented his education. Because the family felt that he was in mortal danger as the namesake of a famous dissident politician who had left the country, Tibor Jr. spent the later war years being shuttled from hiding place to hiding place in Budapest and the countryside by friends of his father and Smallholders Party loyalists. Near the end of the war, while in hiding in a Swedish safe house in Budapest, he was taken prisoner by Russian soldiers, who had just liberated Budapest, and with 20,000 others was placed in a POW camp in Gödöllő on the city's outskirts. The conditions in the camp were extremely harsh. It was January 1945, bitterly cold, and all the windows had been blown out of the building where he was housed. The interned men slept on the floor, so crowded together that they could turn over only in unison.[21]

Eckhardt learned in March of his son's imprisonment and through his high-level connections at the U.S. Department of State began an urgent campaign to secure his son's release. Young Tibor, however, had managed his own escape from the camp at the end of January. On the instruction of a Hungarian interpreter working within the camp, during roll call Tibor Jr. answered to the name of a Ukrainian detainee who was part of a group of Ukrainians and Ruthenians who had been in German slave labor brigades and were scheduled to be released. Thus, Tibor Jr. was allowed to leave the POW camp. Unable to obtain help from the local peasants, who slammed the door in his face, he made his way on foot over one hundred kilometers from Gödöllő to Miskolc, where, earlier in the war, a Miskolc Smallholders party leader, a friend of his father, had helped Tibor Jr. hide out.

New archival documents also show not only that Tibor Sr. received the assistance of the Smallholders officials in Hungary but also that the plan for Tibor Jr.'s release (which had no need for implementation, as Tibor Jr. had already left the camp) was arranged through the intervention of Howard Travers, then chief of the Visa Division at the Department of State, and Ambassador Edwin C. Wilson, a U.S. diplomat who was a close friend of Eckhardt. The highest levels of the State Department were involved in the plan, including intelligence personnel that the U.S. had on the ground in Hungary. Later that spring, Tibor Jr. made his way to Budapest and was reunited with his mother and sister. The U.S. State Department then offered to fund the Eckhardt family's travel out of Hungary.[22]

Tibor Jr.'s mother and sister left Hungary through official channels and traveled to Paris after the post-war elections. Because it was thought that as Eckhardt's son Tibor Jr. remained in mortal danger, the young man could not leave Hungary by conventional means. Eventually, he was smuggled into Italy in a boxcar on a train full of Italian POWs being repatriated from Soviet captivity. Eckhardt orchestrated his son's departure from Hungary with Zoltán Pfeiffer, a prominent leader of the Smallholders Party. Young Tibor arrived in Italy with no papers, having been told to report to the American consulate in Naples, where he would receive a visa to the United States. Although he could not speak Italian, he found his way there only to learn that the diplomatic staff had not been notified to expect his arrival and had no information about a visa for him. He made his way to Rome, having been given the address of the former Hungarian ambassador to Italy, who had remained there after his service ended. The former ambassador arranged for Tibor Jr. to stay at Hungarian House in Rome and obtained a Swedish Emergency Passport for him. His frayed Swedish identity papers, issued on 20 December 1945, still exist and bear immigration stamps from Italy and France; they remain a reminder of the turbulent times that constituted Tibor Jr.'s teenage years and of his family's emigration from Hungary.[23]

Tibor Jr. was able to contact his mother and sister after their arrival in France, and in April he received permission from the French Consulate in Rome to travel to France. Given directions how to make his way from Rome to Paris, he met up with his sister and mother and they all soon departed for the United States. Upon their arrival in New York, the family's visa documents were found to have some irregularity, and they had to spend their first night in the United States on Ellis Island.[24]

Tibor Eckhardt Jr. volunteered for the U.S. Air Force in 1948, and during the Korean War he was based in Japan with the Far East Air Force (FEAF). There, he met his future wife, Myoko Vakui, the daughter of a pharmaceutical manufacturer who had previously served as an official on the Manchurian railroad. The Vakui family was originally from Hokkaido, and Myoko Eckhardt has a sister still living in Japan.[25]

Tibor Eckhardt Jr. served in the Air Force until April 1952, when he returned to the United States with his wife. Thereafter, he worked in various capacities in accounting and office management, first in Seattle and subsequently in New York City. The Eckhardts have no children and in 1985 moved to Florida, where they presently reside.[26]

Tibor Jr. was close to his father and kept in constant touch with him from the time he returned from Japan until Dr. Eckhardt passed away. A few years before his death, Dr. Eckhardt addressed a warm and touching letter to his son. Its text, written to serve as a will, attests to the closeness of their relationship and Eckhardt's realistic and somewhat poignant view of his own legacy:

> Dear Tibi, ... in a few words I would like to tell you what I would like done in the event of my death. ...
> I have no assets so I am not writing a formal will. On my gravestone, please have my name inscribed in Hungarian and the day of my death in English. My books and writings I leave in your care—they are my only assets. ... My only wish: when Hungary is free again, I would like my final resting place to be in my homeland ... in Free Hungary, in Makó ... . With love, your Papa.[27]

Ilona Eckhardt worked at various fashion houses and high-end stores in the United States before marrying Michael Healey, scion of an old and established Bradford, Pennsylvania family. The childless couple moved to Italy in the 1960s, where some years later Michael Healey took his own life. Ilona died in Camogli, Italy in early 1985.[28]

In New York, Ellen Podmaniczky Eckhardt continued to work in the fashion business, as she had in Budapest, holding various sales positions at Saks Fifth Avenue and B. Altman department stores during the 1940s and '50s. She spent her later years working at the Metropolitan Museum Gift Shop in Manhattan, a job from which she derived a great deal of pleasure. She passed away in October 1981 in Denver, Colorado, where she had moved to live with her younger son from her first marriage, Douglas Graham. Douglas, whom Tibor Eckhardt had adopted, graduated from the Technical University of Budapest in 1944 and lived in England immediately after the war, serving the British in military intelligence. After graduating from the London School of Economics in 1952, he moved to United States, where he lived in New York and then Colorado before moving to Florida, where he now resides.[29]

Ellen Eckhardt's oldest child, Robert, left Hungary before the war in the custody of his father, Colonel H.M. Graham, a member of the British military who was said either to have come from Rhodesia or have been posted to that country. Robert is said to have died as a pilot for the Allies in World War II.

After Eckhardt's family joined him in America, he and Ellen came to realize that their marriage was on very rocky ground. They lived together in Manhattan for approximately six months, and when it became clear that the marriage was no longer workable, Eckhardt set up his family in a separate apartment in New York City. He did not divorce Ellen until 1957, almost a decade later and just prior to his third marriage.

Eckhardt's third wife was Judy Alice Dwyer of New York, a beautiful American much younger than he. They married on 29 June 1957.[30] Judy was highly regarded by all members of the family, and by Tibor Eckhardt Jr.'s account this marriage was a happy one, unlike the fractious relationship that prevailed between his parents. The marriage lasted until Judy's untimely death in 1966, six years before Tibor Eckhardt himself passed away. Tibor Jr. recalls that his father and stepmother had met in Washington, D.C., where they both lived in the same hotel or apartment building.

Although he would have been eligible earlier, Eckhardt delayed applying for his American citizenship until 1953, waiting until after he resigned his position on the executive committee of the Hungarian National Council (also known as the Hungarian National Committee)—the leadership of which was composed of émigré leaders who were not American nationals. As his Hungarian citizenship had been revoked in 1941, Eckhardt remained officially stateless until he became an American citizen on 15 April 1955.[31] It was an achievement of which he was very proud and one that the anti anti-communists had been unable to prevent.[32]

Tibor Eckhardt died in his apartment in New York City on Sunday, 3 September 1972 of a heart attack at the age of eighty-three.[33] After a funeral mass held at St. Stephen's Roman Catholic Church in New York the following Saturday, he was buried in Saint Raymond's Cemetery in the Bronx, New York, alongside his wife Judy.

Eckhardt's Political Life and Career in the Inter-War Period

Educated in Budapest, Paris and Berlin, Eckhardt earned his first doctorate, in political science (államtudomány), from Pázmány Péter Tudományegyetem in 1910. In the 1920s he also received a doctorate of laws degree. In Paris he studied at the Sorbonne and in Berlin at the University of Berlin. His early career as a government official began with the position of szolgabíró (deputy sheriff) in his home county, and from 1913 on he served in the division of the Hungarian Ministry of the Interior that was responsible for administering the counties (vármegyei osztály). In his first assignment he was attached to the general staff of the Austro-Hungarian Army, and his last appointment, in 1918, was as főszolgabíró (chief constable or high sheriff) of Torda-Aranyos County.[34] Eckhardt wrote: "At the age of twenty-five, from the first to the last day of WWI, I served for two years as aide to the High Commissioner of Transylvania also in charge of liaison with the 15th (Transylvanian) Army Corps. Then for two more, trying years I was elected as the Administrator of a mountain district in Transylvania, inhabited mainly by Romanians."[35]

Dr. Ottó Hámos, president of the American Hungarian Library and Historical Society in New York, recalls that Eckhardt told him that at the end of First World War he left Transylvania in his horse-drawn coach, riding with a rifle across his knees to protect himself and his coachman from the marauders who preyed on travelers in those chaotic days.[36]

By 1919 Eckhardt was serving as a member of Gyula Károlyi's counter revolutionary government in Arad-Szeged, a region administered by the French as a result of the armistice. Beginning in May 1919, he served in the Arad-Szeged government until its dissolution. He first served as finance minister and then took on the additional position of press secretary, dealing with foreign affairs in the prime minister's office. He held the latter job from the end of May until the middle of July.

After Admiral Horthy became regent of Hungary in 1920, Eckhardt was appointed to a position within the Hungarian Ministry of Foreign Affairs and afterwards served in the premier's office. Regent Horthy became closely associated with Eckhardt politically in 1919, during the latter's participation in the campaign against Béla Kun's Bolshevik revolution. As early as 1920, Horthy was sending Eckhardt on missions and assignments abroad, for which his language skills and travel experience stood him in good stead.[37]

On one of his first trips in 1920, Eckhardt traveled on a sensitive assignment from Regent Horthy to meet with Crown Prince Rupprecht of Bavaria. In Bavaria, he was received in a private audience by the crown prince and heard first hand how Clemenceau had sabotaged Bavaria's plans to create a union of anti-Bolshevik Catholic South-German states. These states would then withdraw from the Reich and liberate themselves from the Marxist Prussian Republic. In their discussion of their countries' respective situations, Crown Prince Rupprecht proved particularly interested in the reconstruction of Hungary following the breakdown of the Bolshevik Kun regime. He asked Eckhardt, as someone who "played a prominent part in the successful fight against Bolshevism in Hungary", for a favor. Eckhardt quotes the request in his memoirs: "'I will ask you, therefore, to do me a favor. Baron Solden,' he turned to his aide, 'will you please see to it that Adolf Hitler visits Mr. von Eckhardt, at his convenience.'"[38]

Eckhardt recalls that it was at this meeting that he heard that name for the first time. The crown prince recognized Eckhardt's ignorance, and Eckhardt writes that the prince explained, "'Do not be surprised when you meet him. He is a simple, Austrian corporal who after the war could not yet find a regular job. But he is an efficient speaker who knows exactly how to handle the working class and their problems. He attends factory meetings in the most turbulent suburbs, according to the reports I get from everywhere, with extraordinary success. He certainly would feel gratified if you could give him advice on our reconstruction work. You may trust him,' concluded the Prince in a whisper, 'I pay him a modest monthly salary.'"[39]

The meeting between Eckhardt and Hitler occurred the next day, and they discussed the issues related to reconstruction in Hungary and Germany. Eckhardt made subsequent trips to Munich because, as he relates, "In those early post-war years, the only place in Europe where some sympathy and a faint echo to our pleas could be found, was Munich. As Chief of the Press Service of the Hungarian Ministry of Foreign Affairs, I visited Munich from time to time to maintain good relations with our anti-communist friends there."[40] On a visit in the fall of 1920, General Franz Ritter von Epp asked Eckhardt to accept an invitation from Hitler to dine in one of Munich's well-known beer cellars. Hitler wanted to introduce Eckhardt to some of his closest collaborators, who by that time had already accepted Hitler as their Führer. A third meeting with Hitler occurred in spring 1923. Eckhardt disassociated himself from Hitler after the brazen attempt of 9 November 1923 to lead the storm troopers to the Feldherrenhalle and the disgraceful end of the Beer Hall Putsch, which revealed Hitler's true intentions to Prince Rupprecht and his loyal anti-Communist supporters. In Eckhardt's view, Hitler "had demonstrated that it was not at the service of a worthy cause, but for the sake of personal power that he was ready to take senseless risks."[41]

Almost a decade later, in mid-September 1932, Eckhardt was again in Munich when "Hitler called me up unexpectedly. 'I read in the papers that you are in Munich. Why don't you come to see me? I want to show you around in my Party's new home, the Braunes Haus; it has just been completed.'"[42] This was to be Eckhardt's last meeting with Hitler, and at it Hitler revealed the extent of his perverted ambition and his plans for Germany. Eckhardt describes the meeting in great detail in his memoirs, saying he came away from it with a horrendous fear of what Hitler would bring upon the European continent in implementing his plans. Recounting some of the dialogue from that meeting, Eckhardt writes that Hitler talked about invading Austria, saying, "The Austrians will belong to Germany! What do I care about sympathies? Do I have time to wait for sympathies to mature? Let me tell you this: sympathy is a very slow motor! And believe me, the most speedy, the most powerful motor of human actions, which brings results, is hatred! Vengeance against a common foe will bring allies and rapid success."[43] Eckhardt was astonished by Hitler's hysteria, but he was also convinced that nothing would stand in the way of his ambition.

Reflecting on the meeting with Hitler, Eckhardt wrote,

> Two hours had passed in lively debate and I had learned enough. I felt that nobody could ever convince Hitler [of his errors], he had no policy, he had fabricated a creed! Success had spoiled him, by hook and by crook, the Austrian Corporal had steadfastly developed into a leader of the strongest nation in Europe and patiently formulated the offensive aims of Nazism. He had reduced the cure of worldwide grave problems into simple slogans, which would appeal to his disgruntled people. My exit was quite unfriendly—he did not escort me downstairs to the door. But as I shortly walked out of the "Brown House," in the descending twilight, I again caught sight of him. He was ruminating in the backyard, impa-

> tiently kicking pebbles with head bowed, deep in thoughts. "A crazy fellow," I muttered, "smitten with sinister complexes of grandeur and national salvation. But what wild energy! The worst about him is that he will act exactly as he says. And we will [be] damned if he arrives at the top!" That was the last time I saw Adolf Hitler.[44]

As a result of this disturbing meeting and what it revealed of Hitler's plans, in October 1932 Eckhardt drafted a detailed memorandum for the Hungarian government. Its main points were: "1) That Hitler's ascendance to the Chancellorship of the German Reich seemed probable; 2) That he was an adventurer and his ambitions were excessive; 3) Austria would become an early victim of Nazi aggression; 4) Hitler might try to come to terms with England but would not shrink away from using force to achieve his exaggerated ambitions."[45] In a final sentence, he explicitly warned the Hungarian government against forming any close ties to Hitler. After Hitler was appointed Germany's chancellor on 30 January 1933, Eckhardt refused to participate in the Hungarian delegation led by Prime Minister Gömbös. Eckhardt relates that after that day he became a favorite target of the Nazi press, particularly the *Essener Zeitung*, Göring's paper, even though Eckhardt believed that Hitler held him in fairly high regard. Eckhardt based the latter belief on the fact that on the day of his appointment, Hitler sent Eckhardt a personal telegram formally announcing the event.[46] Hitler knew of Eckhardt's opposition to him, and it seems more likely that the telegram was fair warning of Hitler's power and what was to come. Eckhardt's opposition was later very much in evidence, as was the Fascists' goal to discredit and destroy him and the Smallholders Party.

Eckhardt in Elected Office

Eckhardt's parliamentary career began when he was elected as a member of the Christian Smallholders Party (Keresztény Kisgazdapárt) in 1922; he joined the Opposition Party in 1923.

Although he is often accused of having been one its founding members in 1918, Eckhardt actually did not join the Ébredő Magyarok Egyesülete (ÉME), a right-wing group, until 1923. He became its president in December of that year.[47] Known as the Fajvédő Párt, it had a strong anti-Semitic ideology and catered to the political views of disenfranchised Hungarians who felt strongly that they were being pushed aside in their own country by the strength of the Jewish financial and industrial aristocracy. In its early years, the group committed atrocities and clamored for anti-Jewish legislation. Eckhardt later explained that he joined the ÉME at the specific request of Prime Minister Count István Bethlen, who had asked him to do so with the express purpose of liquidating the organization.

As journalist Paul Nadanyi, author of *The "Free Hungary" Movement*, wrote in 1942, "This statement is borne out by the fact that one of Eckhardt's first acts as president was to call the Minister of Interior in charge of the police, inform him on where to find the weapons and ammunition to disarm the organization. After Eckhardt took over the Presidency, the terrorist activities of this organization actually ceased. Thus in a measure he helped to break up the most dangerous of all White Terrorist groups, which defamed Hungary in the eyes of the civilized world."

Although during the inter-war years Eckhardt and Count István Bethlen did not see eye to eye and viewed the solutions for Hungary's problems from a different perspective, there is no question that their goals were always the protection and preservation of the Hungarian nation (nemzetvédelem). It was for this reason that Bethlen asked Eckhardt to step into a role with the ÉME organization, to neutralize and control their activities. Eckhardt recognized the damage that the ÉME was causing Hungary, both within the country and in the view of the outside world, and he undertook the assignment. As is evidenced by the actions he took as the ÉME leader and by the fact that the organization ceased its violent activities, he achieved what the prime minister had asked of him.[48]

Eckhardt's Early Trips to America: The Revisionist Movement

Dr. Eckhardt first visited the United States on private business in 1928, and in 1929–1930 he spent five months there lecturing in many U.S. cities under the auspices of the Carnegie Endowment for International Peace, a private non-profit organization dedicated to advancing cooperation between nations and promoting active international engagement by the United States. The endowment was founded in 1910 by industrialist and philanthropist Andrew Carnegie and continues its mission to the present day.[49] Eckhardt's lecture series was entitled "Seeds of a Second World War" and focused on the growing reactions against the post-war peace treaties of Europe.[50] During this period he also lectured at the Royal Institute of International Affairs in London and at the University of Glasgow.

In 1928, the year of its founding, Eckhardt became the executive vice president of the Revisionist League.[51] A centerpiece of his "Peace Treaties of Europe" lectures was to stress the need to revise the Treaty of Trianon. In Hungary Trianon was overwhelmingly the number one political issue during the inter-war period, as it was among the majority of Hungarian émigrés and people of Hungarian extraction living throughout the world. Sentiments against the terms of the treaty had been extremely strong throughout the Hungarian Diaspora even while the Trianon negotiations were still underway. Prior to the actual signing of the accord, Eugene Pivany wrote a major treatise against it on behalf of the Hungarian American Federation; it was published in the United States in 1919.[52] Ladislas Buday, the former director of the Hungarian Central Office of Statistics, protested the treaty in "Dismembered Hungary", which was published in July 1922. Translated into English, it was distributed to university libraries in the United States as gifts of the author.[53]

Observers of events in Central Europe often characterize the Hungarian preoccupation with Trianon as something of a mania, but the fact remains that any number of prominent non-Hungarians who were active participants in the events of the times expressed the same sentiments. For example, as he was leaving his post in Hungary, Major General H.H. Bandholtz, who represented the United States on the Inter-Allied Military Mission in Hungary in 1919–1920, wrote in his diary entry dated 5 February 1920:

> Personally I came here rather inclined to condone and extenuate much of the Roumanian procedure, but their outrageous conduct in violation of all international law, decency, and humane considerations, has made me become an advocate of the Hungarian cause. Turning over portions of Hungary with its civilized and refined population will be like turning over Texas and California to the Mexicans. The Great Powers of the Allies should hang their heads in shame for what they allowed to take place in this country after an armistice. It would be just as sensible to insist also that Switzerland, on account of her mixed French German and Italian population, be subdivided into three states, as to insist upon the illogical ethnographic subdivision and distribution of the territory and people of old Hungary.[54]

While Bandholtz saw both the positive and negative sides of the Hungarians and their situation, which he also addresses in his diary, he makes his sentiments on the issue of Trianon clear. Clearly it is a misrepresentation to assert that only the Hungarians were distressed over Trianon.

Although the topic of treaty revision was in the forefront early on, the Revisionist League itself was not formed until 1928. Under the conservative government of Prime Minister Bethlen (1921–1931), policy was centered on stabilizing the country economically and politically. Despite strong revisionist sentiment, for fear of arousing people's expectations, revision of the Treaty of Trianon was not included in the government program until 1932, when Gyula Gömbös became prime minister. Even in 1932, however, the government only presented a limited program centered on the defense of the rights of the Hungarian minorities under foreign rule.

Despite the overwhelming strength of revisionist sentiment among Hungarians at home and abroad, the worldwide publicity movement in support of revision was initiated neither in Hungary nor by Hungarians. It began when England's Lord Rothermere (Harold Harmsworth, first Viscount Rothermere), a press baron and one of the wealthiest men in the British realm, became interested in the consequences of the Paris peace treaties.[55] His fascination with the subject led him to travel incognito to Hungary along with some of his staff to investigate the impact of the new frontiers. Finding the situation even more devastating than he initially expected, he published his findings in the 21 June 1927 issue of his London newspaper, the *Daily Mail*, in an article entitled "Hungary's Place Under the Sun".

Eckhardt wrote that when word of the article reached Hungary and Hungarians had an opportunity to read it, "the unvarnished truth, coupled with the demand for justice for Hungary and stated by so influential a person, set free an outburst of repressed feelings, of renewed hope and of deep gratitude."[56] The Hungarians, seemingly abandoned by the West and hemmed in by the antagonistic Successor States, had found a champion for the revisionist cause, and the movement spread like wildfire.

Eckhardt was spurred to arrange a meeting with Lord Rothermere in Paris. Eckhardt first of all wanted to convey the Hungarians' thanks and gratitude, but he also wanted Rothermere's input on how to "direct the aroused Hungarian energies toward constructive and realistic national goals."[57] At the meeting, they agreed that the "Hungarians would organize a broad popular movement, based on Article XIX of the Covenant of the League of Nations, to carry out a campaign among the victorious powers for the peaceful revision of the Trianon Treaty through orderly processes of international law."[58] Lord Rothermere pledged the support of his newspaper empire to further the cause of revision.

Within a month, the Hungarian League for Revision (Magyar Revíziós Liga) was established with a broad base of support that transcended political parties, religious denominations and social strata. Labor unions, cultural associations and professional organizations all supported it. The labor unions contributed a large part of the League's funding, as they understood only too well what it meant to be cut off not only from their people but also from the sources of raw materials and potential markets.

Although the government preferred not to sanction the League officially, in order to avoid creating problems with the Little Entente, it nevertheless fulfilled a need. All of the patriotic organizations with irredentist agendas now became part of the League, and their efforts on behalf of revisionism were channeled and controlled through the organization.

Well-known author Ferenc Herczegh was president of the Revisionist League and devoted his considerable energies to its cause. Tibor Eckhardt served the organization, pro bono, as executive vice president from the League's inception until he left for America in March 1941.

Eckhardt felt that the efforts of the League helped to restore legality and order in Hungary. The dispossessed refugees, the former military, the unemployed youth, all grasped onto the idea of revision as the hope for improving their lives. "The ex-officers' groups gave up their plans of armed invasion and no individual attempt at terrorism was ever conceived in Hungary," Eckhardt wrote. "It was the hope attached to Article XIX of the Covenant of the League of Nations, which induced the Hungarians not to take the road the Yugoslavs were soon to choose. No act of violence was committed between the two World Wars by Hungarians against any of their oppressors. But the people of Hungary stood unanimously and firmly by 'their single demand: the equitable revision of the unjust Trianon settlement by peaceful means.' This was not warmongering, it was the only possible peace policy."[59]

Although the cause of revisionism united nearly every political and social faction and eliminated all adventurism in Hungary, the French Little Entente Alliance denounced it as warmongering and provocation. As Eckhardt pointed out, the irony of this was that at the same time Hitler was thumbing his nose at the restrictions of the treaty and preparing his nation for war!

The campaign to stop the program of Hungarian revisionism came about not because revisionism was a threat to peace but because Rothermere's support had brought the mistreatment of Hungary onto the world stage. In 1934 three of the parties in England's House of Commons (a total of 240 members) favored revising the treaty. Revision had the support of prominent figures in Italy and France as well. As early as its 1924 Fifth Party Congress, the Soviet Union had approved the demand "that the Hungarian populated Czechoslovak, Romanian and Yugoslav territories be re-annexed to Hungary".[60] Later of course, as Eckhardt observes, this policy was quickly forgotten when the highway into Central Europe was opened to them during the Teheran Conference.

As a result of his outspoken support, Lord Rothermere became the toast of Hungary and was even spoken of as a possible candidate for election as king of Hungary, although this was not taken seriously by anyone except those who had much to gain by flattery. Eckhardt and the Hungarian leadership chose to view Lord Rothermere's involvement with the revisionist cause in a positive light, for his participation and support had moved their cause into the international spotlight. However, the origins of the Englishman's interest in the cause have been ascribed to various motives: his desire to right an enormous wrong; the influence of his lover and accomplice Princess Stephanie von Hohenlohe; and/or his own incredible ambition. The facts are clear that Stephanie von Hohenlohe influenced Lord Rothermere to support the Hungarian cause, both at the beginning of their acquaintance and during their subsequent personal and business relationship.

Rothermere and the princess met on the French Riviera in 1926, and she made her first trip to Hungary on his behalf sometime in April 1926, as a surviving letter dated 30 April of that year attests. According to the Hohenlohe Papers in the Hoover Institution Archives, she was not financially compensated for her first years of assistance to Rothermere, however in 1931 she encountered some financial difficulties and entered into a financial agreement with Rothermere to work as his paid agent.[61] This arrangement lasted from approximately 19 July 1932 to sometime in late 1938.[62] She not only acted as his intermediary with the Hungarians but also was his emissary to Adolf Hitler and various key German powerbrokers.

Their relationship ended when the princess filed a highly publicized and acrimonious lawsuit against Lord Rothermere, who by then was involved personally with the Hungarians and no longer needed her to act as an intermediary. The scandal resulting from the lawsuit made it difficult for Lord Rothermere to disengage from her, and the situation was made doubly difficult by the media interest in all that transpired between the two of them.[63] The princess's political capital eroded rather rapidly after the suit, and her questionable background, despite her morganatic marriage to a Hohenlohe, added credence to the rather sordid rumors about her double-dealing activities. Whether she was also acting as an agent for Hungary remains to be verified; she did, however, have access to and had personal meetings with Prime Minister Gömbös. In addition, the archival material shows that although she was of Austrian birth, she was travelling in the United States on a Hungarian passport when she overstayed her visa and was interned there as an enemy alien during World War II.[64]

Regardless of Stephanie von Hohenlohe's influence on Rothermere, the fact is that he did visit Hungary in 1927 and happened to be present when Hungarian irredentist groups staged a memorial in front of the Vigadó on the 4 June anniversary of Trianon. In his biography, Rothermere recalls that he was moved by the situation and saw that it was time to take action on behalf of revisionism.

During the 1930s, Eckhardt was viewed as an expert on the unsettled situation in Central Europe and was in frequent demand as a lecturer throughout Europe. In no small part, his ability to function effectively as a spokesperson for Hungary and the Hungarian Revisionist League was due to his ability to converse fluently in French, German and English—unusual for a Hungarian politician, particularly one born outside the higher nobility. He lectured in Milan and Trieste under the auspices of the Foreign Policy Association of Italy and in Vienna by invitation of the Foreign Policy Association of Austria. On 23 March 1934, he spoke on the topic in France, again at the invitation of the Carnegie Endowment. The talk was entitled

"Management of Politics and Economics in the Danubian Basin of Europe" and was delivered at the endowment's Paris headquarters on the Boulevard Saint Germain. That same year, Eckhardt also delivered a series of lectures in England and wrote any number of articles on "The Problem of the Danube Valley". His prescient views on conditions in Central Europe and the threat of Nazi Germany were a harbinger of events to come. As he stated in "The Problem of the Danube Valley", "When the Hitlerist system begins to feel that its existence is threatened from outside, it will turn its increased national energy in the direction abroad [*sic*], and in that case, as the French Revolution has shown us, a long period of war may come upon Europe, in which the German people, fired with revolutionary energy, will be capable of great achievements even in their present disarmed condition."[65]

The Smallholders Party Reorganizes: Eckhardt's Role

In 1930, Eckhardt and Gaszton Gaál founded the reconstituted Smallholders Party, Kisgazda Párt—officially, the Független Kisgazda és Földmunkás Polgári Agrárpárt, a name that was used until 1945.[66] In the autumn of 1932, Gaszton Gaál died. Ferenc Nagy, who was then the Party secretary, recounts in his memoirs that "the National Committee of the Smallholders elected its ablest and most cultured member, Tibor Eckhardt, to succeed him. Always well liked throughout the Smallholders electorate, Eckhardt's popularity mounted when he won an election, on an open ballot in the home district of the minister of agriculture against the minister himself."[67]

The Smallholders Party platform contained some basic points intended to make the life of the rural peasantry more tolerable and to give them an opportunity to participate in the nation's political life. The two key points were first, total suffrage to replace the open ballot system and second, agrarian reform in the form of redistribution of land from the large holdings to the peasantry. By 1935, the Independent Smallholders had become, in terms of numbers of registered voters, the largest party in Hungary. However, they were still having problems getting their candidates on the ballot. According to Ferenc Nagy, they ran candidates in eighty-five election districts, but could not get their candidates on the ballot in another 180 districts. That year, Prime Minister Gömbös "broke his promise to Tibor Eckhardt to submit a new law giving the secret ballot to the whole country, and the elections were held under the old law. … Of Hungary's 2.2 million voters, a half million voted the Smallholders ticket in the eighty-five districts. Accordingly, if Smallholder's candidates had been permitted in the other districts, they would have received a majority of the total vote."[68]

During this period, according to Nagy, what absorbed the party was that the "Independent Smallholders had to shoulder the responsibility of being the only democratic party in Parliament ready to fight Nazism. The Smallholders, under the leadership of Tibor Eckhardt, flung its full strength against the spread of National Socialism; but the party's efforts were ground to nothing between the government party above and the National Socialists below."[69]

Reviewing the international press of the inter-war period, it is evident that by 1937 Germany was flexing its muscles and attempting to influence Hungarian internal politics. By then, Germany's attempts were a topic of discussion not just within Hungary but also in the international press. In each of the articles on the subject that ran in the *New York Times*, Tibor Eckhardt is mentioned as the leader of the anti-Fascist faction. A front page article on 6 March 1937 headlined "Nazi Plot to Rule Bared in Hungary" quotes the Hungarian daily newspaper *Az Est* as saying that "certain extreme reactionary organizations have been trying to control political developments", and adding that "Tibor Eckhardt, leader of the Small Farmers Party, has seen Premier Kálmán Darányi and warned him to take vigorous action." The article goes into detail about pro-Nazi cells within the government and the armed forces that were "lavishly backed with German funds" with the purpose of toppling the government. The *Times* goes on to point out that Eckhardt had revealed this to Premier Darányi five days earlier and provided evidence of the widespread infiltration to the government. Count Stephen (István) Bethlen also associated himself with Eckhardt's warning and "was sufficiently alarmed by the situation to lose his usual calm and speak in the most energetic manner to Premier Darányi concerning the danger."[70]

The next *New York Times* article on the topic appeared on 13 April 1937 and was headlined "Agrarian Denounces Fascism in Hungary: Eckhardt, Party Leader, Calls on Reich to Leave Hungarians Alone to Manage Affairs". This article states, "Tibor Eckhardt, leader of the Agrarian party, who more than anyone else is responsible for the revelation of a Fascist conspiracy in Hungary, with the formation of cells within the armed forces and official bodies, again warned yesterday of the continued danger of a Fascist revolution and declared the Fascist party was receiving foreign support." Eckhardt is reported to have asserted that a "section of the government party … is hand in hand with the dangerous movement, and, under the cloak of combating communism, is organizing military formations and preparing for violence." He is then quoted as saying, "I do not know myself how long the way of evolution will remain open and the way to revolution will not be taken." He points out that the Fascists controlled "thirty-nine newspapers and other publications in the country that shower abuse on Hungary and Hungarians and stir up disorder. Whence comes the money? Part of this country's printed matter comes from abroad."[71]

On 13 November 1937 the *New York Times* wrote in an article headlined "Leniency to Nazis 'Imperils' Hungary": "Two democratic leaders, Hungary's former League representative, Tibor von Eckhardt, who heads the Small Farmers Party, and former Secretary of State Károly Rassay, Chief of the Liberals—today gave their views on the Nazi movement in Hungary and the reasons they regarded it as a growing menace to the Constitution."[72]

Thus, Eckhardt's denunciation of the Fascists was not only common knowledge in Hungary but was also becoming increasingly well publicized abroad. Under the headline "Nazi Propagandists Arrested in Hungary: Pamphlets Containing Attacks on Premier and Opposition Leaders are also Seized", page one of the 27 February 1938 *New York Times* reported on the consequences: "After Major Szálasi and more than sixty friends were arrested a few days ago and then placed under police surveillance, another group of adherents was brought to police headquarters suspected of having launched recent pamphlets against Tibor Eckhardt and other Opposition leaders as well as the British Minister, whom they charge with supporting Hungarian anti-fascist elements."[73]

In his 1942 book, Paul Nadanyi summarized the position held by the Smallholders:

> Eckhardt and his friends constituted the opposition from the right to the Bethlen government. They clamored for drastic and reactionary economic, social and political changes. The moderate nationalistic policy of the government was not satisfactory to this group. As a member of the staff of a newspaper which backed the liberal, left wing opposition to the government, the only good word I then wrote in my newspaper about Eckhardt was that he was the best tennis player among the politicians, beating even his favorite tennis partner and political adversary, the Prime Minister. His ready wit, his knowledge of the Western languages, history and literature, were qualities well appreciated by foreign diplomats, visiting statesmen —among them Ramsey McDonald—at that time head of the British Labor Party and a former Prime Minister of Great Britain.[74]

Nadanyi went on to describe his personal observations about Eckhardt's character during those inter-war years.

> Politically, the newspaper for which I wrote stood far to the left of Tibor Eckhardt, but our opposition to the ideas and policies he advocated in those days didn't lessen my appreciation of the man's character. He could have remained in an important government post and found security in the Government Party, had he been willing to remain a member and cease his sharp open public criticism. He would have retained his right to voice opposition against gov-

ernment measures and plans, but only within the councils of the Government Party. Several other politicians, much more antagonistic to the government's policies, did remain members of the Government Party, because they realized that members of opposition parties always ran risks during election campaigns. Eckhardt courageously took this risk and lost. From 1926 to 1931, he was out of Parliament, but not out of politics.[75]

Chief Delegate to the League of Nations

In 1934 and 1935, Dr. Eckhardt was appointed to serve as Hungary's chief delegate to the League of Nations, following in the footsteps of the Grand Old Man of Hungarian politics, Count Albert Apponyi. Eckhardt's close friend John Pelényi, the accomplished and highly regarded diplomat, had also served under Apponyi in Geneva (1930–1933). The Gömbös government's appointment of Eckhardt to this important and sensitive position, despite his position as a leader of the opposition in Parliament, was a great vote of confidence in him and his abilities. Eckhardt became the architect of Hungary's response to and defense against the charge brought against it in the World Court of having collaborated in the murder, in Marseilles, of King Alexander of Yugoslavia. It is to his lasting credit that Eckhardt's defense was successful and Hungary was vindicated of the charges.[76]

During his service as chief delegate, Eckhardt had the opportunity to work with both Eduard Beneš, then chief delegate from Czechoslovakia, and Anthony Eden, later foreign secretary of Great Britain. Beneš was an avowed and intractable foe of Hungary and Hungarian interests, an architect and proponent of pan-Slavism, and throughout his life a believer in the Soviet Union and the benefit of alignment with it. Although he paid lip service to the concept of a Danubian federation, his plan was for the Czechs and the other Slavs to dominate such an organization at the expense of Austria and Hungary. (After the breakdown by the victorious powers of the centuries-old unified system in Central Europe, and with France leading the charge to keep German influence at bay with the creation of the Little Entente in 1921, Hungary found itself encircled. The Entente, formed with the intention of keeping down Austrian and Hungarian power, had as its members Czechoslovakia, Yugoslavia and Romania.)

In *Recollections* Eckhardt recounts a conversation he had with Eduard Beneš in September 1934, after the Soviet Union had been admitted to the League of Nations. Eckhardt mentions that Beneš was euphoric with the knowledge that his influence would be strengthened by the Soviet presence at to the League of Nations. Beneš "imparted to me his conviction that everything would be perfect in Europe, if only we, the Hungarians, would acquiesce in our fate and give up your demand for a revision of the Trianon Peace Treaty." Eckhardt felt that Beneš really believed what he was saying, that the existing international order, guaranteed by the League of Nations, would exclude the possibility of any major change. Eckhardt writes that he then asked Beneš,

> Are you aware of what dangers threaten you from the North?... Has the time not come for you to consolidate the position of Czechoslovakia, at least on her Southern frontier, with her neighbors? Can you feel safe, while on bad terms with every one of them, not only Germany, but also Poland, Hungary, and Austria? One of them, under a leader called Adolf Hitler, has just started massive rearmament. Who will be his first victim? It will be You [*sic*], Mr. Beneš, with your friends far away and your enemies so near! And don't think that I will feel happy while You [*sic*] are being destroyed, for I know that after you it will be my turn. Would you please give serious thought to the necessity of co-operation on equal terms among the nations of the Danube Valley?[77]

Eckhardt was annoyed with Beneš, for he was acutely aware that Beneš had been the leading opponent of Danubian unity. On the other hand, the spokesperson for Danubian unity in the Prague Parliament, the Slovak leader Milan Hodža, understood as an economist that the small nations of Central Europe could only survive through cooperation with each other.

Eckhardt reports that Beneš then told him, "I know of the plans you have discussed with Hodža. ... You may even be right, but I cannot change my policy—I have gone too far in a different direction." "Gone in a different direction" was a euphemism for having thrown in his lot with his fellow Slavs, the Soviets. In the succeeding weeks and during the time Hungary was defending itself against charges of regicide in Marseilles, Beneš and his allies threw their entire weight at Hungary and at Eckhardt's attempts to defend it against those trumped up charges.[78]

In 1935 Eckhardt withdrew from his position as chief delegate to the League of Nations in order to lead the democratic opposition in Parliament. Having participated in the 1930 reorganization of the Smallholders Party and become its president in 1932, he led the parliamentary opposition from 1935 until his departure for the United States in 1941. During this period he served as a member of the Parliamentary Committee for Foreign Affairs for more than ten years.[79]

In the inter-war period, Eckhardt also served as the vice president of the Society of Hungarians *Quarterly*, editing and publishing its English language periodical, *The Hungarian Quarterly*, for five years. *The Hungarian Quarterly* was founded by István Bethlen, and on its board served such American political luminaries as Nicholas Roosevelt and George Creel, both close friends of Eckhardt.

Eckhardt contributed several articles on international affairs to that periodical as well as to other periodicals and reviews, both in English and in Hungarian. Much has been made of the differences between Bethlen and Eckhardt, stressing that they were polar opposites politically. However, Bethlen had editorial control of *The Hungarian Quarterly*, and had they truly been at loggerheads, he would not have run a profile on Eckhardt in the Spring 1938 edition—an honor previously accorded to only three other people, Regent Horthy, Count István Bethlen and Prime Minister Darányi.[80] During this time period, Eckhardt also served as the vice president of the Anglo-Hungarian Cultural Association.[81]

By 1940, Eckhardt and others in the Hungarian leadership recognized the reality of the European situation and the vise that Hungary found itself in. Evidence of Hungary's precarious position was alarmingly evident, and Eckhardt was asked to undertake a fact-finding tour of the United States on behalf of the government.

Eckhardt was no stranger to the United States, having spent many months there in 1928 and 1929–1930. His first U.S. trip was a lecture tour at various universities under the auspices of the Carnegie Foundation. In 1929 and 1930 he lectured before groups of the Foreign Policy Association–U.S.A. upon the invitation of President Butler of Columbia University. His 1940 visit was billed publicly as a personal trip, but the Hungarian Foreign Ministry Archives clearly show that he was on an official mission for the Hungarian government, and the archives state that the "sake of his objective … [is] to gain friends for Hungary."[82]

Eckhardt arrived in the United States on 6 April and stayed until 15 June. John Pelényi, who was then serving as the Hungarian minister in Washington, D.C., made the arrangements for Eckhardt's tour sub rosa, as it was not an official mission. Nevertheless, it included several high-level meetings. Eckhardt met with the executive committee of the Foreign Affairs Committee of the U.S. House of Representatives on 30 April, with the powerful editors of the *New York Times*, and with all of its overseas writers based in Washington, D.C. In Chicago, Eckhardt met with Colonel Robert McCormick, editor of the *Chicago Tribune*, and the editors of the other Chicago newspaper, as well as with political leaders such as Adlai Stevenson. In New York, he was entertained at a luncheon hosted by the chairman of the Chase National Bank, Mr. Winthrop W. Aldrich, and also including Victor Bator of the Hungarian Commercial Bank of Budapest, László Medgyessy, consul general of Hungary in New York, and Eugene Havas. In a letter to John Pelényi, the vice president of Chase National Bank wrote of the event, "Dr. Eckhardt is a very charming and understanding man and has left a very fine impression with us."[83] Eckhardt was further honored by the entire board of governors of the Federal Reserve System, who were in Washington, D.C., for a meeting. They hosted him and Eugene Havas at a luncheon. In extending the invitation, board member Chester Davis said eagerly, "Our dining rooms are closed on Saturday, but I will hold every other day open until I hear from you."[84]

Eckhardt traveled to Minneapolis–St. Paul in Minnesota and then on to California (Los Angeles and San Francisco) and Oregon (Portland). He took the time to meet Nicholas Roosevelt at his California ranch at Big Sur on the weekend of 25 May and saw George Creel and his wife in San Francisco, where he delivered a well-received lecture at the Commonwealth Club entitled "South-Eastern Europe and the Present Crisis". He returned east via the Grand Canyon, then traveled north to Denver, Colorado, stopped in Des Moines, Iowa, and finally arrived in Pittsburgh, Pennsylvania, on 5 June. He stayed there until 9 June, when he returned to New York.

Eckhardt was well received wherever he went. In a letter to Minister Pelényi, a *New York Times* foreign correspondent commented after their luncheon, "I am sure you would have been proud of the objective, non-partisan discussion of Danubian and Central European affairs which we had." Philip Brown, a former professor at Princeton University, wrote to Pelényi, "Eckhardt made a profound impression. I took Senator Walsh home and he was evidently much impressed."[85]

Professor Brown afterwards hosted a "smoker" for Eckhardt with an illustrious guest list that included several members of the House of Representatives, a senator, an undersecretary of state and a former ambassador. While in the nation's capital, Eckhardt's day and evening program was packed with luncheons and dinners with many power brokers, culminating with the most important meeting of his stay, a visit with Franklin Delano Roosevelt at the White House.

It is little wonder that given Eckhardt's enthusiastic welcome and the contacts he made in the United States in 1940, the Hungarian government had high hopes for his success when he undertook his last and most important journey on its behalf in 1941.

Endnotes

1. Tibor Eckhardt Birth Certificate, Makó, Hungary, #1230/II, Book XVI, p. 338. Duplicate copy issued on 27 September 1939 in author's possession.
2. Tibor Eckhardt, unpublished handwritten "Family History". Document in author's possession.
3. Certificate issued 1 July 1860, Linz, Austria, reading, in translation, "Rittmeister I[ter] Classe, served in the Uhlanen Regiment of Archduke Ferdinand from February 1854". Document in author's possession.
4. Halotti anyakönyvi kivonat. #275 szám. Makó majus 3 1902. Document in author's possession.
5. János Barna and Dezső Sümeghy, *Nemes családok Csanádvármegyében* (Makó: László Gaál Könyvnyomdájában, 1913), pp. 51–52.

Oszkár Eckhardt selected the "előnév" (honorific) of "posonyi" when elevated to the lower nobility. Like "von" in German or "de" in French, his choice means simply "from" Pozsony. The honorific was variously spelled "posonyi" and "pozsonyi" in documents of the day. In the above citation, it is the former, in the following citation it is the latter. I have left it as it reads in these documents, thus the inconsistency in the spelling. The official death certificate of Oszkár Eckhardt (Halotti anyakönyvi kivonat #277, issued 3 May 1902) indicates that the family of Eckhardt's paternal grandmother, néhai pozsonyi Jozefa Eckhardt, also used posonyi as an honorific.

6. Ibid.
7. László Markó, *Ki kicsoda a magyar történelemben?* (Budapest: Holnap Kiadó, 1997), p. 230.
8. Ernő Vermes, *Csanád vármegye tíz évvel Trianon után* (CsanSándord vármegye és az egyelre egyesített Arad és Torontál vármegyék revíziós emlékalbuma, 1929), p. 220.
9. Tibor Eckhardt, *Tibor Eckhardt in His Own Words*, ed. Katalin Kádár Lynn (Boulder and New York: East European Monographs, distributed by Columbia University Press, 2005), p. 36.
10. Sándor Betégh, interview by author, Budapest, 18 December 2004. Also, János Barna and Dezső Sümeghy, *Nemes családok Csanádvármegyében*, p. 52.
11. János Barna and Dezső Sümeghy, *Nemes családok Csanádvármegyében*, pp. 51–52.
12. Tibor Eckhardt Jr., interviews by author, Florida, 9–10 April 2002 and 24 April 2004.
13. Sándor Betégh, interview by author, Budapest, 18 December 2004. Mr. Betégh is the grandson of Tibor Eckhardt's sister Marika.
14. Desi Bognár, *Hungarians in America* (Philadelphia: Alpha Publications, 1971), p. 79.
15. Ellen Eckhardt to John Flournoy Montgomery, 1939, John Flournoy Montgomery Papers, "Correspondence with Tibor and Ellen Eckhardt", Box 1, Vol. II, manuscript #353, Manuscripts and Archives, Yale University Library, New Haven, Connecticut.
16. Tibor Frank, "Conversation with Mr. Tibor Eckhardt et al about going to America. Budapest, November 8, 1940", in *Discussing Hitler: Advisors of U.S. Diplomacy in Central Europe* (Budapest: Central European University Press, 2003), p. 322.

    Eckhardt always denied that he was sent by Horthy and Teleki. In *Discussing Hitler*, Dr. Tibor Frank cites documents from Minister Montgomery's confidential private papers that verify that Eckhardt was on an official mission. Dr. Otto von Habsburg shared with me that he was certain that Eckhardt was on official assignment, but that he was obliged to deny it by virtue of Hungary's alignment with Germany. At the same time that the Eckhardt trip was under discussion, sending Count István Bethlen to England was also a consideration, but ultimately Bethlen refused to leave Hungary.
17. Tibor Eckhardt Jr., interview by the author, 9–10 April 2002. For the complete text of this interview see: Katalin Kádár Lynn, "Tibor Eckhardt Jr., Youthful Recollections of World War II", *Kút* (Budapest: ELTE, BTK II évfolyam 2003 1 Szám), pp. 95–98.
18. Tibor Eckhardt, *Recollections of Tibor Eckhardt: Regicide at Marseille* (New York: The American Hungarian Library and Historical Society, 1964), p. 245. This first book of Eckhardt's memoirs details the politics of the inter-war period, the accusations that Hungary was involved in the regicide of King Alexander I of Yugoslavia, and Eckhardt's recounting of why he went to America in 1941 at the height of World War II.
19. Tibor Eckhardt Jr., interview by the author, 9–10 April 2002.
20. *Tibor Eckhardt in His Own Words*, p. 444.

21. Tibor Eckhardt Jr., interview by the author, 9–10 April 2002.
22. Ibid. Correspondence relating to Tibor Eckhardt Jr.'s release from the POW camp and his family's departure from Hungary is to be found at RG 59: General Records of the Department of State 1945–1949, Central Decimal File, Entry 205J, " Matters of Foreign or Personal Interest", NARA.
23. Emergency passport #210/1945, issued to Tibor Eckhardt Jr. on 20 December 1945, Rome, Italy. Original document in author's possession.
24. Tibor Eckhardt Jr., interview by the author, 9–10 April 2002.
25. Ibid.
26. Ibid.
27. Tibor Eckhardt to Tibor Eckhardt Jr., 19 August 1969, Personal Papers, Box 1, American Hungarian Library and Historical Society Archives, New York.
28. Tibor Eckhardt Jr., interview by author, Florida, 24 April 2004.
29. Desi Bognár, *Hungarians in America,* p. 79.
30. City of New York, Manhattan, Certificate of Marriage #68685, Marriage License #14565, 29 June 1957. Document in author's possession.
31. United States Naturalization Papers #7432920 issued in New York City to Tibor Eckhardt, 15 April 1955. Original document in author's possession.
32. Tibor Eckhardt Papers, Box 1, Folder: Biography–Extension of Stay in the United States, Hoover Institution Archives, Stanford University, Stanford, California.
33. City of New York, Bureau of Vital Statistics, Death Certificate # 156-72-11745, issued 12 September 1972. Document in author's possession.
34. Gyula Borbándi, *Magyar politikai pályaképek 1938–1948* (Budapest: Európa Kiadó, 1997), pp. 113–114.
35. *Tibor Eckhardt in His Own Words*, p. 2.
36. Dr. Ottó Hámos, interview by the author, New York, 19 November 2003. See also Dr. Hámos's introduction to *Tibor Eckhardt in His Own Words.*
37. *Tibor Eckhardt in His Own Words*, p. 1. Horthy was also Eckhardt's second wife's uncle, and he served as best man at Eckhardt's wedding to his niece, Ellen.
38. Ibid., p. 5.
39. Ibid.
40. Ibid., p. 7.
41. Ibid., p. 12.
42. Ibid., p. 14.
43. Ibid., p. 19.
44. Ibid., p. 21.
45. Ibid., p. 22–23.
46. Ibid., p. 23.
47. Hungarian National Archives (Magyar Országos Levéltár), Budapest, Ébredő Magyarok Egyesülete. P1354, 3-dik tétel. Az Ébredő Magyarok Egyesülete alapszabálya és fegyelmi rendtartása. P1354. 3-dik tétel Az ÉME története. Az alakuló Közgyűlés, p. 2. Második tétel, Az ÉME igazgatósági ülésének jegyzkönyvi kivonata, 1925, pp. 1–2.
48. Paul Nadanyi, *The "Free Hungary" Movement* (New York: Amerikai Magyar Népszava, 1942), p. 23.

49. Carnegie Endowment for International Peace Records, 1910–1954, Carnegie Endowment History, p.1, www.carnegieendowment.org/about/index.cfm?fa=history.
50. *Tibor Eckhardt in His Own Words*, p. 73.
51. Gyula Borbándi, *Magyar politikai pályaképek* (Budapest: Európa Könyvkiadó, 1997) p. 114.
52. Eugene Pivany, *Some Facts About the Proposed Dismemberment of Hungary* (Cleveland: Hungarian American Federation, 1919).
53. László Buday, *A megcsonkított Magyarország* (Budapest: Pantheon, 1921).
54. Major General Harry Hill Bandholtz, *An Undiplomatic Diary* (Safety Harbor, Florida: Simon Publications, 2000, reprinted edition), entry of 5 February 1920, p. 261.
55. Viscount Rothermere, *My Campaign for Hungary* (London: Eyre and Spottiswoode Ltd., 1939), pp. 27–28. While the official reason for Rothermere's interest in the Hungarian cause was given as having been related to the injustices of the treaties, the more personal and far more complex reasons for his involvement are explored in the following pages.
56. Tibor Eckhardt, *Recollections*, p. 95.
57. Ibid., p. 96.
58. Ibid.
59. Ibid., p. 97.
60. Endre János, *Trianon: A European Problem* (Zurich: Danubian Press, 1960), p. 14.
61. Princess Stephanie Juliana Hohenlohe-Waldenburg-Schillingsfürst to Mr. Goddard, undated, Papers of Princess Stephanie Juliana Hohenlohe-Waldenburg-Schillingsfürst, Box 1, Folder: 1939, Hoover Institution Archives, Stanford University, Stanford, California. This letter to her solicitor contains a time line of her relationship with Lord Rothermere.
62. Princess Stephanie Juliana Hohenlohe-Waldenburg-Schillingsfürst to Mr. Goddard, 9 January 1939, ibid.
63. Papers of Princess Stephanie Juliana Hohenlohe-Waldenburg-Schillingsfürst, Boxes 1–7, Oversize Boxes 1–2, Hoover Institution Archives, Stanford University, Stanford, California.
64. The Royal Hungarian Legation, London to the Consul-General for America, 24 August 1939, Papers of Stephanie Juliana Hohenlohe-Waldenburg-Schillingsfürst, Box 1, Folder: 1939. The text reads: "The Counsellor of the Hungarian Legation in London presents his compliments to the Consul-General for America, and has the honor to request him to be good enough to grant to the owner of the enclosed passport, Princess Stephanie Hohenlohe, an Hungarian subject, a visitor's visa."
65. Tibor Eckhardt, "The Problem of the Danube Valley", original typescript in English, 1934, Butler Papers, Carnegie Endowment for International Peace Collection, Columbia University Rare Book and Manuscript Library, New York.
66. Ferenc Virágh, *Makótól New Yorkig, Eckhardt Tibor, az államférfi* (Budapest: FKGP, 1998), p. 7.
67. Ferenc Nagy, trans. Stephen K. Swift, *The Struggle Behind the Iron Curtain* (New York: The Macmillan Co., 1948), pp. 24–25.
68. Ibid., p. 31–32.
69. Ibid., p. 32.
70. "Nazi Plot to Rule Bared in Hungary", *New York Times*, 6 March 1937, p. 1.

71. "Agrarian Denounces Fascism in Hungary", *New York Times*, 13 April 1937, p. 7.
72. "Leniency to Nazis 'Imperils' Hungary", *New York Times*, 13 November 1937, p. 8.
73. "Nazi Propagandists Arrested in Hungary", *New York Times*, 27 February 1938, p. 28.
74. Paul Nadanyi, *The "Free Hungary" Movement*, p. 24.
75. Ibid.
76. Tibor Eckhardt, *Recollections*, p. 227.
77. Ibid., p. 75.
78. Ibid., p. 223.
79. Varia Collection, Box 6, Folder 494, ECH–ECO, Georgetown University Library, Washington, D.C.
80. Alexander Pethő, "Tibor Eckhardt", *The Hungarian Quarterly*, Vol. IV, No. 1, Spring 1938, pp. 39–45.
81. Varia Collection, Box 6, Folder 494, ECH–ECO, Georgetown University Library, Washington, D.C.
82. John Pelényi to Dr. Zoltán de Baranyai, Royal Hungarian Consul General, 6 May 1940, Group: Foreign Ministry 106, File Group 125, Washingtoni Követség, Hungarian National Archives (Magyar Országos Levéltár), Budapest.
83. Vice President, Chase National Bank to John Pelényi, 6 May 1940, Group: Foreign Ministry 106, File Group 125, Washingtoni Követség, Hungarian National Archives (Magyar Országos Levéltár), Budapest.
84. Chester C. Davis to John Pelényi, 23 April 1940, Group: Foreign Ministry 106, File Group 125, Washingtoni Követség, Hungarian National Archives (Magyar Országos Levéltár), Budapest.
85. Philip M. Brown to John Pelényi, 23 April 1940, Group: Foreign Ministry 106, File Group 125, Washingtoni Követség, Hungarian National Archives (Magyar Országos Levéltár), Budapest.

CHAPTER 2

Tibor Eckhardt's Fourth Journey to America

After more than twenty years of distinguished, often controversial public service in Hungary, Tibor Eckhardt left his home country in 1941 for what was intended to be an extended (but not permanent) stay in the United States.

The founder (1930) and leader of the Independent Smallholders Party (Független Kisgazdapárt), Eckhardt was the leader of the opposition in Parliament when he took the rather dramatic decision to go abroad; and his motives have been cause for speculation and disinformation ever since his arrival in the United States on 8 August 1941.[1] Eckhardt traveled there without his family, which stayed behind in Hungary,[2] and he took a circuitous and dangerous route that involved stopovers in Yugoslavia, Greece, Egypt and South Africa and lasted over five months.[3]

On each of Eckhardt's previous visits to the United States, he had been well received by the American press and had conferred with political leaders and statesmen, among them President Roosevelt, with whom he met personally in 1940. During his 1940 trip, billed publicly as a personal trip, he was nevertheless on an official mission for the Hungarian government, as the Hungarian Foreign Ministry Archives clearly show.[4] During that visit, Roosevelt invited Eckhardt to return to the United States in the event that the Nazis overran Hungary.[5] Eckhardt was known to be an anti-fascist and no supporter of Hungary's alliance with Nazi Germany. It was a commonly held view that if Hungary were to be occupied by the Reich, the first two leaders sent to a concentration camp would probably be Count István Bethlen and Tibor Eckhardt. (This view is evidenced in a conversation between U.S. Minister J. F. Montgomery and Regent Horthy held in November 1940.[6])

Eckhardt's inter-war activities in Hungary are well documented and include a political shift from the extreme Right, when he was first elected to Parliament in 1922, toward what might be called the political center. After 1931 he espoused many populist causes such as land reform and the use of the secret ballot in all elections. Even those who did not necessarily agree with his political methods or his party's positions regarded Eckhardt highly as a statesman and a patriot. Indicative of this was the fact that at a most critical juncture in the country's political life, the Gömbös government appointed him, as leader of the opposition, to be Hungary's chief delegate to the League of Nations (1934–1935).

Eckhardt's inter-war public life is best viewed in the light of the times. The American leadership's attitude toward the early, far-Right years of his career seems to have been one of "forgive and forget", recognizing his achievements and acknowledging that the values that he once represented had changed. The Americans also doubtless recognized that some of the prejudices prevailing in Hungary immediately after World War I were also to be found in their own society. For example, during that same period, President Roosevelt, who was regarded as a great humanitarian and political pragmatist, chose to appoint southerner Hugo Black to the Supreme Court, knowing full well that in his youth Black had associated with the Ku Klux Klan.[7] The strongest evidence of the American acceptance and support of Eckhardt is the fact that two of his most loyal and vocal supporters and sponsors of his immigration to the United States had both been U.S. ministers to Hungary—John Flournoy Montgomery (1933–1941) and Nicholas Roosevelt (1928–1933).[8]

Given such prominent support, how and why did Eckhardt and the "Movement for Independent Hungary"—which was founded on 27 September 1941 and from which he resigned as chairman a mere ten months later—so quickly become the targets of an organized, virulent and systematic slander campaign? In part, it was because the campaign, which surfaced soon after his arrival in the United States, had actually begun even before he left Hungary.[9]

The Hungary That Eckhardt Left Behind

The aftermath of World War I left Hungary in dire circumstances as the victim of massive wartime casualties and territorial dismemberment by post-war treaties. Two thirds of her former territory was lost, leaving an estimated 3.5 million Magyars as minority populations in lands they had formerly ruled. Political instability and chaos followed the war, resulting in a weak Socialist government, followed by a disastrous six months of Bolshevik government (March–August 1919), followed by a right-wing government. In its attempts to stabilize the nation and its people, the latter instituted a backlash against the supporters of the prior regimes that was later known as the White Terror.[10]

Out of this national trauma, one issue came to the fore and remained there throughout the inter-war years: the loss of historic Greater Hungary and its Magyar population. The solution—overturning the Treaty of Trianon—was an issue that unified and absorbed Hungarians at home and abroad and overrode the domestic issues on the public agenda, many of which were remnants of the semi-feudal system that had operated in Hungary, in particular land reform and the lack of nationwide secret ballot elections. The resulting Revisionist Movement to restore Hungary's pre-Trianon territories was not part of the Hungarian government's stated policy, but it absorbed the political life of the nation and its specter dominated foreign policy considerations during the inter-war years.[11]

The Inter-War Years in America—The Cause of Trianon, a Unifying Force

The Revisionist Movement also provided the first real unifying cause for the Hungarian American émigré community and brought its disparate groups together for the first time. A large percentage of the 1.7 million Hungarians who left Europe during the Great Migration (1880–1914) and emigrated to the United States came from greater Hungary's outlying counties. In the Treaty of Trianon, these areas were made part of the successor states of Czechoslovakia, Romania and Yugoslavia.[12] No matter what their background, social status, profession, education or religion, virtually all Hungarians at home and abroad agreed that revision of the Treaty of Trianon was a just and viable cause. Revision became the rallying cry in the early years after the war, and nowhere more strongly than in America. Prominent historian Eugene Pivány returned to the United States in 1919 (after his repatriation in 1915) specifically in order to lead the Hungarian American anti-Trianon crusade. The major Hungarian-language paper, *Amerikai Magyar Népszava*, and its editor,

Géza Berkó, organized a significant demonstration in Washington, D.C., on 29 March 1920 demanding the application of the Wilsonian principle of national self determination to all of Hungary's arbitrarily detached territories.[13]

The Hungarian American communities continued their demonstrations, petitions and organized efforts throughout the 1920s, but they were also distracted by other important issues such as their assimilation into American society, most of them having decided they would not return to Hungary. Many émigrés still experienced a decided anti-Hungarian prejudice in their communities as a result of Hungary's alliances in the First World War, and there was also a prevailing racial prejudice against East Europeans in much of America. Increasing personal and group rivalries within their own communities and churches provided additional distractions, as did the awareness that by supporting revisionism they were aiding a political regime in Hungary that was far removed from the ideals of democracy and personal freedom that prevailed in America. Particularly disturbing were reports about the chaos and repression during Béla Kun's communist regime and the so-called White Terror that followed its overthrow. Political refugees from Hungary who had witnessed these events would describe them in vivid detail.

During this period, Tibor Eckhardt made his visits to the United States under the sponsorship of the Foreign Policy Association Groups and in his capacity as executive vice president of the Hungarian Revisionist League. These visits provided him with visibility and contacts with Hungarian Americans that other Hungarian politicians did not have.[14]

Despite the decline in post-war political activism among the Hungarian American communities, "the Trianon question continued to be the number one political issue among Hungarian-Americans. It remained a front page issue in most of their newspapers and in much of contemporary Hungarian-American literature."[15] This remained true through the 1920s and '30s and was a focus at the Hungarian National Congress of Buffalo (May 1929) and at the Hungarian World Congresses organized in Budapest by the World Federation of Hungarians in 1929 (22–24 August) and 1938 (16–19 August).[16] The best-known Hungarian American attempt to focus the world's attention on the issue of treaty revision was a trans-Atlantic flight by two young Hungarians, Sándor Magyar and György Endresz. On 15–16 July 1931 their single-engine plane named *Justice for Hungary* duplicated Charles Lindbergh's historic solo route,[17] making the journey from New York to Budapest in twenty-five hours and forty minutes.[18] While such attempts to spotlight the cause of Hungarian revisionism successfully created press coverage, for Hungarian Americans they were primarily consciousness-raising events and served to keep the issue alive within their communities.

In *The Hungarian-Americans*, Steven Béla Vardy writes, "The 1930's brought additional pressures and emotions to Hungarian-American society. News from Hungary was disquieting, the country was falling increasingly under the influence of Mussolini's Italy and Hitler's Germany. While this association brought some long-sought gains for the country in the form of the partial revision of her new frontiers, it also carried the country headlong into the arms of those dictators."[19] The strengthening of the radical Right's political position in Hungary brought with it the passage of increasingly repressive anti-Semitic laws (1939 and 1941) that evoked condemnation for Hungary from around the world. Nevertheless, for many Hungarian Americans the territorial gains of both the first and second Vienna Awards caused great rejoicing because for a large percentage of them it meant their home territories would return to Mother Hungary. In the first Vienna Award, 2 November 1938, the Italian-German court of arbitration returned that part of Czechoslovakia known as the Felvidék, which had a large Hungarian population. In March 1939, Sub-Carpathia (Ruthenia) was re-annexed to Hungary. In August 1940, the second Vienna Award gave back northern Transylvania together with the historic territory of the Széklers, the Székelyföld.

The 1940s—The America that Eckhardt Found

At the beginning of the hostilities that culminated in the Second World War, most Hungarian Americans were assimilated enough to regard the United States as their permanent home, with 50,000 of them serving in the American armed forces.[20] Although their American patriotism was not in question, as it had been in World War I, several branches of the Hungarian Reformed Federation sold war bonds and initiated fund raising drives for donations to buy ambulances for the Red Cross. Under the Federation's auspices, the Hungarian American community even raised the funds to build a U.S. naval ship, the USS *Kossuth*.[21]

By 1940, having been imbued with the cause of Trianon for two decades, it was difficult for Hungarian Americans to view Nazism as an even greater evil threatening their homeland. Hungarian Americans were so thrilled with the Vienna revisions of Trianon that few could see that each territory restored by the grace of Hitler was another tie binding Hungary to the fascists. This blind euphoria contributed greatly to the Hungarian Americans' general apathy toward initial attempts to garner their support for a Free Hungary movement.

The Emergence of the "Free Hungary" Movement

Nineteen forty was a critical year for Central Europe and particularly so for Hungary. A few months after the second Vienna Awards were granted on 30 August of that year, Hungary became a full-fledged member of the Rome–Berlin Fascist Axis. The failure of Mussolini's campaign against Greece made Hitler the sole master of the European portion of the Axis, and his plans to dominate the Balkans were developing in full view of the entire world. On 27 December the Hungarian government announced that the state railway would carry no private passengers for seventeen days so German troops could pass through Hungary towards Romania. At the start of the war, similar permission had been denied the Germans when their army attacked Poland. This change highlighted the reality of Hungary's compromise with fascism and prompted a front-page editorial in *Amerikai Magyar Népszava* calling for a Free Hungary movement.[22]

Headlined "The Hour has Struck", the editorial appeared on 31 December and proclaimed: "It is the historic mission of Americans of Hungarian origin to give voice to the cries of the silenced people of Hungary and to give their wholehearted effort to the liberation of their mother country which is clubbed into submission by the Nazi terror." The final paragraphs called upon the American Hungarian Federation (AHF) in Washington, D.C., to unfurl the banner of a Free Hungary movement without hesitation or delay.[23]

At that time, the American Hungarian Federation represented the three largest Hungarian American fraternal organizations (with an aggregate membership of about 80,000), as well as the major Hungarian religious denominations and local Hungarian organizations throughout the United States. Altogether there were really hundred thousand supporters of this umbrella organization, which attempted to explain Hungary's role on the side of the enemy as that of an "unwilling satellite". Most Hungarian American community leaders and the majority of the Hungarian American newspapers also espoused this view, and it was the theme of numerous memos submitted by the AHF to the United States government.

Founded in 1906, at its 1939 Pittsburgh convention the AHF had been reorganized and moved to Washington, D.C., to be near the seat of American power. From its reorganization until 1948 it was ably led by its national secretary, Professor Tibor Kerekes of Georgetown University.[24] The AHF was the organization most suited to serve as the voice of Hungarian America, for it was the largest and most centrist of their organizations and represented a mainstream cross section of its constituents. On 7 January 1941, the AHF Executive Committee sent a memorandum to President Roosevelt expressing the loyalty of the Hungarian American populace:

> American citizens of Hungarian origin learned with deep regret that the Government of Hungary found it impossible to avoid the signing of the pact with the Axis powers. It is our conviction that by the signing of this pact the Hungarian government lost its power of independent action, that the people of Hungary are no longer free to express their will and that this pact is a direct threat to the ancient independence of Hungary. Therefore, the Executive Committee of the American Hungarian Federation as representative of American Citizens of Hungarian origin, through whom also—as we sincerely believe—the silenced people of Hungary convey their thoughts and desires, consider it our sacred duty to lead a movement for the preservation of an independent Hungary and for the freedom of its people within the limitations of the Constitution and the laws of the United States.[25]

The stage was thus set for the AHF to provide the leadership to establish a Hungarian government in exile, the Free Hungary Movement. The AHF leadership also presented the declaration to Assistant Secretary of State A.A. Berle; and a few days thereafter the editors and publishers of the Hungarian-language publications in the eastern United States, except for those whose sympathies were with the Nazis or Communists, met in New York City and adopted a resolution endorsing it. The resolution emphasized "their unalterable opposition to the forces of Naziism [*sic*], Fascism and Communism and their undivided loyalty to the lofty principles upon which this great nation was founded."[26] Assured of support from the press, the AHF organized a conference to discuss ways and means to promote the "Independence for Hungary" movement.

This meeting revealed a wide range of political outlooks among the participants, but all agreed that such a movement was necessary and put aside their political differences in order to present the "Independence for Hungary" message to Americans of Hungarian origin. But although the Hungarian-language press covered the issue extensively, on the whole the Hungarian American public generally remained apathetic to the cause at this point. "The great masses failed to react. Even the members of the organizations which make up the American Hungarian Federation, were quite indifferent."[27]

In Hungary, the political situation worsened after Prime Minister Pál Teleki committed suicide on 3 April 1941. His suicide was prompted by his inability to hold Germany at bay and prevent its use of Hungary as a staging area for further military action. He was also despondent over his failure to stop the passage through Hungary of German troops to be used against Yugoslavia, with which his government had made an "eternal friendship pact" just a few months before (12 December 1940). After Teleki's death, the urgent need for a strong Free Hungary movement based in the West became increasingly evident. Free governments had already been formed by the Romanians and Czechs, following the British government's recognition of the Free French and Free Poles. The feeling among the Hungarian leadership was that Hungary urgently needed representation in the democratic West. After agreeing that Free Hungary should become a reality, they needed to decide where the organization would be based and whom they would select to lead it.

The Hungarian government considered both Tibor Eckhardt and Count István Bethlen for this assignment abroad. Originally the thought was to send both men to England. However, Eckhardt felt strongly that he could accomplish more in the United States, having already made strong contacts there on his three prior visits. Count Bethlen subsequently decided it would be unwise for him to leave Hungary.[28] Finally, it was decided that Eckhardt would go alone, and he began preparing for his last departure from his homeland.

Eckhardt went abroad as the unofficial, yet "official", representative of the Hungarian government in order to attempt to rally Hungarians abroad to the cause of Hungary. However, among the Hungarian émigrés there were several possible leaders for a Free Hungary organization whose work would not be tied to the Hungarian government. Most prominent among them was Count Michael (Mihály) Károlyi, who was then living in London. President of the short-lived Hungarian Republic after the First World War, Károlyi attempted to form a Free Hungary movement of his own in London in the late summer of 1941 and eventually gained the support of the British Foreign Office and British intelligence, which provided him with assistance and contacts through the Special Operations Executive (SOE), the precursor to the British intelligence agency MI-5. Although the British did not have much confidence in Károlyi or much hope for the positive outcome of his efforts, they gave lip service to his group, the New Democratic Hungary Movement. The SOE even attempted to help Károlyi and his wife obtain an exit permit to travel to the United States and tried to secure funding for their trip through a foundation sponsored by the American government. The purpose of the trip was for Károlyi to marshal support in person for his UK-based movement.[29] Károlyi, however, was not well esteemed in U.S. diplomatic circles. He was viewed as the leader who handed over the Hungarian government to communist Béla Kun in 1919, and the Americans didn't want one more visiting Hungarian émigré leader stirring the political pot. The Károlyis never made the trip, as the United States would not issue them visas.

British intelligence encouraged a merger between the two London based groups of Hungarian exiles, Károlyi's organization and the Antal (Anthony) Zsilinszky group (National Association of Hungarians in Great Britain). The group formed by Zsilinszky had made an alliance with the Eckhardt group in the United States once it was formed. As a criterion for the merger, Károlyi wanted Zsilinszky to disassociate himself from Eckhardt, which Zsilinszky was unwilling to do, and so the merger came to naught. Shortly afterwards, Zsilinszky committed suicide, however even Károlyi mentions in his book that its cause was personal. Originally, Károlyi's group also had the support of Count Lónyay, but they had a falling out, and Lónyay continued with an organization of his own so that for a time, there were at least three Hungarian exile groups operating in London.

Károlyi's group had supporters in America as well, including Oszkár Jászi, Rusztem Vámbéry, Pál Kéri and László Fényes. Jászi and Vámbéry were both part of the liberal Left and great advocates of social change in Hungary. Jászi had served in the Károlyi cabinet, and Vámbéry headed the criminal law department at the University of Budapest during the Károlyi administration.[30] Kéri and Fényes, Károlyi loyalists from Hungary, had a more questionable past. They had been tried for the murder of Count István Tisza, prime minister of Hungary from 1912 until 1917, who had been shot to death on the second day of the Károlyi revolution, 31 October 1918. Kéri and Fényes were both convicted. Kéri was subsequently freed from jail through an exchange agreement with the Soviet government. Fényes was also released, but details of the trial and subsequent releases are murky and controversial to this day.

The prevailing view in Hungarian America at that time, however, was that the weak Károlyi government had handed Hungary over to Béla Kun's Communist government, and Kun supporters abroad got little support from the Hungarian émigrés. Nevertheless, the United States was seen as potentially fertile ground for the Hungarian Communists' political activities. In fact, beginning in December 1941 the notorious Mátyás Rákosi, a former Kun cabinet member who had been living in exile in Moscow since his release from prison in Hungary, repeatedly pressed Georgi Dimitrov to petition the U.S. embassy to allow him to go to America to work among the Hungarian émigrés there. On 26 January 1942 Dimitrov noted in his diary, "Rakosi on Hungarian business. Again he insists on petitioning the American embassy to allow him to go to America to work among Hungarian émigrés there." This is followed by the words "Not feasible!" Although Dimitrov, Stalin's close associate and the head of the Comintern, rebuffed Rákosi's appeals, the Hungarian's continued insistence on going to American indicates how important the views and the political clout of the American Hungarian population were considered to be in the global plan to win over public sentiment among immigrants of Hungarian extraction in favor of the USSR and communism.[31]

In fact, there was real distaste for left-wing politics in the mainstream Hungarian American community, which tended toward conservatism. Prominent historian Steven Béla Vardy refers to these and subsequent émigré politicians as "heads without bodies", alluding to their lack of support among Hungarian Americans.[32] "The majority of Hungarian-Americans," Vardy writes, "were still believers and supporters of the down-to-earth Kossuthist nationalism of their immigrant forefathers and believed that Hungary's demand for territorial revisionism was simply an attempt to implement the Wilsonian principle of national self-determination. Thus they were not about to accept the leadership of persons and organizations that failed to stand up for these principles."[33]

Károlyi, however, did have the support of the Hungarian anti-monarchists, who feared the restoration of the Habsburgs to the Hungarian or Austrian throne, of the Communists, with whom he had cordial relations, and of Eduard Beneš. Beneš, president of the Czechoslovakian Government in Exile, was a powerful political force. Located in London, he was influential in West European circles and was a shrewd politician. It was clear to him that his country had a great deal to fear if the revisionist movement succeeded even in part, or if a Habsburg was ever restored to power. The Károlyi supporters and the Beneš government therefore understood that any Hungarian government in exile with royalist ties and potential populist support had to be discredited. That Beneš had close ties to Moscow was public knowledge. What was not known at the time and has been corroborated by recently uncovered documents cited in this chapter is that the USSR, which had plans for the countries on its periphery, encouraged and monitored the Czechs' efforts to discredit any strong exile movement that could return to govern post-war Hungary.[34] As early as 1942, Nadanyi also speculated about the Soviet intent, writing, "or is it that the Soviet regime is using Beneš as a tool to create chaos in central Europe; which will make it an easy prey for bolshevist revolution ... We are not fighting against the Nazis to let another totalitarian system take its place."[35]

An additional cause for alarm among the anti-monarchists was that Archduke Otto von Habsburg, the heir to the Austro-Hungarian throne, was living in the United States during the war and had ongoing contact with President Roosevelt, who made it clear to his political circle that he held the young heir in high regard. Roosevelt met with the archduke regularly, and his political confidants knew that the president entertained the idea of solving the region's problems by creating a Danubian federation or perhaps reinstalling the Habsburg dynasty in Austria and Hungary. This would, of course, de-legitimize the newly created post-Trianon states.[36] The British were very concerned about Archduke Otto and his influence and mention him regularly in their communications. An internal Special Operations Executive memorandum sent on 16 January 1942 by Major Boughey (DH 70), the head of the Hungarian desk in London, stated, "Otto now making propaganda for Eckhardt, and it seems all the more important that Eckhardt's influence should be combated in some way."[37]

While the Károlyi group did not have the support of the Hungarian Americans or the American Hungarian Federation, it was supported by left-leaning intellectuals and for a while also gained trust and support in various American political circles. These included the Movement for a New Democratic Hungary, the Federation of Democratic Hungarians and The Hungarian American Council for Democracy. "All of these, however," writes Steven Béla Vardy, who best describes their role, "were the brainchildren of recently arrived intellectuals who had no real connections with the Hungarian-American community, and whose views—however commendable in many instances—were so far removed from those of the Hungarian-American majority that they had no hope for any sort of mass support from among the latter's ranks."[38]

Clearly, all of these fringe groups and the Károlyi Free Hungary movement based in London played their most significant role as "spoilers". Their goal was to discredit and destabilize the AHF and its newly conceived Free Hungary movement and to discredit its leadership.

Eckhardt's Arrival in the United States

Eckhardt recalls that on 7 March 1941, the day he left Hungary for the United States, "more than one hundred Gestapo agents crowded the railway platform in Budapest with orders to prevent my departure, if need be, even by force." He managed to get away thanks to his friend József Sombor, the chief of the Budapest police force, who provided twice as many detectives as the Gestapo had agents.[39] As a mark of their regard for Eckhardt, American Minister to Hungary John Flournoy Montgomery and the staff of the American legation were on the platform to see him off.[40] While the number of Gestapo agents referred to by Eckhardt may be an exaggeration, it was indeed difficult for him to depart Hungary and then Europe, as evidenced by his circuitous, nearly six-month-long route through Egypt and South Africa. Herbert Pell, the last pre Pearl Harbor American minister in Budapest, reported to the State Department in October 1941 (after Eckhardt had arrived in the United States) that Eckhardt's "proposed departure and reason therefore were known, debated and largely approved in informed circles, including the Regency and the Government."[41]

From the time of Eckhardt's arrived to the present day there has been constant speculation as to whether or not he was in the United States as the Horthy government's official emissary to establish a Hungarian government in exile. For decades after 1941, Eckhardt repeatedly denied having traveled in an official capacity or with government funds, saying he was there simply to "become the spokesman of the nation that was unable to speak for itself anymore."[42] However, in his later memoirs, published as *Tibor Eckhardt in His Own Words*, he acknowledges that he was on a mission for his government. Also, secret documents of Minister J. F. Montgomery, dated 8 November 1940, show that Eckhardt went to the United States as a result of an agreement with the Hungarian leadership and that it was common knowledge within Hungarian government circles that he was on an official mission. Eckhardt had even officially requested a three-month leave of absence from his position as a member of Parliament in order to take on the assignment.[43]

In his own words, Eckhardt's stated goals in going to America were "to continue the fight against Nazism which had become impossible in Hungary", but his immediate goal was also "to bring over at the earliest opportunity Hungary and her armed forces to the Allied side".[44] He expanded on the topic of his motivations in a memo to the U.S. Department of State some six months after his August 1941 arrival in the United States: "My decision to come here was largely due to the influence of Mr. John F. Montgomery, the United States Minister to Hungary, who for months repeatedly had urged me to do so. My first move in the United States was to inform Mr. Sumner Welles about my intentions as stated above."[45]

Eckhardt's denial that he was on an official mission arose from the need to disassociate himself and his mission from the government of Hungary, which had allied with the Germans. The U.S. Department of State accepted Eckhardt's position; in fact he received a considerable amount of official support immediately after his arrival in the United States. But from the onset of his trip, the British, particularly British intelligence, viewed Eckhardt's purpose with skepticism that shortly became a full-blown anti-Eckhardt campaign. The official reasoning that launched the campaign against Eckhardt may never be totally clear, but it is evident from the available SOE archival documents that very much in the forefront of the campaign were both Major Basil Davidson, who had been posted to Budapest in 1940 by British intelligence, and George Pálóczy-Horváth, a Hungarian who had already been recruited by the prior British agents in Hungary and who remained with SOE as an operative throughout the war. In the late 1930s, Hungarians already viewed Pálóczy-Horváth as a Soviet agent; Eckhardt even mentioning it in his memoirs.[46] In addition, in his posting after leaving Hungary in 1941 Davidson's aide was none other than James Klugmann, a member of the Communist Party of Great Britain (CPGB) since 1933, when he was at Cambridge. Klugmann was later identified as a Soviet agent by Anthony Blunt, one of a group of Cambridge spies that included Guy Burgess, Donald Maclean and Kim Philby.[47] While Davidson is always referred to as "leftish", the fact remains that two of his closest aides were agents in the service of the Soviet Union. The SOE files show that much of the secret correspondence regarding activities related to Hungary was written by him or forwarded to him for his comments and approval and that he was very influential in formulating that policy.

The campaign against Eckhardt that was orchestrated and funded by the Czechs in collaboration with the Soviets was also being directed on another front by the British as they invested a large number of resources against Eckhardt beginning in 1941. The immediate goal of this campaign was to discredit and remove the anti-Soviet Eckhardt from the Hungarian émigré political leadership.

However, the long term effect of the SOE's work, as Nigel West so aptly states in the introduction to *Secret War*, was that the SOE, "a small covert sabotage service, financed from the British Government secret vote and a mining magnate's private fortune, was transformed into a global organization that actively assisted despotic tyrannies to seize power in so much of Eastern Europe [after World War II]".[48]

On 21 October, shortly after Eckhardt's arrival in the United States, an internal Special Operations Executive document from Major Davidson noted that Eckhardt "has sold himself very successfully to the State Department, who went so far as to place an official in his entourage for the purpose of writing his speeches, preparing press receptions and generally assisting in the launching of his Free Hungarian movement. This is totally against the policy of G50000, who thinks of Eckhardt in the same terms as we do." Within a few weeks, a cipher telegram written by Major E.P. (Peter) F. Boughey and routed from Istanbul noted, "Exposure of Eckhardt our main card. We shall need the help of BBS [British Broadcasting Service] and Miniform. ZP could contribute valuable evidence for exposure ... Calculated exposure from official British sources of Eckhardt as reinsurance agent of present government."[49]

The British were pragmatic and knew that Eckhardt was the figure behind whom most of the Hungarian Americans or Hungarians abroad would rally. A memo in the SOE files from "D/HV [Lt. Col. J.S.A. Pearson] to D/HY [T.S. Masterson] both London based" dated 21 December 1941[50] observes that the "only two candidates who command any support in our opinion are Bethlen and Eckhardt. Both of these, I know, are undesirable and it is for this reason that we feel the political question should be put in the background for the time being." The memo continuous, "It is agreed that in most cases for subversive work one should go as far to the left as possible as they are likely to produce most action. ... It is thought here to be unwise to expose Eckhardt, as he probably commands more support in Hungary than Bethlen, and so our policy in this direction should be to damp him down and see that he gets as little support as possible. The Karolyi-Vambery crowd command no support in Hungary and scarcely any support outside, though it is agreed that they are intelligent and honest people."[51]

The British also consulted some experts on Hungary before they set their policy, however by then the campaign against Eckhardt was in full swing. These included historian Paul Ignotus, who wrote a long, strictly confidential report on 13 January 1942 addressed to The British Broadcasting Corporation, European Intelligence Department outlining for SOE decision makers the deficiencies of the two different kinds of free movements. "Behind Karoli [*sic*] there is no real movement only a compromising but brilliant past.... In America and here such old refugees as Jaszi, Vambery, Fenyes are spending their time grumbling and playing on old grievances as Karolyi does, and around them there is nobody but at best Czechoslovak minority leaders or Communists, who use them as shields, and at worst little inefficient careerists, blackmail journalists etc. who had been chucked out of the Czechoslovak Civil anti-chambres, and the Communist cells as well as from the Hungarian press rooms when they begged for subsidies.... As there are, I am afraid, neither in America or Britain, outstanding Hungarians who have not been compromised either by the past errors of the Karolyi set, or by at least passive participation in the criminal Hungarian Counter-Revolutionary regime over the last twenty two years, it would be absolutely hopeless to try to build up a movement of men completely beyond reproach."[52]

The Movement for Independent Hungary (Független Magyarországért Mozgalom)[53] *Becomes Reality*

Unaware of the full extent of the campaign being mounted against him, Eckhardt's arrival in America provided the AHF with the leader they needed for their Free Hungary campaign. With its policy in place and its intentions made clear to the U.S. State Department, the American Hungarian Federation threw its resources behind Eckhardt's leadership. In a letter to the editor of the *Washington Post* on 7 October 1941, Dr. Tibor Kerekes lauded the AHF decision:

> May I express the appreciation and thanks of all Hungarian organizations united in the American Hungarian Federation for the splendid editorial "New Hungary" in your September 28th issue. Our Federation representing the large majority of Americans of Hungarian descent in this country expressed already its full approval of Tibor Eckhardt's movement for "Independent Hungary". We did this after careful consideration of the character and political past of the man, who took upon himself the task to free his country from forceful subjugation and restore its ancient and rightful independence and sovereignty. Were not Eckhardt the only possible leader of "Independent Hungary," he would not have with him John Pelényi, who resigned the post of Hungarian Minister to the United States when Hungarian politics fell under Nazi influence, or Anthony Balasy and Anthony Zsilinszky who rather gave up their diplomatic posts in London than remain in the service of the present Hungarian government which today is under Nazi domination.[54]

After meetings at the State Department to determine the parameters for his political activities in the United States, Eckhardt set up his executive committee, all the members of which were at that time Hungarian citizens, primarily former Hungarian diplomats. They included John Pelényi, who resigned as minister to Washington when Hungary joined the Axis; Antal Balasy, who resigned as counselor of the Hungarian legation in London because he wanted no ties with a Hungarian government that could make any kind of deal with Hitler; Antal Zsilinszky, secretary of the Hungarian legation in London; and Dr. Victor Bator, well known in the legal profession in Hungary.[55]

On 27 September 1941, the Movement for Independent Hungary issued its first proclamation, which was strongly anti-Nazi, patriotic, devoid of real specifics and did not address Hungary's recent territorial gains. The proclamation made a strong impression in Hungarian American circles, especially among those who until then had focused on regaining lost territories as the most important issue for the Hungarian people—not realizing that in regaining portions of historic Greater Hungary, the country had lost her even most precious independence.[56]

As Hungarian Americans who had been indifferent to the AHF movement or were not part of organized Hungarian American activities became aware of Hungary's crisis, they "expressed in great numbers their willingness to support the Free Hungary Movement of Eckhardt."[57] In Eckhardt's own words,

> I succeeded in obtaining the support of all these groups (religious and secular) except the Jewish groups which split into two factions. The moderate faction, led by Rabbi George Lányi of New York City decided from the onset to support me. This caused a split in the Jewish organization, the radical pro-Bolshevik elements taking a stand against all pro-Hungarian organizations. According to the views of the State Department, coinciding fully with my own views, I did neither seek nor did I accept the support of the small pro-Nazi or pro-Communist groups.[58]

Eckhardt's correspondence from the period includes innumerable requests for him to make personal appearances as well as expressions of interest in the movement from Hungarian American groups throughout the United States and abroad.[59] The result was that Eckhardt's presence in America helped to unify the Hungarian Americans against Nazism and, as his contemporary Paul Nadanyi put it, "completely obliterated the small group of isolationists and pro-German Hungarians, even before Pearl Harbor".[60]

The proclamation of September 27 was broadcast to Hungary a few days after it was issued and caused such a political storm that Tibor Eckhardt and his associates were deprived of their Hungarian citizenship. Ironically, so was Rusztem Vámbéry, who had aligned himself with the Károlyi movement in the meantime and ultimately became a source of much anti-Eckhardt propaganda.[61]

During his stay in the United States in 1940, Eckhardt had met with Vámbéry, whom he knew well from Hungary and who had immigrated to the States in the late 1930s. An archliberal and distinguished legal scholar, Vámbéry was already established and teaching at the New School for Social Research in New York City.

At their meeting, the old time Hungarian liberal and Eckhardt discussed the fact that if Eckhardt failed in his fight against the Nazis in Hungary, he would return to the United States to continue his campaign. "Vámbéry assured him that he could count upon his assistance in such a campaign", according to Paul Nadanyi.[62]

Upon his return to America in 1941, Eckhardt contacted Vámbéry to let him know that he was ready to start a Free Hungary movement. Vámbéry informed Eckhardt that he, Eckhardt, could no longer count on his, Vámbéry's, support, that he was now aligned with the group headed by Count Michael Károlyi and could not participate in Eckhardt's movement, although they would work harmoniously with each other. Vámbéry's willingness to cooperate was also personally expressed to Paul Nadanyi, then editor of *Amerikai Magyar Népszava*, who quotes Vámbéry as having told him, "Hungarians who would not heed my warning of the dangers Nazism means to Hungary would believe it when coming from the lips of Eckhardt."[63]

Vámbéry's cooperation had been sought by the British, who in all probability knew of his connection to the Czechs but nevertheless were still mulling over the possibility of an Eckhardt (and thus Zsilinszky)/Vámbéry/Károlyi collaboration long after Vámbéry had clearly thrown his lot in with the Czechs. A cipher telegram sent to New York on 31 October 1941 stated, "Interested to know how the understanding between Eckhardt and Vambery is progressing … don't want to close door on any elements of the right. Eckhardt stands well with the State Department. He enjoys more support from elements of the right in Hungary than seemed at first to be the case as they regard as insurance in case we win…. Our view that he should not be supported by us at the expense of Vambery is therefore somewhat modified by the above."[64]

When it appeared to the founders and participants of the Free Hungary movement that they had their organization in place, their next step was to meet with the AHF leadership, whose endorsement they had already obtained, to organize the AHF support committee. American support for the Movement for Independent Hungary was organized on 28 November 1941, two months after the proclamation was issued and just a day after the AHF convention had elected a new board of directors and adopted a new, more liberal platform. Joseph Darago, president of the Verhovay Fraternal Insurance Association, was elected chairman. During the organizing meeting, Eckhardt presented the six-point program that outlined the objectives of the Movement for Independent Hungary. Nadanyi summarized the points:

1. That Hungarians join the fight against the new paganism of the Nazi system which threatens the very foundation of Christian civilization and is a danger to the whole world. That the Hungarians stay in the battle line until the final victory is won.

2. "The History of the years between the two World Wars proved once more that the peoples of the Carpathian basin and more generally the peoples living in the Danube valley cannot singly and separately assure their existence. To insure the security and economic prosperity of all peoples living in this region, the Free Hungary movement favors the organization of a Danubian Federation.
3. The Hungarians must combat all oppressive or imperialistic ambitions, irrespective of whether they originate outside of or within the Danube area. They must insist upon the integral application of true democratic principles to the relations among the Danubian nations.
4. Politically satisfactory and economically workable boundaries which respect the principle of nationality, can only be drawn within the framework of a Danubian Federation.
5. Apart from the indispensable limitations imposed by Danubian cooperation, every state must be sovereign and free to chose [*sic*] its form of government. Nevertheless, a totalitarian or anti democratic system of government cannot find place within such a Federation. (To this point, the democratic transformation of Hungary was also stressed.)
6. To pave the way for a general limitation of armaments and for European peace, the establishment of a general European collaboration is favored to safeguard the vital interests of the continent.[65]

What was so radical about this program that it would inspire such extreme efforts to destabilize and eliminate it?

The goals included many issues that were agreed upon or proposed for consideration by the leadership of the Hungarian American communities and by individuals other than Eckhardt. Dr. Oszkár Jászi, for example, was a great proponent of a Danubian federation. Clearly other forces were at work, forces whose intentions were formulated before World War II as part of a long-range plan to dominate Central- and Eastern Europe.

Attacks on the Movement for Independent Hungary

Most historians date Eckhardt's becoming the target of the other "Free Movements" (headed by rival Czech, Yugoslav and Romanian exiles) and of various leftist movements holding different views concerning the Soviet Union to the issuance of the September 27 proclamation. However, the personal attacks on Eckhardt actually started in the United States while he was still in Africa en route to America. An article by Ludwig Lore published by the *New York Post* on 21 July 1941 alleged that Eckhardt was coming to the United States as an ally of

"Mr. Hitler and his Hungarian accomplices".[66] These charges supposedly originated in certain "Hungarian" circles, on whose behalf a Mr. Terebessy had called upon various editors requesting that they print the accusations, which he handed over in typewritten form. Later investigation of Mr. Terebessy and his group found that he was a Czechoslovak citizen and a former member of the Communist Party.[67] His action was the beginning of a systematic campaign by Czechoslovaks partnering with Rusztem Vámbéry. They waged a propaganda war against Eckhardt with increasing intensity throughout the life of the movement and even after the movement's demise.

The early nature of this collaboration and the extent of the support given to Vámbéry is revealed in a letter from Vámbéry to Jan Masaryk in London requesting funds from the Czechoslovakian Government in Exile in order to establish a fortnightly publication to discredit the Eckhardt movement in the United States. This letter is dated 13 July 1941, several months *before* Eckhardt's arrival in the United States. More than any other of his writings, this private and confidential letter to Masaryk revealed what Vámbéry feared from Eckhardt and his Hungarian American allies. "I found," Vámbéry wrote, "that the overwhelming majority of Hungarian Americans are either revisionists, the term being a convenient cloak for Nazism [*sic*] or Communists." He then continues with his reasons for requesting funding. "Our propaganda seems all the more important as the Hungarian government is making an effort through their emissary Dr. Eckhardt, using American revisionist organizations to establish a pseudo-exiled Hungarian government which would secure in case of an Allied victory the continuation of the post-war reactionary regime in Hungary. These efforts would find powerful support in the major part of the Magyar newspapers published in this country. It seems to us, therefore, of greatest importance to establish a literary foothold in support of our democratic, liberal and progressive movement." The letter goes on to request $1000 per month for this purpose.[68] Subsequently, *Harc!*, an "anti-fascist" paper, was funded and began publishing scathingly critical views of Eckhardt, the Free Hungary Movement and its American supporters.[69]

The pro-Károlyi group presided over by Vámbéry met in Cleveland in the latter part of September 1941. This group, the American Federation of Democratic Hungarians (Demokratikus Magyarok Amerikai Szövetsége), headed by citizens of Hungary, the United States and Czechoslovakia; all of them radicals and some of them discredited leaders of the 1918–1919 Hungarian revolutions. They all accepted the leadership of Count Michael Károlyi, who had just issued a position paper in London inspired by communist ideology.[70]

The Vámbéry-orchestrated campaign to discredit the Movement for Independent Hungary continued with an article by Ignac Schultz, a Czechoslovak member of the Vámbéry committee, which appeared in *The Nation* on 27 September 1941 under the title "Budapest's Fake Mission".[71] That article was followed a week later by an editorial in *The Nation* attacking Eckhardt and the U.S. State Department. These two articles placed in a prominent left-leaning publication further illustrate the wide-ranging effort the Vámbéry organization put into the anti-Eckhardt campaign. This editorial agitation failed to have much impact on the Hungarian American community, however. The failure of the attack campaign's opening salvos was so evident that even the pro-Communist Hungarian section of the International Workers Organization (IWO) refrained from endorsing the Vámbéry group. Indeed, in Pittsburgh the IWO sought admission into a Hungarian American group that supported the Eckhardt movement. (The IWO's more accurate name was IWA, International Workers Association, but both names were used interchangeably.)

The Vámbéry organization also covertly published a virulent anonymous newsletter called *Igazmondó*, which was funded by the British Center of Information. The publication was SOE's idea, and the organization was very proud of its effectiveness as a propaganda tool. Many SOE agents had been recruited from the field of journalism, and they and other SOE operatives used that profession as a cover. As the organization grew, these "journalists" continued to seek out members of their profession to act as SOE agents. As an example, from 1940 to 1941 SOE agent Major Davidson, originally a journalist, was based in Budapest under the guise of running a western news bureau.[72] It was Davidson who developed much of the network of agents related to Hungary. Known to be left of center and anti-Horthy, he was influential in all British policy decisions related to Hungary throughout the war. After Hungary, Davidson went on to SOE postings in Belgrade, then Istanbul and then Cairo.[73] Eckhardt became aware that the SOE was operating out of the Middle East when, while in transit from Budapest to New York, he encountered Colonel S. William Bailey (DH 2, another agent) in Cairo. The colonel, whom he had known in Budapest, informed Eckhardt that "the British had acquired the services of the best Hungarian political leader, a Count Karolyi, expected to take over power at the war's end ... he is a friend of Benes and will again revolutionize Hungary—he did it once at the first World War's end." Eckhardt commented that it was Karolyi who had turned over Hungary to the communists, and Colonel Bailey's response was "Maybe he will do it again!"[74]

The British Center of Information was a public propaganda arm for Great Britain, but it was also an intelligence arm of the SOE. Even while policy makers in London were debating what direction to take in regard to their subversive activities among Hungarian émigré communities (and even in Hungary itself),[75] the SOE was working behind the scenes to destroy the Eckhardt movement and discredit the American Hungarian Federation, whose leadership they generally viewed as pro-fascist. In addition to supporting the Czechs' activities through the British Center of Information, the SOE had agents in the United States who monitored not only Eckhardt's activities (submitting reports even from some of his more private meetings) but also the secret sessions of the AHF Board. The SOE intercepted the correspondence between Eckhardt and the head of his organization in England, Zsilinszky, and thus the SOE reports also included the details of their correspondence. Beginning in early 1941, the SOE regularly produced a "Progress Report on the Hungarian Communities in the United States", which detailed all meetings of the Eckhardt organization, the AHF and the Vámbéry group as well as the activities of their various leaders.[76]

For their part, the Hungarian Americans not only had no idea who the SOE decision makers and operatives were, they had no idea the SOE existed.[77] Undetected by the Hungarian Americans, the SOE network of agents infiltrated and reported back to British intelligence on all activities and secret meetings of not only the AHF but also all the other Hungarian-American organizations operating in the U.S. The SOE records clearly attest that the British infiltration was not only widespread but also served a purpose that went beyond that of simple observation. SOE agents were involved in the active spread of disinformation and propaganda,[78] and the British Center of Information sought to discredit the Eckhardt movement and create discord among Hungarian Americans by voicing the Czechoslovakian Government in Exile's complaints about Hungary.[79] SOE documents indicate that the British Center had offices side by side with the Czech Center of Information in New York's Rockefeller Center, and certainly the British Center served to support British foreign policy in Central Europe. The undisguised intent of that policy was to ensure the continued survival of the small nations that were the successor states of the Austro-Hungarian Empire and to make certain that Archduke Otto was neither restored to the vacant throne nor the Empire reconstituted.

The Vámbéry campaign took a new tack at the beginning of 1942, when it became evident that it was not succeeding in changing the viewpoint of mainstream Hungarian Americans. The leaders of the campaign turned instead to a costly propaganda machine, through which they systematically tried to influence English-language publications and American public opinion against the Movement and to discredit Eckhardt and his committee's efforts.[80] To accomplish this goal, the Czechoslovakian Government in Exile established several different organizations, some openly and some under another pretext. According to an article in the 6 January 1942 issue of the New York publication *Dennik*, a Czech Center of Information similar to the British Center of Information had been established in New York under the direction of Dr. Jan Papanek, a "personal envoy of Mr. Beneš". The center's purpose was to "counter-balance German and Hungarian propaganda" in the United States, with its chief task being "to disrupt the Hungarian and Austrian Free Movements constituted in America".[81]

A principal organ spreading anti-Hungarian propaganda was *Newsflashes from Czecho-Slovakia Under Nazi Domination*, published by the Czecho-Slovak National Council of America. In the 19 January 1942 issue, a Professor Klecanda authored an article in which he accused Hungary of double dealing and Tibor Eckhardt of fascist and terrorist activities.[82] Each issue of this paper contained at least one item that was anti-Hungarian. The publication was supplied to every newspaper in the United States, many of which frequently reprinted items from its pages. Another source of false information about Hungary and Hungarians was the Czech agency Telegrafic Kurir (CTK). Its semi-official character gave the false information and slander it spread an appearance of authenticity. The "news" released by the CTK was published not only in the Czech and Slovak papers but in the English-language press as well, with little or no attempt to verify the accuracy of the information. Eckhardt made a summary of false information about the Movement for Independent Hungary that he found while perusing the Czech and Slovak press in America at random. In a single month's publications, January 1942, he found seventeen articles that included deliberate falsification of the "Program for the Reconstruction of the Danubian Area". That program had been adopted the previous November by the American Committee of the Movement for Independent Hungary at a joint meeting with the American Hungarian Federation in Pittsburgh.[83]

As a result of this propaganda campaign, a number of virulent protests against the Movement for Independent Hungary appeared in various newspapers. Additionally, the Reverend Pelikan, president of the Slovak National Federation of America, protested to the U.S. president and secretary of state against the activities of the Movement, accusing its leaders of preparing to reestablish Hungarian domination over the enslaved Slovak nation.[84] Collaborating with the Czechoslovak Center of Information, the British Center of Information helped foment the anti-Eckhardt activities, but the SOE's primary tactic in these activities was Ignac Schultz's newletter *Igazmondó*. The newsletter consistently attacked the Movement, Eckhardt and the AHF but had enough content of value that it was heavily read and distributed in American Hungarian circles. In fact, the SOE files contain a fascinating exchange of letters between Paul Nadanyi of the *Amerikai Magyar Népszava* and Joseph Darago of the AHF revealing that each thought that the other knew the identity of *Igazmondó*'s mysterious editor and was cooperating with the rogue publication.[85]

The attacks against Tibor Eckhardt found their way into many other newspapers in the western press. Mr. Schultz's article from *The Nation* was reprinted in the 15 November 1941 issue of *Forum*, published in Capetown, South Africa. The Association of Hungarians in Great Britain also reported the publication in that country of numerous attacks on Eckhardt and the Movement, including an article in *The Christian Century* entitled "Free Hungarians Will Support Károlyi". The author of that piece mentions that "one group under the leadership of Tibor von

Eckhardt had in view a Habsburg restoration. But that group has now broken up and Eckhardt has disappeared from the country. ... A much larger group under Dr. Rustum [*sic*] Vambery ... has now unanimously joined Károlyi's movement, which includes all reliable anti-Axis Hungarian forces in England, the United States and South America."[86] (The journalist who wrote the article was clearly under the impression that the Vámbéry group had mass popular support, not realizing that their meetings seldom had more than several dozen attendees and they counted their supporters in the hundreds rather than the hundred thousands, as the AHF did.[87]) The *Central European Observer*, published in London under Czech auspices, published an article by one Walter Angel in its issue of 9 January 1942. Entitled "Tibor Eckhardt—Fascist in Disguise", it added a new dimension to the attacks by accusing Eckhardt of being a member of long standing of the Deutscher Volksbund in Hungary. Some of the articles exceeded even the expectations of the intelligence operatives. SOE Istanbul reported to SOE Cairo on 7 August 1942 that he had placed an article in a local French language paper and that "I am afraid that the editorialist, in rewriting the piece I gave him, has rather overdone himself, and painted Eckhardt in colours a good deal blacker than he deserves; but the general effect is perhaps not an inaccurate one."[88]

When the Movement for Independent Hungary was contemplating beaming radio broadcasts to Hungary, both the Czechoslovak and Yugoslav governments protested to the Overseas News Agency. The news agency used its influence with the U.S. government to prevent the broadcasts. While Eckhardt was denied access, however, not too many months later, on 6 October 1943, Oszkár Jászi broadcast to Hungary through the auspices of the Office of War Information. Jászi had been living abroad for several decades and was not an active participant in the more populist Hungarian émigré circles, although he had agreed to serve as chairman of the Vámbéry organization. An article in *Harc!* states that the purpose of Jászi's talk was to convey the message of the Demokratikus Amerikai Szövetsége and its president (Vámbéry) to the Hungarian public.[89]

The Vámbéry/Károlyi/Beneš faction's highly scripted and well-organized attack continued with a lengthy memorandum sent to the British Embassy in Washington, D.C., and to the British Center of Information.[90] The faction consistently referred to Eckhardt as Tibor von Eckhardt in their communiqués, even though he himself never used the German honorific. This quirk made it easier to track the source and dissemination of the slanderous attacks, for unwary editors who published all or part of the memorandum continued to use "von" when referring to Eckhardt thereafter. Given that the SOE operated the British Center of Information, widespread distribution of the anti-Eckhardt propaganda supplied by the Vámbéry faction was assured, with publications from as far afield as South Africa publishing the material distributed by them.

The memorandum alleged, among other things, that Eckhardt had initiated a scheme to counterfeit French francs that had involved several prominent political figures; that he was connected with the murder of King Alexander of Yugoslavia; and that he was related to Horthy.[91] It contained numerous other statements that distorted Eckhardt's role in a number of extremely complex historic events.[92] Among other accusations the memorandum contended: 1) The counterrevolutionary "White Terror" that raged in Hungary from 1919 until 1922 was chiefly originated and led by Eckhardt. 2) Eckhardt, though a member of the opposition, was chiefly responsible for the Hungarian government's foreign policies, as proven by the fact that he was Hungary's chief delegate to the League of Nations. 3) Eckhardt was a counterfeiter, thief and cheat and misused his official position. 4) Eckhardt was the chief revisionist directing the movement for revision of the Treaty of Trianon. 5) Eckhardt's support by the liberals, the Hungarian language press and the AHF was all due to the fact that the Hungarian government had subsidized these organizations, all of which were made up of reactionaries, Nazis or Nazi sympathizers. 6) Eckhardt was funded by Victor Bator via the Hungarian government, which had expropriated the assets of the Manfréd Weiss family and transferred them to Bator. 7) And finally, all of the individuals supporting the Movement for Independent Hungary, including Eckhardt, were only pretending to fight Nazism but were actually serving it.

The authors of these blatant untruths wanted the recipients to believe that all supporters of Eckhardt and the Movement for Independent Hungary were fascists, reactionaries, Nazi sympathizers and subsidized agents of nazism. Contrary to what its critics wanted the press to believe, the participants in the Movement for Independent Hungary were prominent leaders of the Hungarian émigré community such as Eckhardt and Pelényi, neither of whom was a fascist. The Movement's organizational supporters, for example the American Committee of the Movement for Independent Hungary, included the most prominent American Hungarians in the United States including AHF officers Joseph Darago, Francis Deák of the faculty of Columbia University School of Law and Tibor Kerekes of Georgetown University. The AHF and its member organizations, none of them pro-fascist, including secular, academic and religious organizations numbering many hundreds of thousands of members who wholeheartedly supported the Movement's mission statement and its work.[93] In addition, the Movement had the support of both the daily newspapers published in the U.S. in the Hungarian language and of all the weekly papers (approximately forty-five) save the few that were pro-Bolshevik or pro-Nazi.[94] It would seem impossible that the lies of a few provocateurs could damage the Movement for Independent Hungary. However, because Hungary was an ally of Germany and because Hungary's political situation was little known, it actually proved relatively easy to spread the discrediting information.

The memorandum to the British Embassy was signed by Rusztem Vámbéry and László Fényes representing the Association of Democratic Hungarians (Demokratikus Magyarok Amerikai Szövetsége), the organization they had formed in 1941. The founding members of the organization also included two emigrant politicians from Czechoslovakia, with the balance consisting of Hungarians. The Hungarian members had either emigrated from Hungary after the Bolshevik regime was toppled in 1919 and had not been in their homeland since or had never been active in political life in Hungary, despite the fact that the Social Democratic Party and other liberal democratic groups had always had a substantial number of representatives elected to the Hungarian Parliament.[95]

Effect of the Attacks on the Movement and Eckhardt

Looking back at these events, it is clear from today's perspective that the propaganda and disinformation campaign used to discredit Eckhardt and the Movement for Independent Hungary was of a type regularly employed by the Nazis under the direction of Joseph Goebbels and by the Communist Party worldwide, even when its members were fighting on the side of the Allies.

Some insights into the campaign's deeper aims and the origins of its funding come from a copy of a Secret Service report Eckhardt received after he arrived in the United States. It recounts the details of a meeting of the Communist International in Mexico City in 1941 and outlines the program of action to be taken by communist organizations in order to destabilize the political situation in Western democracies. Key action points included establishing national "Freedom Movements" to be funded secretly by the communists and concerted plans to discredit all opposition leaders, whether political, religious or secular, who would not cooperate with the communists. The campaign against the Movement and the Hungarians' efforts followed the general outline of this program of work set forth for the Western Hemisphere's communist parties.[96]

In the chaos of those days, it was very difficult to separate the truth from the carefully crafted fiction that was both widely distributed and passionately reinforced by the propagandists. Few newspaper editors outside of the Hungarian-language press had enough background in foreign affairs and the issues in Central Europe to assess the information that they received with any accuracy. In many ways, the negative press Hungary received in the United States was totally understandable, given that it had fallen into the Nazi camp and declared war on the United States.

That Moscow had Eckhardt in its sights and saw him as an anti-communist force that needed to be eliminated or neutralized is also evident in a negative article written by Ralph Parker, Moscow correspondent for the *New York Times* and a prime example of a journalist who was influenced by the Soviets. In a *Times* article on 25 July 1942, Parker deals at length with the Movement for Independent Hungary. According to his dispatch, "it causes surprise here that such a Hungarian as Tibor Eckhardt should find any support in the United States as a representative of 'Free Hungarians', who, in Soviet eyes are better represented by true democrats driven from Hungary, such as Rustum [*sic*] Vambery, Professor Jaszi or Matyas Rakosy [*sic*]."[97]

Who were the three men Parker felt were better qualified to lead than Tibor Eckhardt? Rusztem Vámbéry had both proponents and detractors within Hungary, and while never persecuted in Hungary (even though he was the defense attorney at the trial of notorious Communist Mátyás Rákosi), he was nevertheless not a political leader.[98] He left Hungary of his own volition and spent a great deal of time writing mercilessly critical commentary on his homeland and its leadership. However, as Paul Nadanyi points out, he did enjoy "the friendship of some outstanding liberals in America and England, he is a contributor to many liberal periodicals in this country and has a reputation as a scholar."[99] Vámbéry left Hungary, as others did, because he recognized the inevitable and knew that the spread of Nazi domination would threaten his interests and his livelihood.

Oszkár Jászi did not leave Hungary during the Horthy regime but during Béla Kun's terroristic Bolshevik rule, having exhausted his political potential during the Károlyi regime. He cannot be accused of vindictive and vitriolic action against Hungary, although he was and remained a critic of the Horthy regime throughout the inter war period and agreed to associate himself with the Vámbéry faction and its efforts. Nonetheless, Jászi does not deserve to be lumped with the likes of Vámbéry and Rákosi, as he was a fine scholar and a man of integrity who only wished for the best outcome from the war for Hungary and the Hungarians.

The third potential leader Parker named, Mátyás Rákosi, was living in exile in the Soviet Union and was Moscow's Hungarian politician of choice. Once a "People's Commissar", he would never be remotely acceptable to Hungarians as a leader of their Free Hungary Movement and "was a detested personality, known to the Hungarian people as the notorious propagandist of the Soviet regime".[100] Few individuals other than Parker would have been so misguided as to refer to him as a "true democrat". Fewer than ten years later, the Hungarians would learn what leadership by Rákosi meant, and it did not have a great deal to do with freedom.

The propagandists did their dirty work quickly and efficiently, as evidenced by their success even with a writer for the prestigious and well regarded *New York Times*. While the Movement was organizing and unifying, those who opposed it kept up the negative campaign. Influential American friends of the Movement such as Nicholas Roosevelt, John Flournoy Montgomery and Anne O'Hare McCormick, as well as prominent Hungarian Americans such as Francis Deák and Paul Nadanyi, were kept busy writing letters to the editors of various publications in response to the tenacious disinformation campaign.[101] Eckhardt's American friends were astonished that anyone would spread or believe such lies. Former U.S. Minister Montgomery defended Eckhardt in a letter to Paul Nadanyi that was widely published. It first describes the history of his and his predecessors' relationships with Eckhardt and goes on to state emphatically,

> "We came to rely a great deal on what he told us, and never once did he deceive us and never once did he give us any misinformation. ... I was, therefore, quite astonished to learn that Doctor Eckhardt was accused of being a Nazi and a Fascist and even anti-Semitic. As all of this is so contrary to the facts, it did not occur to me until I received your letter that anyone would pay the slightest bit of attention to it, particularly since I knew that the Honorable Nicholas Roosevelt, my predecessor, had refuted all these charges in an editorial in the Herald Tribune, and that Ann McCormick had likewise come to Doctor Eckhardt's defense."[102]

Montgomery then rebuts at length the three major accusations against Eckhardt:

> Doctor Eckhardt as a Nazi: It would be just as absurd to discuss Winston Churchill as a Nazi, for each played the same role in the [*sic*] respective countries. Eckhardt was the outstanding anti-Nazi in Hungary. I know personally that there were a number of threats made against him, even written on the wall of his house, and it was because I had believed that he would the first man killed when the Nazi took possession of the country that I began last fall to urge him to get out while he could. ...[103] I saw him off in Budapest and any statement that he was aided and abetted in any way by the German Government is complete perversion of the truth. If they had wanted him to leave, he could have been here five months sooner by going through Germany or Italy.
>
> Doctor Eckhardt as a Fascist: As far back as the reports I read extended and during my stay in Budapest, Eckhardt was fanatical in his demands for land reform and extension of the ballot. To my knowledge he could have gone into any ministry that was formed while I was there if he had been willing to sacrifice a little on these two issues. ... I consider him a democrat as we understand the term in America, but whatever he is, he certainly not a Fascist.

> Dr. Eckhardt as an anti-Semite: I kept in touch with all the leading Jews in Hungary. Every time anything came up on the Jewish question, I went to them before I saw anyone else and I never once heard Doctor Eckhardt mentioned as an anti-Semitic. In fact, he was so outstanding in his championship of the Jews that it hurt his career considerably… I certainly would not call Doctor Eckhardt anti-Semitic and I know that my Jewish friends in Budapest wouldn't either because never did one express anything but praise for him and his conduct.
>
> I saw somewhere since I have been home the statement that Doctor Eckhardt had something to do with counterfeiting Czech currency or something of that kind. If he did, I never heard anyone mention it while I was in Budapest. I was a particular friend of the Czech Minister and knew all of the other in the Legation very well. I often discussed Eckhardt with various members of the Legations and no one ever mentioned anything of this kind. I know that Doctor Eckhardt and his wife went to the Czech Legation and entertained the Czech Minister and others in their home. From all the expressions of opinion I heard, they considered him a man of integrity as did everyone else.
>
> Being a public man and one who was generally on the popular side, there were a lot of things said from time to time about Doctor Eckhardt, but I never heard anyone seriously dispute his honesty or integrity nor did I ever hear anyone say he was a Nazi, a Fascist, or anti-Semitic until I came back to America this spring and read a letter someone wrote to one of the New York papers.
>
> You suggest it is Czech propaganda. To me it sounds more as if it originated in Berlin. From what I have seen of the Czechs, I can't believe that they would be so silly as to say such things about Tibor Eckhardt because they are so easily disproved. … During the time I was in Budapest, I observed the methods of Doctor Goebbels. He seemed to work on the theory of making absurd charges against onyone [*sic*] with the idea that someone would believe them. Strangely enough, they did."[104]

Montgomery wrote the above letter from the perspective of someone who, while in Hungary, had known Eckhardt much better than he had known anyone else. He often said that Eckhardt was his closest friend in Budapest, and as they had spent eight years working and socializing together, they were aware of each other's shortcomings. Montgomery made an undated biographical note on Eckhardt while Eckhardt was forming the Movement for Independent Hungary; it reveals Montgomery's level of insight: "The stormy petrel of Hungarian politics … A brilliant man, more like an American politician than a Hungarian. Generally considered an opportunist, but actually more of an idealist. While I was in Hungary, every time he had a chance to go in the Government or make some progress, he did something to make it impossible. He seems to be a great patriot and since he is now in America and the head of the movement for Free Hungary, he may do his country considerable service unless he does something to spoil it. Incidentally, he was the greatest duelist in Hungary during my time."[105] In this short sketch, Montgomery acknowledges Eckhardt's idealism, integrity and patriotism as well as his shortcomings.

That Eckhardt and Montgomery might not be thinking in tandem during the period when these biographical notes were written is also revealed in his memoirs. There, Eckhardt recounts that he and John Pelényi met with Montgomery at the latter's residence in Manchester, Vermont, immediately after Eckhardt's arrival in the United States and found him at odds with their own views on the war and what the United States' role in it should be. Eckhardt comments that since Montgomery had returned to America, "our friend had turned not only into an 'America First-er' but into a determined isolationist".[106]

The Result of the Disinformation Campaign

Soon after the Movement for Independent Hungary's program for reconstruction of the Danubian area was published (the Movement was then but a few months old), the disinformation program escalated and continued to do so. No matter that mainstream Hungarian Americans supported the Movement, no matter that the AHF recognized its necessity and supported it, the bitter attacks continued, and Eckhardt's supporters spent a great deal of time countering them. Despite Eckhardt's excellent command of the English language and, as a former press chief for the Hungarian government, his undoubted public relations skills, he would not counterattack. When asked why, Nadanyi reports that Eckhardt replied,

> I regard myself as a guest of America, I deem it my duty to behave as such. I came to America to further the interests of a truly Free Hungary, to help promote the victory of the democracies as a means of attaining it. In my estimation Hitlerism spells enslavement for Europe and the world and I watched its growth and spread. ... Nationals of other countries who come to America owe it as a duty to the country which extends its hospitality to do everything in their power to promote the unity which America needs in its most crucial hour if it is to save Europe and the world from barbarism. If others in my position choose to do otherwise, that is no reason why I should violate America's hospitality. I have utmost confidence that truth will prevail.[107]

While this was his public position, Eckhardt was a shrewd enough politician to realize that privately he must try to counter the smear campaign. He authored any number of confidential memoranda addressing this issue. One of these, dated 11 February 1942 and addressed to the U.S. Department of State, is twenty-six pages long. In it he indicates that those who were slandering him were having their successes, as "I am reliably advised that even high United States Government officials have made statements to the effect that Mr. Eckhardt and his organization have to be 'smashed'." He closes the memo, "In my present status, I find it difficult, if not impossible to counteract this unconscionable propaganda conducted by the Czechs with all the resources of their government. I have been advised by the State Department to refrain from polemics."[108]

Eckhardt's memo focuses on the Czechs, for although he was aware of the British activities, he did not realize the extent of British involvement in the campaign against him, and until his death he remained unaware of the complex web of activities mounted by the British.

By the middle of 1942, Eckhardt realized that if the Movement for Independent Hungary were to survive and be effective, he would have to step down from its leadership. The war of words by a small, very vocal group of individuals working on behalf of anti-Hungarian interests to discredit Eckhardt and the Movement had won—at least against Eckhardt. As a result of their ongoing agitation and behind the scenes pressure from their British allies, the U.S. State Department felt compelled to express its official view toward so-called "free movements" in the United States, stating that they did not operate with the government's approval. The Overseas News Agency circulated the official State Department document to publications and radio stations on behalf of "the democratic nations of Central Europe, Czechoslovakia and Yugoslavia who considered it dangerous to their future peace and safety" if Eckhardt were allowed to continue with his Movement. The document states, in part:

> In general, the Government of the United States does not favor "free movements" or groups representing such movements which carry on activities contrary to the established policies, domestic or foreign, of the Government of the United States, and prefers that the governing committees of such movements shall be composed of citizens of the foreign country rather than of American sympathizers. It disapproves of any attempt to enlist the support of American citizens of like racial background on the theory that they are "fellow nationals." Though it recognizes that because of common race background, American citizens, acting as Americans and with full allegiance to the United States, may nevertheless be sympathetic to the national aspirations of their country of racial

> origin, and may organize in sympathetic and friendly support of such aspirations.[109]

Thus, the disinformation campaign led to the de facto suspension of the Movement and Eckhardt's retirement from political activities until after the war. "Deprived of Eckhardt's leadership, the same political orientation continued to be represented by the AHF, although with few tangible results," Steven Béla Vardy observed.[110] Just one year after his arrival in the United States, Eckhardt realized that he "had to vanish to escape constant harassment by the communists and their protagonists". Eckhardt notes in his memoirs that he then "went underground" and left New York City for Washington, D.C. He remained there until the end of the war years, mistakenly thinking that he was removing himself as a target of a Red conspiracy.[111]

Despite Eckhardt's self exile, the Soviets continued to support the efforts of the Czechs, as their agents in the propaganda war, to discredit what the USSR viewed as the Hungarian establishment. This continued throughout World War II and into the Cold War years. Eckhardt continued to charge the perpetrators, and he protested the disinformation campaign to various government agencies, including the Office of Strategic Services (OSS), but with no results. Of course, Eckhardt also believed that like other U.S. government agencies, the OSS had been heavily infiltrated by the communists. The path taken by the damaging "Document on Free Hungarian Plans" seems to strongly substantiate this view.

"Document on Free Hungarian Plans" was the title of a six-part message sent from the KGB New York Resident to Moscow on 29–30 November 1944. The routing of the message provides substantive proof of the Czech–Moscow connection in regards to Hungary. The information it contained was sent to Soviet agent Vladimir Sergeevich Pravdin ("Sergej") in New York by none other than Dr. Jan Papanek of the Czech Center of Information. "Sergej" then forwarded the information in a memorandum to "Viktor" at the KGB in Moscow. Two copies of this report are in the VENONA Archives, and the original decoded transcript identifies "Viktor" as Pavel Ivanovich Fedosimov, a KGB major and head of the First Chief Directorate. A later notation on another copy of the report, stamped "Top Secret", suggests that the major might have been Stepan Zakhareneh Arresyan, KGB New York Resident in 1944.

Made public as part of the VENONA Archives (which began to be released in 1997), this sensational document identifies the following provenance for the "Document on Free Hungarian Plans" in its report sent to Moscow. "PAPANEK has passed on to Sergej an English translation of a note in Hungarian which Tibor ECKHARDT lost in a taxi among a number of other documents. The driver (unidentified) handed the find over to the Khata [FBI] and the latter through IZBA [OSS] entrusted the translation to a Hungarian (we will try to find out his name) from VAMBERY'S group who then passed the translation to PAPANEK."

The New York KGB Resident states to Moscow that the notes found in the taxi were in Eckhardt's handwriting and were an outline of his advice to the Hungarian government as to their actions in the critical days of November 1944. Having been passed on to the Soviets by the Czechs, the Soviets dissected and analyzed the entire document of Eckhardt's recommendations to the Hungarian government, and as a result many of the Hungarian members of Eckhardt's anti-communist, anti-fascist group within and outside Hungary were identified.

The VENONA document also provides evidence that the Vámbéry-Károlyi alliance with the Czechs, and Eduard Beneš's crusade against Hungarian interests that were not closely aligned with his pro-Soviet policy were both actually serving Moscow. It gives further proof that in addition to disseminating propaganda, the Czech Center of Information and its head, Dr. Papanek, ran an intelligence operation that reported to Soviet intelligence.

In tracing these connections, it becomes clear that Eckhardt and his collaborators were the targets of a Soviet disinformation campaign using the Czechs as agents. The fact that the disinformation campaign against Eckhardt continued until Hungary became a Soviet satellite shows that while the Czechs did not want Eckhardt to return to lead the Smallholders Party in Hungary, discrediting Eckhardt and keeping him in America also served the Soviets' interest in consolidating their power in Central Europe. Thus the "evidence" of Eckhardt's "fascism" and all the damaging information about him that began to appear in 1941 were no coincidence but a propaganda campaign.[112]

The intent of the campaign became clear in the light of post-war events. The Soviets wanted to neutralize anyone who had the potential to be a strong post-war political leader, particularly one with close ties to the Habsburgs and to the Roman Catholic Church. The Czechs, Slovaks, Yugoslavs and Romanians wanted to make certain that the cause of Hungarian revisionism and its advocates would be silenced, thus ensuring the existence of their countries and their borders.

The charge that Eckhardt had been a representative of the Horthy government when he arrived in the United States in 1941 never died down during Eckhardt's lifetime. Current documents and his memoirs both amply attest that the assertion was correct, although Eckhardt was reluctant to acknowledge the fact until the last few years of his life. He traveled to America understanding that he could succeed only if he were not viewed as a representative of the German-allied Horthy government.[113]

The issue of financial impropriety also continued to be raised in some circles. It was asserted that the Horthy government had entrusted Eckhardt with five million dollars to form a government in exile and pave the way for the Horthy government's withdrawal from Hungary but once in the United States, he kept the money but did not implement the plan. This rumor, untrue on both charges, was fueled by the SOE and its sources—Major Davidson having been the author of two of the three internal memos on the subject that were circulated that commented on Eckhardt's embezzlement of funds. The first report, dated 6 December 1941, was from a Professor Peterfy, a Hungarian university professor stationed in Istanbul. He claimed that Eckhardt absconded with seven million dollars of Hungarian government funds. The second report, dated 23 December 1941, is a cipher memo from DH V (Lieutenant Colonel Pearson) to DH 2 (Colonel S. William Bailey): "Various conflicting reports have come in concerning Eckhardt's finances. One of these reports states that Teleki deposited between five and six million dollars in the USA for Eckhardt's use. It occurs to me that now America is in the war it might be possible to ascertain Eckhardt's income so that we can clear up these rumours once and for all. Will you give this matter your consideration."[114] Three months later, SOE's discussion of the topic continued in a letter from DH 18 (Davidson) in Istanbul to SOE Cairo opining, "I shudder to think what Eckhardt will do with those 9,000,000 dollars. Someone ought to open a night-club in Washington in the Allied interest; such changes do not occur every day of the week."[115]

Clearly, Eckhardt's situation, his support and his funding were compelling areas of interest for British intelligence, which was on constant lookout for methods to compromise or bring him down. Ruining Eckhardt's reputation was thought to be one way to neutralize him, thus the interest in his finances.

Some accused Eckhardt of dishonorable behavior in abandoning Hungary and the cause for which the funds had been provided just in order to resettle in the West. Speculation on this issue might have gone on forever if John Pelényi, the Hungarian minister to the United States from 1933 to 1940, had not published an article in the June 1964 issue of the *Journal of Modern History*.[116] Entitled "The Secret Plan for a Hungarian Government in the West at the Outbreak of World War II", it describes an official government plan for a Hungarian government in exile and lists who was involved in the plan to withdraw the legitimate government of Hungary to the West as the Nazis grew close to gaining control of the country.

In the article Minister Pelényi writes that he proposed the plan to Prime Minister Teleki and Count Csáky, the foreign minister, at a private luncheon in September 1938. After broaching the topic, Pelényi followed up with a 17 April 1939 confidential memorandum to Teleki and Csáky outlining the details of the proposal, the timing and the merits of the action. Using Eduard Beneš as a then-current example, Pelényi explains how Beneš maintained a power base first in France and then in Great Britain for himself and for Czechoslovakia after the

German occupation of his country. Calling on his government to make a decision, Pelényi said, "Events are happening so fast that what would be still feasible today may become impossible tomorrow. It seems, therefore, that immediate action is imperative, lest all our efforts prove to be a 'coat after the rain', as in 1918–1920, when they could no longer prevent the fatal [Treaty of] Trianon."[117]

In the spring of 1940, Minister Pelényi received an unexpected visit from Andor Teleki, the prime minister's nephew, who was traveling outside of regular diplomatic channels. Teleki brought a letter dated 17 March 1940, which began as follows:

> By order of Hungary's Regent I inform Your Excellency of the following.
>
> The President of the Hungarian National Bank will turn over to you for safekeeping five million dollars in bank notes or securities for the purpose of your placing these funds in a safe to be rented in the name of the Hungarian National Bank but to be at the disposal of Your Excellency. You are to keep the key to the safe with you or in some other safe place and you are to keep the funds at your disposal in accordance with the orders of Hungary's Regent. Furthermore you are to turn them over, in the situations defined and specified below by the Regent to the persons designated by him and listed here for the purposes of the Hungarian emigration, which is to be led by the Regent in person or by his appointee or appointees.[118]

Pelényi learned that the emissary had been sent solely to deliver instructions regarding the five million dollars to be placed in his, Pelényi's, safekeeping. To assure the greatest secrecy, Prime Minister Teleki had not entrusted the documents to a regular diplomatic messenger but had sent his nephew instead. Pelényi wrote in his 1964 article that to his knowledge, Prime Minister Teleki made only one reference to the secret plan. In a letter dated 18 March 1940 to György (George) Barcza, the Hungarian minister in London, Teleki instructed the minister to turn to Pelényi "should a certain situation arise".

Further instructions in the Hungarian regent's letter directed Pelényi to turn over the funds not only to the regent but also to certain gentlemen designated as the leaders of a possible Hungarian emigration. "First of all to Count Julius [Gyula] Károlyi, or to Count Paul [Pál] Teleki, who are also authorized singly and individually to take over the funds and to dispose of them for the defense of our national freedom: second to Count Alexander Khuen-Hédervári, to Messrs. George de Barcza, Leopold Baranyai, Count Stephen Bethlen and Francis Keresztes-Fischer of whom any two together with your Excellency as the third are jointly authorized to take over the funds for their free disposal." If only one of the above gentlemen was available, Mr. Royall Tyler, an American citizen,[119] was designated as the third person authorized to draw on the fund. Further details charged Pelényi with leaving instructions in his last will as to how the funds should be disposed and clarifying that the funds did not constitute his personal property.

This weighty responsibility turned out to be short lived. Four days later, Pelényi received a cable instructing him to transfer the funds in his safekeeping to the Federal Reserve Bank in New York to be credited to the Hungarian National Bank. Pelényi immediately complied with the request, and the funds were thus returned to the Hungarian government's accounts. In a letter written in his own hand and dated 21 May 1940, Teleki thanked Pelényi on behalf of Regent Horthy for taking on this task.[120]

Pelényi states in his article that he was never informed of the reasons for the directive and only could surmise that in view of the total collapse of the Allied Front in the West, "it was felt that the secret plan no longer fitted the international situation".[121].

Having succeeded in its mission as a spoiler, British intelligence helped ruin Eckhardt. After he left the leadership of the Movement for Independent Hungary, SOE was left with the Vámbéry organization, which it and the Czechs had so avidly supported. By then, however, their enthusiasm for Vámbéry and his group had evaporated. In a private SOE cipher sent from London to Cairo and Istanbul on 8 October 1942, the writer notes that "all are in agreement that Karolyi and Vambery should not (repeat. NOT) appear as successors to Eckhardt."[122]

Endnotes

1. Biographical Notes, Tibor Eckhardt Papers, Box 1, File 1, Hoover Institution Archives, Stanford, California.
2. Tibor Eckhardt Jr., correspondence with the author, August 2000. Eckhardt's 1941 journey is also covered in *Tibor Eckhardt in His Own Words*, pp. 96–98.
3. Paul Nadanyi, *The "Free Hungary" Movement*, p. 19.
4. John Pelényi to Dr. Zoltán de Baranyai, Royal Hungarian Consul General, 6 May 1940, Group: Foreign Ministry 106, File Group 125, Washingtoni Követség, Hungarian National Archives (Magyar Országos Levéltár), Budapest.
5. Biographical Notes, Tibor Eckhardt Papers, Box 1, File 1, Hoover Institution Archives.
6. Tibor Frank, ed., *Discussing Hitler: Advisers of U.S. Diplomacy in Central Europe 1934–1941* (Budapest: Central European University Press, 2003). See: Conversation #173, J.F. Montgomery with HSH the Regent, Budapest, 8 November 1940, p. 323.
7. Arlington National Cemetery Website, "Hugo Lafayette Black, Captain United States Army, United States Senator, Alabama, Associate Justice of the United States Supreme Court", www.arlingtoncemetary.net/hlblack.htm.

8. Tibor Frank, ed., *Discussing Hitler*, p. 323.
9. Attacks Against Tibor Eckhardt, 11 February 1942, Tibor Eckhardt Papers, Box 1, Hoover Institution Archives; Ludwig Lore, *New York Post*, 21 July 1941; Rusztem Vámbéry to Jan Masaryk, 13 July 1943, Rusztem Vámbéry Papers, Box 2, File: Jan Masaryk 1941, Hoover Institution Archives. This Vámbéry letter is marked "Confidential" and addressed to Masaryk in his capacity as Czechoslovak Minister of Foreign Affairs in the London exile government. Sent many weeks *prior* to Eckhardt's arrival there, it requests funds to counter his efforts in the United States—this correspondence is covered in detail in Chapter 4.
10. Tibor Hajdú and Zsuzsa L. Nagy, "Revolution, Counterrevolution, Consolidation", in Peter F. Sugar, Peter Hanák, Tibor Frank, eds., *A History of Hungary* (Bloomington: Indiana University Press, 1990), pp. 303–309.
11. Mark Imre Major, *American Hungarian Relations 1918–1944* (Astor Park, Florida: Danubian Press, 1974), pp. 164–165. "A journalist needed to be in Hungary but a few hours to realize that the whole nation was in mourning for its lost territories."
12. Julianna Puskás, *From Hungary to the United States: 1880–1914*, p. 59. The population migration tables in this work clearly illustrate this point.
13. Steven Béla Vardy, *The Hungarian-Americans*, p. 101.
14. Paul Nadanyi, *The "Free Hungary" Movement*, p. 24.
15. Steven Béla Vardy, *The Hungarian-Americans*, p. 102.
16. Emil Lengyel, *Americans From Hungary* (Philadelphia and New York: J.B. Lippincott, 1948), p. 173. The proclamation invited "the people of Magyar America" to send representatives to an assembly to "establish the long desired American Hungarian unity, express everlasting loyalty to America, and lay down the lines along which a just revision of the Treaty of Trianon can be rendered possible."
17. Ibid., pp. 173–174.
18. Steven Béla Vardy, *The Hungarian-Americans*, p. 106.
19. Ibid., p. 109.
20. Ibid., p. 110.
21. George Dozsa, ed., *One Hundredth Anniversary Album 1896–1996*. (Washington, D.C.: Hungarian Reformed Federation of America, 1996), pp. 85–86.
22. Paul Nadanyi, *The "Free Hungary" Movement*, p. 8.
23. Ibid.
24. Steven Béla Vardy, *The Hungarian-Americans*, p. 110.
25. Paul Nadanyi, *The "Free Hungary" Movement*, p. 10.
26. Ibid.
27. Ibid., p. 12.
28. *Tibor Eckhardt in His Own Words*, pp. 98–104. See also: Tibor Frank, ed., *Discussing Hitler*, pp. 322–323.
29. SOE memorandum, 16 January 1942, Records of the Special Operations Executive, Eastern Europe [hereafter SOE Records], Registered File: Hungary, HS/4/95 Political Groups and Freedom Movements for SOE activities, National Archives of the United Kingdom.
30. Commentators (Nadanyi, Fenyő) writing on Jászi's association with Michael Károlyi's movement speak of his support for it. Vardy, however, says, "Moreover, Karolyi's London-based movement was so pro-communist and pro-Soviet that it was

even rejected by his longtime friend and political ally, the noted progressive liberal sociologist and ex-politician Oscar Jaszi." *The Hungarian-Americans*, p. 111.

31. Ivo Banac, ed., *The Diary of Georgi Dimitrov 1933–1949* (New Haven and London: Yale University Press, 2003), p. 207.
32. Steven Béla Vardy, *The Hungarian-Americans*, p. 111.
33. Ibid.
34. John Flournoy Montgomery, *Hungary, the Unwilling Satellite* (New York: Devin-Adair Company, 1947), pp. 94–98; Mario D. Fenyő, *Hitler, Horthy, and Hungarian-German Relations 1941–1944* (New Haven and London: Yale University Press, 1972), pp. 112–113.
35. Paul Nadanyi, *The "Free Hungary" Movement*, pp. 45–46.
36. Mark Imre Major, *American Hungarian Relations*, pp. 241–242.
37. SOE Records, HS/4/95, National Archives of the United Kingdom.
38. Steven Béla Vardy, *The Hungarian-Americans*, p. 111.
39. Tibor Eckhardt, *Recollections of Tibor Eckhardt: Regicide at Marseille* (New York: American Hungarian Library and Historical Society, 1964), p. 245.
40. *Tibor Eckhardt in His Own Words,* p. 506.
41. Mario Fenyő, *Hitler, Horthy and Hungary-German Relations*, p. 111.
42. Steven Béla Vardy, *The Hungarian-Americans*, p. 110.
43. Tibor Frank, ed., *Discussing Hitler*, p. 322.
44. *Tibor Eckhardt in His Own Words*, p. 146.
45. Tibor Eckhardt to the United States Department of State, 11 February 1942, memo, p.1, Tibor Eckhardt Papers, Box 1, File: Attacks against Tibor Eckhardt, Hoover Institution Archives. Also referred to here as the State Department Memo, this is Eckhardt's response to the "attacks" against him.
46. *Tibor Eckhardt in His Own Words*, pp. 127–128.
47. Barrie Penrose and Simon Freeman, *Conspiracy of Silence: The Secret Life of Anthony Blunt* (London: Grafton Books, 1986), pp. 77–78.
48. Nigel West, *Secret War: The Story of SOE, Britain's Wartime Sabotage Organisation* (Great Britain: Coronet Books, 1992), p. 8.
49. Cipher telegram #0184, headed "Addressed to ? Cairo? 226 Repeated London 184 Following from DH 18", SOE Records, HS/4/95, National Archives of the United Kingdom.
50. SOE Records, HS/8/985, National Archives of the United Kingdom.
51. SOE Records, HS/4/95, National Archives of the United Kingdom.
52. Ibid.
53. The Movement for Independent Hungary was also referred to as the Free Hungary Movement in contemporary references and the two names were often used interchangeably. Journalists and historians writing in Hungarian often refer to the Movement as Független Magyarországért rather than Magyar Szabadság Mozgalom, which is how it was most often referred to in the United States.
54. Tibor Kerekes, executive director American Hungarian Federation, "New Hungary", letter to the editor, *Washington Post*, 4 October 1941, p. 10. The letter is quoted here in its entirety.
55. Paul Nadanyi, *The "Free Hungary" Movement*, p. 34.

56. Ibid., pp. 34–36. A copy of the original proclamation of 27 September 1941 is reprinted in the Appendix.
57. Paul Nadanyi, *The "Free Hungary" Movement*, p. 37.
58. State Department Memo, p. 3, Tibor Eckhardt Papers, Box 1, File: Attacks Against Tibor Eckhardt, Hoover Institution Archives; "Hungarian Leader Summons Magyars to 'Freedom Fight'", *Washington Post*, 27 September 1941, p. 11.
59. Tibor Eckhardt Papers, Box 20, Personal Correspondence, Hoover Institution Archives.
60. Paul Nadanyi, *The "Free Hungary" Movement*, p. 34.
61. Ibid., p. 36.
62. Ibid.
63. Ibid., p. 37.
64. Unknown to "G" in New York, Cipher telegram #2775, 31 October 1941, SOE Records, HS/4/95, National Archives of the United Kingdom.
65. Paul Nadanyi, *The "Free Hungary" Movement*, pp. 37–38.
66. State Department Memo, p. 4, Tibor Eckhardt Papers, Box 1, File: Attacks against Tibor Eckhardt, Hoover Institution Archives.
67. Ibid.
68. Rusztem Vámbéry to Jan Masaryk, 13 July 1943, Rusztem Vámbéry Papers, Hoover Institution Archives. Marked "Confidential", this letter was written to Masaryk in his capacity as Czechoslovak Minister of Foreign Affairs in the London-based exile government.
69. Beginning with its initial issue on 25 December 1941, *Harc!* made Tibor Eckhardt one of the prime targets of its propaganda campaign. One of the ironies of the attacks was their transparent inconsistency. The first issue declared on page 12 that "it is with Jewish money that he [Eckhardt] supports his party and his own propaganda". Having exhausted that accusation, which seemed not to have any negative impact on Eckhardt's efforts, six months later, 25 July 1942, *Harc!* branded Eckhardt as an ardent anti-Semite. Eckhardt's accusers were to obtain a great deal more mileage from this accusation in their campaign to discredit him.
70. Rusztem Vámbéry Papers, Box 3, File: Speeches and Writings "Free Hungary Movement" in the U.S., 12 October 1941, Hoover Institution Archives.
71. *The Nation*, 27 September 1941 and *The Nation*, Letters to the Editor, 10 October 1941, Rusztem Vámbéry Papers, Box 8, File: Eckhardt, Tibor, Hoover Institution Archives.
72. According to Nigel West in *Secret War: The Story of SOE, Britain's Wartime Sabotage Organisation* (pp. 26–27), Davidson had been sent to Budapest by the precursor to the SOE, Section D of British Secret Intelligence Service, the SIS. (Section D was folded into the SOE when it was established on 19 July 1940.) The "press office" in Budapest had been opened in 1939 by two journalists who were hastily pressed into intelligence work and who bumbled the assignment so badly that Davidson was sent to replace the two of them in 1940. In his memoirs (pp. 127–128), Eckhardt notes that Davidson inherited as one of his agents, a Hungarian named George Pálóczy-Horváth, a double agent suspected by the Hungarians even in the late 30s of being in the service of the Soviets.
73. Basil Davidson, *Special Operations Europe: Scenes from the Anti-Nazi War* (London: Grafton Books, 1987), pp. 80, 115–119.

74. *Tibor Eckhardt in His Own Words*, p. 128.
75. For example, a cipher telegram from Cairo on 20 November 1941 states, "Meanwhile do you think moment is propitious attempt initiate negotiations with Horthy through Eckhardt with a view to compromising former more fully? This could be done from America and Istanbul." SOE Records, HS/4/95, National Archives of the United Kingdom.
76. SOE Records, HS/4/95, National Archives of the United Kingdom.
77. Like the OSS, whose activities were not known to Americans during the war, the activities of SOE agents seem not to have been a concern to the U.S. government. It appears that very few in the U.S. save the intelligence community knew of the SOE's existence or of the extent of its intelligence operation within émigré communities in the U.S.
78. *Igazmondó* issues dated 5 August 1941, 8 September 1941, 29 September 1941, 6 October 1941, 20 October 1941, 27 October 1941, 17 November 1941, 21 November 1941, 1 December 1941, and 24 December 1941, Tibor Eckhardt Papers, Box 1, Folder: *Igazmondó*, Hoover Institution Archives.
79. Rusztem Vámbéry to Donald Hall at the British Information Service, 7 December 1942, Rusztem Vámbéry Papers, Box 1, Folder: Correspondence, Donald Hall 1941–1943, Hoover Institution Archives. The letter begins, "I enclose a copy of our statement of adherence which I mailed last night."
80. Gordon Brook-Shepherd, *Uncrowned Emperor: The Life and Times of Otto von Habsburg* (London and New York: Hambledon and London, 2003), p. 158.
81. State Department Memo, p. 7, Tibor Eckhardt Papers, Box 1, File: Attacks Against Tibor Eckhardt, Hoover Institution Archives.
82. Ibid. Professor Klecanda was vice-chairman of the Czecho-Slovak State Council in London.
83. Paul Nadanyi, *The "Free Hungary" Movement*, p. 37. See also: Francis Deák to the editor, *New York Post*, 16 March 1942, Tibor Eckhardt Papers, Box 1, File: Defense of Tibor Eckhardt, Hoover Institution Archives. Deák, of the Columbia University Law School Faculty, refutes charges against Eckhardt and the Movement for Independent Hungary.
84. State Department Memo, p. 9, Tibor Eckhardt Papers, Box 1. File: Attacks against Tibor Eckhardt, Hoover Institution Archives.
85. SOE Records, HS/4/95, National Archives of the United Kingdom. The Darago letter in this file is marked "Copy" and has no date. The Nadanyi letter is marked "Strictly Confidential" and also has no date. The correspondence can, however, be tentatively dated as it is referenced in a report entitled "Translation of a Report from Editor of 'Igazmondó'" (Hungarian Bulletin) and is marked Appendix "D". This entry is a portion of Special Operations Report 559, entitled "Fourth Progress Report on the Hungarian Communities in the United States" and dated 25 November 1941. All of these reports are contained in HS/4/95.
86. Rusztem Vámbéry Papers, Box 8, File: Károlyi, Mihály 1942–1946, Hoover Institution Archives.
87. "Jöjjön, aminek jönni kell", *Magyar Jövő*, 13 June 1941, Rusztem Vámbéry Papers, Box 8, File: Clippings 1941, Hoover Institution Archives. This article detailing the formation of the Demokratikus Magyarok Amerikai Szövetsége (Association of Democratic Hungarians), the Vámbéry and Fényes organization, mentions that only

twenty-two people were present and that there was real intent to exclude the working class element from the organization.

In *The Hungarian-Americans* Steven Béla Vardy refers to all the groups formed by Hungarian Americans save the American Hungarian Federation as being "heads without bodies" for their lack of constituency and support in the United States (p. 111). On page 113 he writes: "Of the nearly half a dozen organizations, councils and committees that tried to pass themselves off as the true representatives of the Hungarian-American community and of Hungary's national interests only the American Hungarian Federation survived the war. The others failed to survive because they had very few followers among Hungarian-Americans." Vardy also notes the composition of the AHF membership (p. 110) and says that altogether there were several hundred thousand supporters of this umbrella organization. Clearly they had major resources within their membership, given that they were able to raise all the funds to build the USS *Kossuth* for the United States Navy.

88. SOE Records, HS/4/96, Independent Hungarian Movement, National Archives of the United Kingdom.
89. "Jászi Oszkár rádióüzenete Magyarország népéhez", *Harc!*, 13 November 1943, p. 1.
90. Rusztem Vámbéry to the British Embassy in Washington, D.C., memorandum, pp. 1–3, Tibor Eckhardt Papers, Box 1, File: Attacks Against Tibor Eckhardt, Hoover Institution Archives.
91. If his attackers had done their research, they could have accurately stated that Eckhardt was related "by marriage" to Horthy, who was Eckhardt's wife Ellen's uncle.
92. Rusztem Vámbéry to the British Embassy in Washington D.C., memo, pp. 1–13, Tibor Eckhardt Papers, Box 1, File: Attacks Against Tibor Eckhardt (see also, File: Defense of Tibor Eckhardt), Hoover Institution Archives.
93. Paul Nadanyi, *The "Free Hungary" Movement*, pp. 8–9.
94. Ibid., p. 11. Vámbéry recognized that the Hungarian-language newspapers were in support of Eckhardt, as his correspondence with Jan Masaryk shows: "Dr. Eckhardt, using American revisionist organizations to establish a pseudo-exiled Hungarian government ... these efforts would find powerful support in the major part of the Magyar newspapers published in this country." (Vámbéry to Masaryk, 13 July 1941, Rusztem Vámbéry Papers.)
95. "Jöjjön, aminek jönni kell", *Magyar Jövő*, 13 June 1941, Rusztem Vámbéry Papers, Hoover Institution Archives. This article in *Magyar Jövő*, the Communist Hungarian-language newspaper, states (in Hungarian) that "Rusztem Vámbéry had done nothing for the last twenty years and now suddenly he has political ambitions. It is not like even one worker is longing to join this burnt out professor's political action group, because all they are going to hear is warmongering."
96. Count H. Degenfeld to Tibor Eckhardt, 23 February 1942, Tibor Eckhardt Papers, Box 1, File: Archduke Otto von Habsburg, American Hungarian Library and Historical Society, New York.
97. Ralph Parker, *New York Times*, 25 July 1942.
98. This is amply illustrated by the less than enthusiastic opinions expressed by the communist *Magyar Jövő* on 13 June 1941 in a report on Vámbéry entering the political arena with his organization. A portion of the text is translated and quoted in endnote 95, above. The Hungarian-language extracts, with English translations, are quoted in endnotes 22 and 23 in Chapter 4.
99. Paul Nadanyi, *The "Free Hungary" Movement*, p. 9.

100. "Who Can be the Torchbearers of the Free Hungarian Movement?", *Amerikai Magyar Népszava*, 27 July 1942.
101. Anne O'Hare McCormick was the noted British-born European correspondent for the *New York Times* during the inter-war years and in 1937 was the first female recipient of a Pulitzer Prize.
102. Minister John Flournoy Montgomery to Paul Nadanyi, undated letter in response to Nadanyi's letter of 22 January 1942, Tibor Eckhardt Papers, Box 17, File: Correspondence, John Flournoy Montgomery, Hoover Institution Archives.
103. Ibid. See also, Tibor Frank, ed., *Discussing Hitler*, pp. 322–325. These pages reproduce two entries in Montgomery's diaries, both dated 8 November 1940—"Conversation with Mr. Tibor Eckhardt et al about going to America" followed by "Conversation with H.S.H., The Regent".
104. Minister John Flournoy Montgomery to Paul Nadanyi, undated letter in response to Nadanyi's letter of 22 January 1942, Tibor Eckhardt Papers, Box 17, File: Correspondence, John Flournoy Montgomery, Hoover Institution Archives. For the complete texts of Nadanyi's letter to Montgomery and Montgomery's reply, see Appendix.
105. Tibor Frank, ed., *Discussing Hitler*, p. 53.
106. *Tibor Eckhardt in His Own Words*, p. 157.
107. Paul Nadanyi, *The "Free Hungary" Movement*, p. 40.
108. Tibor Eckhardt to the U.S. Department of State, memo, "Protest Against Systematic Attacks against the Movement and its Leadership from Czecho-Slovak Quarters", 1 February 1942, Tibor Eckhardt Papers, Box 1. File: Attacks Against Tibor Eckhardt, Hoover Institution Archives.
109. Overseas News Agency, Report #480 "Exile Nations Warn Washington of Eckhardt's Activities Here", 9 February 1942, Tibor Eckhardt Papers, Box 1, File: Attacks Against Tibor Eckhardt, Hoover Institution Archives.
110. Steven Béla Vardy. *The Hungarian-Americans*. pp. 110–112.
111. *Tibor Eckhardt in His Own Words*, p. 157.
112. Document on Free Hungarian Plans, 29–30 November 1944, New York to Moscow #1669–1672, 1674–1675, VENONA Archives, www.nsa.gov/venona/venon00113.cfm.
113. Mario D. Fenyő, *Hitler, Horthy, and Hungarian-German Relations 1941–1944*, p. 111. For his part, Admiral Horthy declared during an interrogation he underwent in Wiesbaden after the war that although Eckhardt had been the leader of an opposition party, he considered Eckhardt a "correct" man (later clarified as meaning "honorable"). Horthy "denied ... that the trip to the United States had an official purpose."
114. SOE Records, HS/4/95, National Archives of the United Kingdom.
115. SOE Records, HS/4/96, National Archives of the United Kingdom.
116. John Pelényi, "The Secret Plan for a Hungarian Government in the West at the Outbreak of World War II", *Journal of Modern History* (June 1964), pp. 170–179. (See also: Papers of John Pelényi, Box 1, File: Miscellaneous Papers, Hoover Institution Archives.)
117. Ibid.
118. Ibid., Document II, pp. 175–176.

119. Royall Tyler was the representative of the League of Nations in Hungary in connection with Hungary's League of Nations loan. Later in the war years he was to be revealed as an agent of British interests.
120. John Pelényi, *Journal of Modern History*, p. 171.
121. Ibid. Photocopies of all the financial documents in this transaction and the original documents related to the transfer of the five million dollars to Pelényi in the United States are archived in Box 1 of the Papers of John Pelényi at the Hoover Institution Archives. This topic was also covered by Nandor Dreisziger in "Bridges to the West: The Horthy Regimes' Reinsurance Policies in 1941", *War and Society* (May 1989), pp. 1–23 and by this author in "Eckhardt Tibor és a Szabad Magyarországért Mozgalom", in *Tanulmányok a XIX–XX. századi történelemből* (Budapest: ELTE BTK., 2001), pp. 195–210.
122. SOE Records, HS/4/95, National Archives of the United Kingdom.

CHAPTER 3

Eckhardt and Archduke Otto von Habsburg

One of the first individuals to contact Tibor Eckhardt upon his arrival in America on 8 August 1941 was Archduke Otto von Habsburg, the heir to the Austro-Hungarian throne. "Graciously, he had sent a message to the pier in Brooklyn, when I arrived, asking to see me urgently. The British had lost no time following the Nazi invasion of Russia to start promoting Soviet aims against our nations and the archduke wished to give me a warning against these machinations."[1]

The archduke and Tibor Eckhardt had first met shortly after the 1936 World Scout Jamboree, held in Holland. Paul Teleki had arranged for them to meet in Lyon, France, thinking it important for the two of them to get together to discuss Central European affairs.[2] The initial meeting went very well, and from then on they were in regular contact. It needs to be made clear that Eckhardt was not then a Legitimist, nor did he ever become one, however he was very impressed with the young archduke's depth of knowledge regarding the world, Hungary and the precarious peace on the continent, and he appreciated Otto von Habsburg's insights. "He impressed me most favorably," Eckhardt wrote, "with an unbiased knowledge of world affairs and the understanding of conditions, even in Hungary."[3]

Archduke Otto was already living in the United States by 1941, as were other members of his family, including his mother, Empress Zita, who initially resided in Canada and later moved to Tuxedo Park, New York. Eckhardt observed that the archduke, through his contacts and by virtue of "his quick wit and amiable personality had fortunately ingratiated himself with the President on his very first visit to the White House in 1940. As a result he was courteously received in the State Department as well, particularly by Sumner Welles. Outstanding Americans sincerely befriended him, prominent individuals such as Supreme Court Justice Frank Murphy, and the former Ambassador to the Soviet Russia and later to France, the remarkable William C. Bullitt. The Archduke was not only kept well informed, he also knew his way in the jungle of official Washington. He was unbiased and youthfully sincere, therefore generally liked. Of course, he also knew the difference between a real friend and a snob."[4]

The issue of mutual interest that Archduke Otto wished to discuss with Eckhardt at their first meeting in the United States was related to the British Broadcasting Corporation's propaganda broadcasts to Hungary, which a friend of the archduke had characterized to him as "only helping Goebbels". Eckhardt wrote in his memoirs, "On this and all other questions of mutual interest, I was happy to find that I was in complete agreement with the Archduke. Thereafter for three tormented war years we collaborated without a trace of dissent. I value very highly the Archduke's loyalty to the cause of the nations whom he legitimately represented amidst the most trying of circumstances."[5]

The Third International in Mexico

At their initial New York meeting, the archduke told Eckhardt that he had organized a committee to handle Austrian affairs and the problems of a future peace treaty, and he asked Eckhardt to stay in touch with him concerning Hungarian affairs. For his part, the archduke was pleased to have a partner to fight against the scheming of Beneš and Károlyi, and Eckhardt hoped that the archduke's friendship with President Roosevelt would bode well for the future of Hungary at the end of the conflict.

Soon, another area of mutual interest surfaced—the meeting of the Central Bureau of the Third International, which was held in Mexico from 16–19 November 1941. On 23 February 1942, Count Degenfeld, the archduke's secretary, forwarded a full report of the meeting to Eckhardt in order to forewarn him of the incredible effort the USSR was mounting against democracy and democratic institutions. The report had originated with the Mexican government's secret service, which had infiltrated the meetings. One of the archduke's brothers had been supplied with a copy and made it available to Archduke Otto, who immediately submitted it directly to President Roosevelt, in late November 1941.[6]

The report detailed the workings of the Communist International meetings and the general orders issued at the meetings, which formed the "basis for future action of the different communist parties and other organizations in the Americas". First and foremost, the always existing ideology of the Third International remained untouched. Point number one in the report is that "the present war is an important incident but nothing else in the achievement of the ultimate goal of the Third International. The single object of the Communist International is the destruction of the capitalist regimes and the creation in all countries of communist governments." Another major point is that although German aggression against Russia had made Nazism and Germany the primary enemy, "it should never be forgotten, that there exist two bourgeois capitalistic regimes, which although helping Russia to destroy Nazism, must in their turn be destroyed by an international revolution immediately at the conclusion of the hostilities. Taking for granted an allied victory and the destruction of Nazism, this victory must coincide with communist movements in England and the U.S.A. until the destruction of the present regimes and the way of living of these countries."[7] The report goes on to say that the USSR and the Red Army must appear to everybody to be humanity's saviors, the power thanks to which alone England, the United States and the other Allies are able to fight.

Another statement in the report was frighteningly predictive of the future: "Propaganda must be aimed at creating the impression that groups and organizations or persons, who are nationalists, monarchists, conservatives, and militarists as well as industrialists and financial leaders or churchmen, are in all countries friends, sympathizers or contributors to Nazism or fascist, actively or passively. The impression must be created that all these friends including religious groups are fascist. Thus it will be possible to bring it about that the destruction of Nazism will also mean the destruction of all these powers and ideologies opposed to communist aims."

The report further stated that in most of the European countries the Communist Party would create "Freedom Movements" that would "have to act apparently independent of each other and will not have to show that they are in reality controlled by the Third International. The Third International and the communist parties will only support these movements in an invisible way."[8]

By the time he received the report, Eckhardt had already been in the United States for four months, and he already had ample evidence of the campaign against him and his efforts. In learning the details of the meeting in Mexico, he could see the genesis of the campaign being waged against him and all others who would not side with communism. As explained in Chapter 2, in addition to the concerted and extensive efforts of the Czechs and the Russians, the British, too, had an early and extensive involvement against the Eckhardt movement. The British regarded the movement as a "re-insurance" attempt to return the Horthy regime and its allies to power after war's end and were also determined to keep Archduke Otto von Habsburg from having any influence or rebuilding a power base in Central- and East Europe.

Genesis of the Austrian and Hungarian Legions

By the summer of 1942, after the American declaration of war on Hungary, both Eckhardt and the archduke sensed that a change of policy was in the offing regarding the countries bordering Russia. "The Archduke Otto, never a victim of wishful thinking, noticed and discussed with me the main issues resulting from the unsteady situation," Eckhardt wrote. "We agreed that clarification of American policy concerning Central Europe was badly needed."[9] On 17 September, Archduke Otto called on the White House, asking to introduce his brother Felix to the president, and the two archdukes were received kindly. The president gave detailed and most favorable responses to their questions about matters of interest to them. Foremost was the dilemma of how the small European nations forced into the Axis camp would fare. Would the Allies hold on to their constructive peace aims despite pressure from the Soviets? According to Eckhardt's memoirs, Archduke Otto told him that Roosevelt answered empathetically, "We want a lasting peace, not a peace based on the facts of this war. We have no other purpose but lasting peace. This is why Germany will have to pay a heavy price. But no other nation shall be placed into the same category."[10] Archduke Otto told Eckhardt that he asked anxiously whether the United States would have to accept Soviet demands that might interfere with the Americans' highly commendable plans. According to the archduke, President Roosevelt replied, "Don't be worried, by the time the war comes to an end, the Russians will be much weaker and no serious menace to Europe any more."[11]

At this meeting, the president also discussed his views about the necessity of a federal system in the Central-Danubian Valley. He told Archduke Otto that he felt that "nations with a Western culture should not be united with Pravoslav in the Balkans. ... The Danubian Federation should certainly comprise Austria, including the Italian-Tirol, Slovenia and Istria with Trieste, Hungary with all of Transylvania and also a separate Croatia. The President then declared that he had definitely recognized the Polish-Czechoslovak Federation, although Slovakia could decide later, by plebiscite, whether she preferred to join a Northern or rather the Danubian Federation."[12] As part of the discussion regarding Czechoslovakia, the president also said that he had recognized Beneš as that country's temporary prime minister. Continuing the discussion with the archduke regarding Central- and East Europe, the president went on to condemn Romania, saying that he felt it should be placed under international administration for at least ten years and adding that the "present war also did prove that there was no Yugoslavia, there only existed a Serbia and Croatia, he told this to King Peter of the Serbs and the King did not protest."[13]

The archdukes' meeting with President Roosevelt lasted for more than an hour, and the final ten minutes, according to Eckhardt, produced an "outright sensation".[14] Roosevelt declared that he had not become reconciled to the idea that all the European governments in exile and free movements should be located in London. He felt it would allow the British to influence strongly the future policies of those nations. "He explicitly authorized the Archduke Otto to initiate and organize an Austrian and also a Hungarian Legion in America." If only one thousand volunteers will join each Legion, concluded the President, you can immediately form governments which I will then recognize. Quickly, the Archduke accepted the President's offer. This happened four months before the Soviet victory at Stalingrad."[15] The president recognized that armed forces must be placed under the guidance and control of a political authority and on 17 September 1942 authorized Archduke Otto to organize the two legions on American soil. President Roosevelt promised that if the initiative proved successful, he would recognize an Austrian and a Hungarian government in exile.[16]

According to Eckhardt, it was a "sweltering hot afternoon when returning from the White House, the Archduke Otto stopped at my nearby one-room apartment on K Street."[17] Eckhardt recounts that his pleasure on hearing the good news was tempered by the fact that the offer seemed to have been an improvisation caused by "British meddling with the fate of Central-Europe".[18] Eckhardt knew that Roosevelt's plan would meet with stiff opposition by the English and the Soviets, as well as from within the U.S. administration. Archduke Otto offered to put Eckhardt in charge of the Hungarian Legion, while he himself would personally take charge of the Austrian unit. Having reservations about the plan, as Hungary had already declared war on the United States and was in a different position than Austria, Eckhardt demurred; but having agreed to the president's request, the archduke had to follow through with the creation of the Austrian Legion. Eckhardt urged him to conclude an agreement in writing with the secretary of war and proceeded that night to draft a document regarding the aid required for setting up an Austrian Legion on American soil. "With only slight changes, that agreement was signed within a few days by both the War Department and the Archduke Otto."[19]

By 2 November 1942, Eckhardt had noted in his diary that effective organization of the Austrian Legion was already facing serious difficulties. However, thanks to strong military support, provided on the president's instruction, the work to establish the legion had begun. Three of Archduke Otto's brothers joined the organization as volunteers on the first day it was announced, and gradually the State Department accepted the idea. Fortunately, President Roosevelt had commented favorably and in public on the legion and the success of the Austrian initiative. By the end of January 1943, the Austrian Legion had formed at a military camp in Indiana. Archduke Otto's brothers were among the first trainees. By the end of February 1943, the first Austrian battalion, composed of 1,000 volunteers, had been set up, and preparations were made for forming a second Austrian battalion.[20]

Eckhardt's diary reveals that to his thinking, the fact that President Roosevelt informed Sumner Welles in the State Department of the comments he made to the Habsburg archdukes, indicated that what the president said at the meeting was not an "expression of a passing mood", as was sometimes Roosevelt's wont.[21] The president's comments were prompted instead by his annoyance with British interference in the Danubian area, an area in which he had not abandoned his own interest. However, Eckhardt notes that on 2 November 1942, entirely counter to the plans for Central Europe that Roosevelt shared with the archduke, "Sumner Welles informed the Archduke Otto that Stalin intended to set up puppet governments for the neighboring countries, including even Austria. This was planned in full agreement with Beneš, whom Welles sharply criticized as an 'intrigeur and a liar.' He also condemned continued British appeasement, ready to sacrifice all of Romania, Serbia, Bulgaria, even half of Poland, all of them to be reconstructed under Soviet auspices."[22]

On 28 May 1943, following visits to Washington, D.C., by Anthony Eden and Eduard Beneš, George Creel, a friend of long standing of both Eckhardt and Archduke Otto, shared with them a long conversation he had had with his friend Secretary of State Cordell Hull. [23] Based on the evidence of his diary, Eckhardt notes in his memoirs that Hull had strongly advised Creel that "it was of primary importance to keep Soviet Russia in the war, for Russia was carrying the main burden of the fighting. America … must therefore accept the Russian demands."[24] Upon hearing this, the archduke then shared with Creel and Eckhardt the news that the Austrian Legion had been ordered to disband as a consequence of the Americans having given in to Soviet pressure. The commander of the Legion, General Edwards, who had signed the original agreement approved by Secretary of War Stimson, had suddenly been moved to another command. His successor, General West, then refused to observe any pledge the War Department had made. So after just three months of service in the U.S. Army, the Austrian volunteers were granted citizenship and dispersed without fanfare among various

American regiments. Thus, the Austrian Legion ceased to exist. Eckhardt notes that among all the disappointments that Archduke Otto had to endure, this was the one occasion when he saw him almost lose his composure.[25]

In his biography of Otto von Habsburg, Gordon Brook-Shepherd writes of the anti-Habsburg opposition's desire to destroy the Austrian Legion, noting that the archduke's efforts were "no match for the formally constituted Czech Provisional Government, headed by the world famous Beneš. The Czech statesman's promotion of his own cause carried with it a determination to destroy that of the Habsburgs, with their programme of a post-war conservative-led federation along the banks of the Danube. The Kremlin was equally resolved, for its own purposes, to block this concept and, after Russia's entry into the war, backed a joint Czech-Soviet propaganda campaign run from offices in New York's Rockefeller Centre. They were thought to have found (or bought) sympathetic outlets in up to four hundred newspapers or local radio stations throughout the United States and the collapse of the 'Austrian Battalion' project was due not least to their efforts."[26]

This information coincides with information in the Eckhardt papers that details the complexity of the attacks and gives a perspective on the magnitude of the effort.

Direct proof of the Czechoslovakian Government in Exile's financial involvement in funding propaganda efforts against the Hungarians is furnished in the already-noted correspondence between Rusztem Vámbéry and Jan Masaryk that is located in the Hoover Institution Archives. The on-going monthly financial payments to Vámbéry to fund his work against "Eckhardt and his like" are specifically discussed. Access to these papers was formerly restricted.[27] The connection between the Soviet KGB and the Czechoslovakian Government in Exile and its New York press office, run by Dr. Papanek, is also proven in secret Soviet communications intercepted by the Americans and decoded in the VENONA Archives (see Chapter 2).

In regards to assistance for Hungary, at the suggestion of Count Sigray, the Hungarian senator, a plan had been proposed in April 1942 to organize a regular channel between America and her friends in Hungary for political contact and information. Archduke Otto had passed on this request from Hungary to Colonel William Donovan of the OSS, hoping to initiate cooperation between the two countries. In October 1942 the Hungarians again contacted the archduke, insisting that the time had come to discuss what policy changes should be made in Budapest. The archduke spoke to any number of his friends in the State Department, among them Sumner Welles, but never received an answer substantive enough to relay to his anti-Nazi contacts in Hungary. There seemed to be a desire at the State Department to forestall making any commitment of which the Soviets might not approve; this was similar to the tactics the British SOE used in regards to the Eckhardt movement and Eckhardt's activities.

Collaboration with U.S. Intelligence and the State Department

However, in late 1942 following the Allied landing in North Africa, the archduke and Eckhardt were unexpectedly invited to a conference at the Pentagon. In contrast to their meetings with the State Department, the Pentagon group was composed of a dozen professional military officers of the General Staff. The visitors were informed that the Allied Expeditionary Army in Africa needed current, reliable information regarding Central Europe and were asked to name contacts who would help obtain the needed intelligence.

This meeting had come out of left field. Neither Eckhardt nor Archduke Otto knew the individuals involved, nor could they judge how secure the information would remain, if passed; and so they did not divulge the names of any contacts. Torture and death awaited Allied collaborators, and they could not risk revealing this type of information. Archduke Otto handled the situation diplomatically, but after the meeting a young major approached Eckhardt and suggested they have lunch the next day. "That is how we became friends," Eckhardt writes, "come rain or shine, for a life-time with John V. Grombach, who retired from the U.S. Army as a General."[28]

As a result of this initial meeting with Major Grombach, in February 1943 Eckhardt and Archduke Otto began to work actively with the American intelligence community and to collaborate with it on behalf of Austria and Hungary. For Eckhardt, the collaboration would continue even after the archduke returned to Europe at the end of the war. It has been said that Eckhardt "ran" a group of intelligence agents on behalf of the U.S. government and reported directly to Allen Dulles, director of the OSS (later the CIA). Eckhardt's memoirs reveal that his and the archduke's affiliation was in fact with the Department of the Army Counter Intelligence Corps (the CIC) and the War Department, not the OSS.[29]

It may be instructive at this point to give the details of Eckhardt's work on behalf of the U.S. government. The information that follows and the letters reproduced in the Appendix have not previously been available, and it seems appropriate to include it at this point, given that the collaboration between Eckhardt, Otto von Habsburg and J.V. Grombach dates from their first meeting in the fall of 1942.[30]

Ample proof of Eckhardt's wartime collaboration and the value placed on his work by the Department of the Army is provided by photocopies of original letters to Eckhardt from the War Department thanking him for his contributions. The first, dated 15 November 1943, is from Hayes A. Kroner, a brigadier general in the US Army and chief of the Military Intelligence Service (MIS). Brigadier General Kroner thanks Eckhardt for his work on behalf of the MIS and for his "highly important contributions to the war effort, which you, and many others through and because of you, have made and are making, often at great personal risk." Kroner goes on to say that he commends Eckhardt "for your unselfish and steadfast refusal to accept any pay or compensation whatever for your own work, though it was repeatedly offered because of a feeling that your high-minded and idealistic attitude in this respect was working undue hardship on you."[31] On 15 September 1947, Major General Stephen J. Chamberlin, then the director of military intelligence on the War Department's general staff, wrote Eckhardt to congratulate him on his service as a consultant for "a World War II secret project of the M.I.S. from February 1943 to this date. The leadership, judgment, tact, security, technical knowledge, general efficiency and research and analysis abilities exhibited by you during this period were of a superior nature and most worthy of my commendation."[32]

These original documents not only confirm Eckhardt's contribution to the U.S. war effort but also reaffirm his idealistic and patriotic choice to work without compensation. This arrangement continued for the better part of a decade, and his contributions were again acknowledged in a letter supporting Eckhardt's application for U.S. citizenship in 1954. That letter is from J.V. Grombach, who had risen to the rank of brigadier general since he, Eckhardt and Archduke Otto first met. Writing that he had worked with Eckhardt "for more than twelve years",[33] Grombach recounts Eckhardt's contributions and reaffirms his loyal efforts on behalf of Hungary and the United States. "During the war years, because of his double responsibilities and loyalties, he refused point blank all U.S. efforts and all my efforts to take any compensation or to accept any financial help even though he was working full time for us. This is just to give you a further idea of the man." Written at the height of the Cold War, Grombach's letter goes on to say, "the reason why I am writing you again on this matter is that I am informed that there have been penetrations in the Immigration and Naturalization Service, and I do know that there have been cases where there have been delays and handicaps which mysteriously appeared against people active in fighting Communism, Socialism and Marxism. Naturally, our friend, who had a price on head by both Hitler and Stalin, would be a target of the anti anti-Communists."[34]

Dr. Tibor Frank, who has researched and written extensively on John Flournoy Montgomery, offers a different perspective, based on Montgomery's secret correspondence, on the topic of Eckhardt's collaboration with the U.S. government. Frank postulates in *Discussing Hitler* that Eckhardt might have been serving U.S. intelligence even before his 1941 move to the United States and raises the question of why Eckhardt was assigned a code number when the information he supplied to Montgomery was recorded. (Although he notes that a number was assigned only once between 1934 and 1941.) Frank observes that "one nevertheless wonders whether the Hungarian party leader knew that what he

[Eckhardt] said about politics at home and abroad would be recorded, ending up, through various channels as reports on Washington, D.C., desks … and might we perhaps identify this or that one of his partners in conversations as agents? Paid agents, perhaps, at least in some cases?"[35] Although one cannot dismiss this idea out of hand, there is no evidence to support Frank's theory in any archival material related to Eckhardt found to date.

Eckhardt's collaboration with U.S. intelligence has been clarified in his own recounting of it in his memoirs, *Tibor Eckhardt in His Own Words* (2005), which contain material not previously available; there is ample documentation that the arrangement in question began either in late 1942 or early 1943, just as Eckhardt states. It is also reasonable to assert that Frank's speculation in *Discussing Hitler* that Eckhardt may have been in the pay of the U.S. intelligence services is unfounded. Both of the Army generals quoted above stated in writing (see Appendix) that Eckhardt refused all pay or financial compensation while working with Army Intelligence. Their correspondence also indicates the dates of Eckhardt's collaboration with the U.S. Army MIS.

Eckhardt details his collaborative activities with the archduke in his memoirs:

> On January 27, 1943, we decided on a basic requirement to be observed if our collaboration with the War Department was to last and become successful. The Archduke must have known something about "bugging," for he had the radio blasting and the water running while we discussed our problems. The first thing we agreed upon was to offer our gratuitous collaboration with the U.S. Army dependent on a single pledge, namely on complete secrecy not only toward the Bolsheviks and the British but also concerning American Governmental Agencies, particularly the OSS and OWI.[36] We had to insist that no subversive activities and no revolutionary policies be promoted through our channels to our homelands. We accepted a future change of the regime in Hungary, but only if carried out by orderly, constitutional processes. If this basis for cooperation was accepted we were prepared to immediately contact three factors in Hungary: 1) the anti-Nazi political and religious leaders; 2) properly selected chiefs in the Foreign Office; 3) reliable high-ranking offers in the Army and in the Police. While serving our country we also wished to serve America well. We never deviated from this firm resolve.[37]

Eckhardt wanted to be helpful to the archduke and the president by supplying them with reliable information on European affairs. He had contacts all over Central- and East Europe who were anxious to provide him with high-level reliable information for the United States without receiving remuneration. All his contacts were convinced that they were serving the cause of human freedom and the independence of their respective nations. By organizing a network of such informants and utilizing the resources of the War Department, Eckhardt, through John V. Grombach, maintained a lasting and friendly relationship with the Army General Staff. A secure mode of communication was made available through the Hungarian government in various legations abroad and their couriers. Eckhardt also obtained the invaluable help of the Polish underground, which generously extended its help and resources to the Eckhardt/Habsburg network. Indeed, the Polish underground proved an invaluable and heroic communications network, especially given the numerous instances when the U.S. State Department did not deliver or held up documents, or when communication channels were compromised for a variety of reasons. Using this network of resources, Eckhardt was able to communicate all over Europe across hostile frontiers, including with his family and friends during the second half of the war. At the war's end, he received clear, written expressions of the War Department's gratitude.[38]

While the working relationship they established with the MIS went on quietly and with some success, Archduke Otto and Eckhardt also continued their attempts to work with the State Department and President Roosevelt. President Roosevelt made the U.S. Naval Code Books available to the archduke so that the latter could communicate secretly with his brother Charles, who lived in Lisbon, Portugal, and with other European contacts. Access to the code books facilitated the funneling of information back and forth on behalf of the Allied efforts in Europe, and Archduke Otto, his brother Charles and Eckhardt all used this manner of communication throughout the war.[39]

For his part, Roosevelt continued to reinforce his often-expressed opinion that the small nations of Europe that had been forced into partnership with the Reich were not in the Fascist camp. In a report to Congress after the Italian fleet surrendered and came over to the Allied side, Roosevelt stated, as reported in the Washington, D.C., *Evening Star* on Friday, 17 September 1943: "I believe that equal jubilation and enthusiasm will be shown by the people of the other nations now under the German heel when Nazi gauleiters and native quislings are removed through force or fight. ... We have reliable information that there is definite unrest and a growing desire for peace among the peoples of these satellite countries—Romania, Hungary, Finland and Bulgaria. We hope that in these nations the spirit of revolt against Nazi dominance which commenced in Italy will burst into flame and become a consuming fire." However, after the debacle of the Austrian Legion, it was extremely difficult for Eckhardt and the archduke to find common ground with the U.S. administration.

While Eckhardt's and Otto von Habsburg's full-time collaboration in attempting to bring Hungary over to the Allied side yielded mostly frustration, a different, somewhat unexpected connection brought about the prospect of a breakthrough in Hungary's negotiations with the Allies. In Istanbul, the British made contact with a senior Hungarian official, László Veress, who had been attempting to open negotiations. Veress was abruptly summoned to the yacht of the British envoy, Sir Hugh Knatchbull-Hughessen, and was presented with a list of preliminary conditions for opening official talks with the Hungarian government. Since he was not entrusted with the actual document, Veress had to take down the points from dictation. Foreign Minister Anthony Eden had instructed Knatchbull-Hughessen that details of the agreement could not be made known "before the Allies reached the frontiers of Hungary". Although there was little that was unexpected in the terms outlined, when Veress presented them to Hungarian Prime Minister Kállay, there was a major sticking point—the entire agreement was predicated upon "unconditional surrender" to the Allies, and to that the Hungarians would not agree.

Nevertheless, the agreement was signed in Lisbon, without agreement on that clause, with Andor Wodianer[40] signing for Prime Minister Kállay and Sir Ronald Campbell, the British minister to Portugal, signing for the Allies.[41] As Lisbon had been the main channel of communication for both the archduke and Eckhardt, it is possible that their efforts played a role in the trans-Atlantic pact.

Unfortunately, on 19 August 1944, just three weeks before the signing, far reaching discussions on all issues of primary importance had gotten underway at the Second Anglo-American Quebec Conference. Central Europe was certainly not at the top of the agenda. During the conference, on 18 September, Roosevelt received the archduke to discuss an outspoken letter the latter had sent him seven days earlier. In addition to attempting to clear up some issues regarding the U.S. State Department's belligerent attitude toward Austria, the archduke had used the letter to ask for armaments and funds for the anti-Nazi underground in Austria. Roosevelt's explanation for denying the aid shocked the archduke. The Three Great Powers, Roosevelt said, had agreed in Quebec "that underground movements could only be helped when all the Three Great Powers agreed on giving it."[42] What this meant was that the underground communist parties in Italy and France had been aided with armaments and funds granted by the "British and the Americans who had decided on a policy of never refusing any such demand."[43] But the president advised the archduke that this was not the view of the Soviets, and "it was quite possible ... that in certain countries only the Left of the Resistance would get help."[44] Roosevelt said he deplored the situation, but there was nothing that he could do about it. In his memoirs, Eckhardt quotes the archduke as remarking that as far as the Austrian underground receiving help from the Allies to battle Hitler was concerned, "we might as well have asked for it from a stone wall."[45]

Eckhardt makes it clear that President Roosevelt was the only individual inside or outside government who realized that he and Archduke Otto were working with both the State Department and the Department of the Army MIS.[46] Eckhardt and the archduke were politically savvy enough to understand the problems within the State Department and American intelligence services and to recognize that while they could and should cooperate with them, there were clear limits to their work in that arena. They were also acutely aware of Roosevelt's grand ambitions and in addition were among the only realists when it came to understanding Stalin's plans for the post-war years and England's role in fulfilling them. Both men were jolted into reality when they realized to what extent the Allies were willing to compromise in order to keep the Soviet Union fighting on their side. Quick studies both, they decided to cooperate to the best of their ability but never to compromise or expose their collaborators in the actual theater of war. The example of the Soviet veto on assistance to underground movements that were not communist-sponsored showed them that the Soviets would be the deciding factor in all the Allied powers' decisions. While careful to protect their sources and collaborators, however, Eckhardt and the archduke continued to work closely with each other and with the State Department in the slim hope that there might be a diplomatic solution to the situation in which Austria and Hungary found themselves.

In a dialogue with Gordon Brook-Shepherd, Otto von Habsburg recounted the story of his affiliation with Eckhardt, a reminiscence the archduke later also shared personally with this author.

> In Washington, I was working mainly with Mr. Tibor Eckhardt, the former President of the Independent Smallholders Party in Hungary, who left the country when he saw the direction Horthy was taking in order to build up a Hungarian representation abroad. Eckhardt was a man of great courage and intelligence and, furthermore, an expert on foreign affairs since he had been very active in the League of Nations. I first met him in 1937 and we had remained in close contact ever since.[47] He had, for obvious reasons, no political connections in the United States and I was able to provide him with these. In return, he did much of the actual planning and representation as to how Hungary could be saved by changing sides.[48]

Dr. von Habsburg further reinforced the above statement when elaborating to me in a personal interview on his close three-year collaboration with Eckhardt. "Of course, you see whenever I went to talk to the key decision-makers in the Roosevelt administration, I would talk first to Eckhardt," he said. "We worked very closely with each other. He knew what I was doing; I knew what he was doing. We coordinated our actions completely in all aspects of contact with the United States government and on efforts on behalf of Hungary."[49]

Archduke Otto and Eckhardt were to continue their friendship and working relationship long after the archduke returned to Europe after the war. Eckhardt's memoirs show that he developed enormous respect for the archduke's intelligence and integrity and felt genuine affection for the man. He also valued the archduke's friendship and his efforts on Hungary's behalf and in the tumultuous rough and tumble world of émigré politics. Eckhardt often turned to him for advice and counsel, particularly at the height of the Cold War when he, Eckhardt, served on the Hungarian National Council (1948–1954).

Given the myriad activities in which Eckhardt was involved from the moment he stepped off the gangplank in New York, it is clear that he and Archduke Otto were the fulcrum around which revolved all the major diplomatic efforts in the United States on behalf of Hungary during World War II. Their access to diplomatic circles and the executive branch would not have been possible without the archduke's contacts and energetic efforts. Eckhardt worked to coordinate all of the efforts on behalf of Hungary and attempted to stay in touch with all interested individuals and organizations in the United States and abroad regarding Hungary's situation. It was a full-time job, and in addition to receiving no compensation, it often seemed he got very little support except from his royal partner. Unfortunately, the Hungarians remained unwilling to consider the Allies' demand for "unconditional surrender" and/or to act on Eckhardt's frank suggestion that "now is the time to open secret negotiations with the Russians."[50] Hungary was overrun before either of those diplomatic options was exercised.

The War's End

While Tibor Eckhardt was working full time with Otto von Habsburg and the counter-intelligence unit of the U.S. Department of the Army, he was literally without personal funds. His assets had been frozen in Hungary, he refused financial compensation from the U.S. government, and he lived primarily on financial assistance from friends, although he did some lecturing and writing. In Washington, D.C., he lived in a studio apartment and in equally modest circumstances in New York.

At war's end Eckhardt found he was unable to return to Hungary, and he claimed that that was due to direct intervention by Soviet Foreign Minister Molotov himself.[51] Regardless of who was instrumental in the decision, it is a fact that pressure was applied in both the United States and Hungary to prevent him from returning and resuming the leadership of the Smallholders Party, which had captured a sizeable majority in the 1945 Hungarian elections. Stateless, without a passport and virtually without resources, Eckhardt continued his mission in the United States, firmly believing that others would eventually share his conviction that the Soviet Union intended to impose its will on Central- and East Europe, thus further intensifying the tragic outcome of World War II.

Endnotes

1. *Tibor Eckhardt in His Own Words*, p. 157.
2. Dr. Otto von Habsburg, interview by the author, Pöcking, Germany, 28 October 2003.
3. *Tibor Eckhardt in His Own Words*, pp. 157–158.
4. Ibid.
5. Ibid., p. 158.
6. Count H. Degenfeld to Tibor Eckhardt, 23 February 1942, "The meeting in Mexico of the Central Bureau of the Third International, November 16th to November 19th 1941", Tibor Eckhardt Papers, Box 1, File: Archduke Otto von Habsburg, American Hungarian Library and Historical Society, New York.
7. Ibid.
8. Ibid.
9. *Tibor Eckhardt in His Own Words*, p. 433.
10. Ibid.
11. Ibid., p. 434.
12. Ibid.
13. Ibid.
14. Ibid.
15. Ibid., pp. 434–435.
16. Ibid., p. 435.
17. Ibid.
18. Ibid.
19. Ibid.
20. Gordon Brook-Sheperd, *Uncrowned Emperor: The Life and Times of Otto von Habsburg* (London and New York: Hambledon and London, 2003). In this unauthorized biography of Archduke Otto von Habsburg, the history of the Austrian Battalion is described as a virtual disaster (pp. 155–156). Otto von Habsburg supports the Eckhardt history but does say the battalion did not have 1,000 members. Author's correspondence with Otto von Habsburg, 27 September 2004.
21. *Tibor Eckhardt in His Own Words*, p. 435.
22. Ibid, pp. 436–437.
23. George Creel was a member of Franklin Roosevelt's "Kitchen Cabinet" and served as one of his most trusted advisors until 1940, when he opposed Roosevelt's decision to run for a third term of office. Originally a newspaperman, Creel headed Woodrow Wilson's Committee on Public Information during World War I. He served as chief of the Western Division of the National Recovery Act (NRA) during the 1930s and was chairman of the Advisory Board of the Works Progress Administration (WPA). Creel served as Wilson's representative to Central Europe immediately after the Paris peace talks, toured Europe for a month and assessed the Károlyi government for Wilson. The closest friend of John F. Montgomery, Creel was instrumental in obtaining Montgomery's appointment to the post of U.S. minister to Hungary, and his political clout was the major reason Montgomery remained in that post from 1933–1941. Creel traveled to Hungary in 1936 and served on the advisory board of the *Hungarian*

Quarterly from its inception in 1936 until 1941. His term coinciding with Eckhardt's service on its editorial board. Creel also competed against Upton Sinclair for the Democratic nomination to run for governor of California in the 1930s. Creel and Eckhardt remained cordial friends and political allies until Creel's death in 1953.

24. *Tibor Eckhardt in His Own Words*, p. 437.

25. The Austrian Legion, officially the Austrian Battalion (101st Atterbury Infantry Battalion), was part of the United States Army, which also contained one Czech Battalion and one Norwegian Battalion. The Austrian Battalion trained at Camp Atterbury, Indiana, from the time of its formation on 7 December 1942 until it was deactivated on 27 May 1943.

26. Gordon Brook-Shepherd, *Uncrowned Emperor*, p. 158.

27. Rusztem Vámbéry to Jan Masaryk, 13 July 1941, Rusztem Vámbéry Papers, Hoover Institution Archives. It is worth noting once again that this date *precedes* Eckhardt's actual arrival in the United States.

28. *Tibor Eckhardt in His Own Words*, p. 442. In his memoirs Eckhardt refers to the Grombach organization as part of the CIC (Department of the Army, Counter Intelligence Corps). In fact, the Grombach organization was part of MIS (Military Intelligence Service) for part of its existence, but was not part of CIC, according to the records found to date by Mark Stout (see endnote 30).

29. Ibid., p. 444.

30. Mark Stout, formerly at the CIA's Directorate of Intelligence and as of this writing an analyst at the Institute for Defense Analyses (IDA), shared his written analysis of the Grombach organization with this author. (See also *Studies in Intelligence, Journal of the American Intelligence Professional* Vol. 48, No. 3 (2004) pp. 69–82 and www.cia.gov/csi/kent_csi/docs/v48i3a07p.htm.) Entitled "The Pond: Running Agents for State, War and the CIA", Stout's study states that the J.V. Grombach organization in fact was never a part of the Department of the Army Counterintelligence (CIC). Instead, it was a secret intelligence organization run by Grombach as part of the Military Intelligence Service (MIS) from 1942–1947, and was later sponsored by different government agencies. MIS was part of MID, the Military Intelligence Division, and the CIC to which Eckhardt refers reported to the MIS. In an email to this author of 25 May 2006, Stout writes that the Grombach organization "due to its nature had purposely obscure cover names and did not appear on most wiring diagrams. And, one of its names was very similar to the name of another quite different branch of War Department intel." Stout verifies that John Patrick Finnegan's standard official history, *Military Intelligence* (Washington, D.C: Center of Military History of the United States Army, 1998), lists Kroner as head of MIS for a period during the war and Chamberlin as head of all War Department intelligence, under a slightly different name, just after the war.

31. Hayes Kroner to Tibor Eckhardt, 15 November 1943, Tibor Eckhardt Papers, Box 1, Manuscript of memoirs, American Hungarian Library and Historical Society. The original letter is reproduced in the Appendix.

32. Stephen Chamberlin to Tibor Eckhardt, 15 September 1947, Tibor Eckhardt Papers, Box 1, Manuscript of memoirs, American Hungarian Library and Historical Society. The original letter is reproduced in the Appendix.

33. John Valentine Grombach was a complex character and his secret "independent" intelligence organization was in fact looked at askance by the official intelligence

bodies. Mark Stout is the authority on J.V. Grombach and his organization and is researching and writing a book on the subject.

34. John V. Grombach to Robert C. Alexander, 11 August 1954, Tibor Eckhardt Papers, Box 1, Folder: Biography–Extension of Stay in the United States, Hoover Institution Archives. The original letter is reproduced in the Appendix.

35. Tibor Frank, ed., *Discussing Hitler: Advisers of U.S. Diplomacy in Central Europe 1934–1941* (Budapest: Central European University Press, 2003), pp. 52–53.

36. Office of War Information.

37. *Tibor Eckhardt in His Own Words*, p. 444.

38. The original letters are reproduced in the Appendix.

39. Dr. Otto von Habsburg, interview by the author, Pöcking, Germany, 28 October 2003.

40. Andor Wodianer was minister of the Royal Hungarian Legation in Lisbon from May 1939 until 27 April 1944.

41. Gordon Brook-Shepherd, *Uncrowned Emperor*, p. 164.

42. *Tibor Eckhardt His Own Words*, p. 438.

43. Ibid., p. 439.

44. Ibid.

45. Ibid., p. 440.

46. Ibid., pp. 445 and 465.

47. The date Eckhardt and Otto von Habsburg first met is often stated as 1937. However in a personal interview with the author, Dr. von Habsburg stated that it was immediately following the Scout Jamboree in Holland, the year therefore would have to be 1936.

48. Gordon Brook-Shepherd, *Uncrowned Emperor,* p. 163.

49. Otto von Habsburg, interview by the author, Pöcking, Germany, 28 October 2003.

50. *Tibor Eckhardt in His Own Words*, p. 471.

51. Tibor Eckhardt, *Recollections, Regicide at Marseille*, from the flyleaf.

CHAPTER 4

Hungarian Émigré Organizations in America, 1941–1945

Despite the failure of Tibor Eckhardt's short-lived (1941–1942) Movement for Independent Hungary, the Hungarian leadership in America and elsewhere in the West was unwilling to abandon the idea of forming a strong Hungarian organization. Key individuals continued to plan for a group that would assume a prominent role in the development of post-war Hungary.

The Secret Barcza-Pelényi Committee—The Committee of Ministers/Követi Bizottság

Eckhardt had contacts within the U.S. Department of State and a strong relationship with former minister to Hungary John Flournoy Montgomery. However, John Pelényi, the former Hungarian minister to the United States, had even greater access to key U.S. government decision makers. In his final and most important posting, Pelényi had served as Royal Hungarian Minister from 1933 until Hungary entered an alliance with Germany on 22 November 1940. That day, Pelényi notified Count Pál Teleki that he was resigning his post.[1]

The *New York Tribune* article written at the time of Pelényi's resignation reflects the extent of his American contacts and the high regard in which the administration held him.

> While never for a moment surrendering any of his qualities as Minister from Hungary, and always faithfully reporting about Hungarian affairs and interpreting them to Americans, Mr. Pelényi established such close personal contacts with persons in all walks of American life and in all parts of this country that he came to know and understand the United States better than most Americans know and understand it. He made it a point to meet not only officials and Washington correspondents, but professors, writers, bankers, business men and labor leaders in all parts of the country. The wide range of Mr. Pelényi's friendships in this country make his resignation of more than ordinary interest. He will be missed in Washington and New York, and by all those persons in different walks of life who, during the last quarter-century, had come to look on him as virtually "one of ours." It is good news that he plans to spend at least a part of his retirement here in the United States. He will thus continue as unofficial ambassador, and can be counted upon to further the cause of close Hungarian-American relations.[2]

The *New York Times* report of the resignation was similarly effusive:

> No member of the Washington diplomatic corps knows this country better, or understands it more thoroughly, than Mr. John Pelényi, whose resignation as Minister of Hungary to the United States ends a useful and distinguished diplomatic career. ... It is due largely to his tact, character and personal popularity that there has been so much American sympathy for Hungary in all its trials and vicissitudes. To those who have learned to admire and respect Mr. Pelényi, his retirement at this time will be as deeply regretted as the new tie-up forced upon his unhappy and unwilling country.[3]

In a letter to his good friend Tibor Eckhardt explaining his decision to resign, Pelényi said, "If a clear cut issue arises one has to take a stand, one has to be one thing or another, one cannot be a stradler [*sic*]." He went on to quote the powerful words a friend had recently said to him: "I realize that your men at home must remain at their posts, but if you stay on as Minister it can only mean that you have sacrificed your principles for the retention of a comfortable berth." Pelényi acknowledged to Eckhardt that if he stayed at his post he would lose his creditability with the contacts he had built so carefully and thus the possibility to be of future use to Hungary and the Hungarian cause.[4]

Pelényi joined the faculty at Dartmouth College in Hanover, New Hampshire, in 1941 as a professor of political science, but he continued to maintain his diplomatic contacts and his involvement in Hungarian-American relations. He was also often called to Washington for consultations with various government officials and to be briefed on top-secret matters relating to Hungary and the conduct of the war. His privileges as an unofficial ambassador made it possible for him to provide support and information to his Hungarian contacts and to serve as a conduit for communication between the Hungarian government and the United States.

Though Hungary was officially an Axis state, it is widely known that the Hungarians made several diplomatic attempts to remove themselves from the German side as the war progressed. Pelényi received a confidential letter from Hungary in May 1943 thanking him for his insights and advice and providing a status report on the resistance movement within Hungary:

> We could give considerable practical help to promote Anglo-Saxon occupation and several instruments for this purpose have already been created. I can inform you that we have organized groups all over the country which at the approach of Anglo-Saxon troops are instructed to give them all assistance. On the other hand, it is clear that due to our geographical position we cannot initiate any action before the approach of the troops of occupation. Premature or ill advised action on our part might even retard the Allied military action. For the time being we keep our railroads, bridges and roads prepared for all eventualities awaiting the future approach of Allied Divisions.[5]

The writer observes that the only roadblocks to cooperation with the Allies could come from the Hungarian-German minority, which had been heavily armed by the Germans and the Romanians. The letter also makes the point that the "Hungarian Revisionist League is destined to play an important role in Hungary. Since you left, it has built up an efficient organization in every community of the country and is today the strongest organization. The Boy Scouts Organization has merged into the Revisionist league and has refused to join the Hitler Jugend in Vienna, as the Germans had requested." The writer closes with a request that Pelényi send further news. Clearly, in early 1943 the Hungarians still held the hope that they could escape being crushed between the Germans and Russians in the coming battle on their soil.

Given his long diplomatic career, it is to be expected that Pelényi would have access to information within Hungary. What was extraordinary was his access to confidential American information at the height of the war. This can best be illustrated by some rather astonishing notes that he took during a 7 July 1943 conversation with William C. Bullitt, the former U.S. ambassador to the USSR.

Bullitt's awareness of the consequences of appeasing the USSR during the course of the war is patently evident, and the raw candor of his remarks to Pelényi about Hungary's future was ominous.

> B: [Bullitt] cannot understand anything of British policy—lay down completely to Russians.
>
> Russia will have to be satisfied for some years to come with Roumania, Bulgaria, and Yugoslavia—minus Croatia which they don't want.
>
> Europe divided between British in West and Russian in East—two 'unselfish powers."
>
> Hungary is included in the Russian sphere of interest.
>
> B: "that little s.o.b." sold out completely to Russia.
>
> He pursue Pontius Pilate policy washing on hands [*sic*]—I am at 100% disagreement with our policy and told the Pres. so.
>
> If we cannot make our views prevail now—we have missed the boat.
>
> Can there be any peace on this basis?
>
> With this policy there can be no Federat [*sic*] of Europe and no regional federations.
>
> Conversation that he refused to ever consider Hungary the enemy and was talking in that vaine [*sic*].[6]

Ambassador Bullitt's remarks make it clear that it was known within U.S. diplomatic circles as early as 1943 that Hungary was to be sacrificed to the Russians. (This was long before the Yalta Conference, 4–11 February 1945, to which most historians date the Allied decisions regarding the post-war spheres of influence in Europe.) In 1942, almost immediately after realizing that the Movement for Independent Hungary was not going to succeed without Eckhardt's leadership, and with the situation in Hungary becoming more critical by the moment, former Ambassador Pelényi and other Hungarian diplomats and leaders began to talk about forming a group of leaders to encourage and support resistance in Hungary and to prepare for the post-war period. However, they were not able to organize officially until 1944. On 3 April of that year, key émigré figures—led by the dean of Hungarian ministers, György Barcza, in Europe and by John Pelényi in the United States—agreed in strictest confidence to form a Committee of Ministers. Barcza was the former Hungarian minister in London; his anglicized name was George Barcza or sometimes George de Barcza, in Hungary he was György nagyalasonyi Barcza. He had been corresponding with key Hungarian diplomats since the previous spring about the possibility of forming a diplomats' committee.[7]

In a letter to Pelényi, Baron György Bakach-Bessenyey (Hungarian minister to Switzerland until his resignation on 24 March 1944) describes the proposed committee's composition and mission:

> [A] committee comprising all ministers and heads of missions who have not recognized the Sztojay government, will undertake to group those Hungarian diplomats, employees and other patriots who may be relied on, and to function, as suits the occasion, as an advisory and informatory organization relative to any matters concerning Hungary for the United States, Great Britain, and the Allied nations generally. The committee will seek to promote the organization of civil and military resistance to the German in Hungary. The committee represents no political party and assumes no standpoint regarding matters of internal policy, but its persistent aim is the reestablishment of Hungarian sovereignty and independence, based on constitutional democracy.[8]

Information about the new committee was sent to all the most trustworthy Hungarian diplomats; those who agreed to participate in it were to so signify by sending a telegram reading "J'accepte". Minister Bessenyey was among the many Hungarian diplomats who refused to recognize the new Hungarian government and resigned his post. Having forfeited his citizenship as well, he joined the fledgling organization led by Barcza and Pelényi.[9] With few exceptions, membership in the new organization was limited to diplomats who had resigned their posts before March 1944, a group that included the crème de la crème of Hungarian ministers and many at the consular, vice-consular and secretarial levels.[10]

Barcza was counting on Tibor Eckhardt's participation in the group and included him in his original membership invitation, but Eckhardt declined, citing his ongoing status as a primary target of the Vámbéry/Károlyi faction's slander campaign. Eckhardt sent Pelényi an undated, handwritten personal note saying, "I wellcome [*sic*] and shall readily support much needed action for resistance but ask not to put my name on the list of the Council members as no practical result could be obtained at present here by my inclusion."[11]

On 18 May 1944, as the new committee—to be known as the Committee of Ministers (Követi Bizottság)—was being formulated,[12] Pelényi received a call at Dartmouth from Howard Travers of the State Department. Travers wanted to stop by the next day on his way back to Washington, D.C., and Pelényi thought it must be in reference to gaining admission to Dartmouth for his son. Much to the professor's surprise, "he said he was coming to me on official business by order of his superiors."[13] The message Travers brought was in code and first had to be transcribed. According to Pelényi's notes, the gist of the message was that "while the Dept could not recognize my committee it looked with favor on the proposed activities and was ready therefore to facilitate the intercourse between the Hungarians in questions (all cable expense) provided it goes through State Dept. As he was speaking about the State Dept. as 'they' I asked who 'they were'? He said the only people who knew about it beside himself were Hull, Stettinius, [?], and Cannon."[14] Travers also said that the State Department was trying to get in touch with Count István Bethlen. The matter was discussed thoroughly, and Pelényi noted that Travers "immediately realized that certain elements would attack anyone figuring in Hung. movement and that I would loose [*sic*] all usefulness in case of publicity."[15]

Pelényi accepted the proposed arrangement with the State Department, but he told Travers that the president of the United States would have to approve it, as he, Pelényi, had pledged when he resigned as minister in 1940 to consult with the president before engaging in any kind of political activity. Pelényi said that he would draft a memo on the matter for the president's approval. Travers also asked for and received Pelényi's authorization to show the memo intended for the president to Tibor Eckhardt immediately.

Eckhardt saw the memo the next day, 20 May. When they spoke on the phone the following night, Pelényi noted that Eckhardt advised him to keep their activities confidential and "that nothing would be gained by exposing me to attacks—particularly since the nyugat communist pope had already come out with an attack against all former ministers including myself."[16] That day Pelényi drafted his statement of intent for the new organization and, as per his request, sent it to Travers at the State Department, where it was approved by Travers's superiors.

The dissident diplomats who formed the Committee of Ministers were the leaders in whom the hard-pressed Hungarian government put its greatest faith, for they were the most aware of the untenable situation in which their country found itself. Throughout 1943, a faint hope remained that the Hungarians could control the situation. The Germans had, for example, not taken over the major government agencies, thus leaving open certain possibilities for the future. However, the low point in an already disastrous situation for Hungary came in March 1944, when the Nazi puppet government was installed and set about implementing the German policies of ethnic cleansing that the Horthy government had succeeded in putting off. This, coupled with the progress of the war, served to make Hungary's situation even more untenable.

The Revisionist League, which was active in Hungary, had indicated to the leaders of the Committee of Ministers that its members were hopeful that they could take some steps to avoid the apparently inevitable disaster for Hungary. However, by the autumn of 1944, the leaders of all the anti-Nazi parties in Hungary had been dragged to Germany. A letter to György Barcza from the Hungarian legation in Rome dated 19 September 1944 stated that "these leaders represent the totality of anti nazi organizations and in any case represent the overwhelming majority of the country. For that reason the leaders dans L'espirit de la constitution may well act as pars pro toto and form a regency-council/provided by the constitution and so maintain Hungarian soverignty [*sic*] until time will be propitious for, them to act, name a government and reestablish law and order."[17]

The Committee of Ministers had unofficial support and even some financial assistance from the U.S. government. The key contact at the State Department was Howard Travers, and Tibor Eckhardt was his conduit and chief source of information regarding both the Committee of Ministers' efforts and other national and international events with respect to Hungary.[18] Why then did the United States neither support the Committee's efforts publicly nor provide more assistance? Perhaps the answer can be found in the disinformation being dispensed by an émigré group with a completely different agenda for Hungary's future.

The Vámbéry Faction

What the dissident Hungarian diplomats sought was to preserve the Hungarian political status quo after the war. They sought it first through Eckhardt's Free Hungary movement and when that failed through the Committee of Ministers. Another group of Hungarian émigrés and their supporters were working at cross-purposes to this goal. The "nyugat communist pope" Eckhardt referred to when speaking with Pelényi on 20 May was probably Eduard Beneš or perhaps even Rusztem Vámbéry. Until their deaths, these two leading power brokers in the movement for post-war change in Hungary continued to be Eckhardt's nemesis.

Vámbéry was convinced that every evil that had befallen Hungary was a result of the Horthy regency's reactionary leadership and the perpetuation of the rights of the nobility and petty nobility. He was intractable on this issue. In a 2 October 1942 draft of an article for *Harc!* entitled "After Horthy What?", he writes of political parties that might be willing to join the Horthy-Kállay-Bethlen coalition government: "... if they willingly enter such marriage not even the Almighty could dismiss the charge that by saving the political setup of 1919 they attempted to prevent the democratic transformation of Hungary. However only people with a limited intelligence can imagine that amidst peoples striving for democracy Hungary could survive as an island of feudal organization."[19]

Vámbéry arrived in the United States in 1938, having recognized the path that Hungary was taking by allying itself with Germany and having anticipated even greater political upheaval in Europe in the future. Already elderly, Vámbéry was a controversial figure with prodigious intellectual powers, a small but vocal left-wing political base, a rigid view of Hungary and Hungarian politics and a definite political agenda. He soon settled into a teaching position at the New School for Social Research in New York City and continued his activities as an influential force against the Horthy regime. He wrote for left-wing publications such as *The Nation*, lobbied for political change in Hungary and the Danubian Basin, and tried to influence American foreign policy through his network of colleagues on the Left.

It is not difficult to understand why Vámbéry was highly regarded for his scholarship in the field of criminal law or why his left-wing views found public support in America during this period of time. He exerted a disproportionate influence as a result of his prolific writing and networking, especially in some university and intellectual circles, as the Communist cause and its political ideology had a substantial number of supporters in the English-speaking world—particularly in England and the United States. Vámbéry had little support within the Hungarian émigré community, except in communist and socialist circles, and even they were suspicious of his elitist background, as articles about him in the communist newspaper *Magyar Jövő* readily demonstrate.[20]

Vámbéry was well aware of the sentiment within the Hungarian American communities regarding his views on the Horthy government. Before the United States entered World War II, a Professor Wrong had suggested to a leader of the Hungarian community in Canada that Vámbéry help counter pro-Nazi propaganda by giving a series of lectures. (This should be understood as countering pro-Horthy regime propaganda). One of the Canadian community leaders replied, "According to about six or seven leading Hungarian gentlemen in Toronto, and I too share their opinion, it would be mistake to bring Prof. Vámbéry to Toronto or even to Canada to lecture to the Hungarians 'to counteract Nazi propaganda' since there is no Nazi movement or propaganda among the Hungarians here. As a matter of fact, the Hungarians are very against Naziism [*sic*]! We have more difficulty with the Communistic elements here!"[21]

Anticipating Tibor Eckhardt's arrival in America, Vámbéry wanted to form his own group in order to counter Eckhardt's potential impact. Vámbéry and the newly-arrived László Fényes founded the American Federation of Democratic Hungarians (Demokratikus Magyarok Amerikai Szövetsége) on 6 June 1941 at a "közgyülés" at the *Magyar Jövő* offices. Twenty-two people attended.[22] The writer of the *Magyar Jövő* article on the meeting was quick to note that regardless of the founding members' professed liberal values, attendance had been by invitation only, with the intention of keeping out the element considered undesirable—working class Hungarian Americans.[23] Contrary to Vámbéry's expectations, the formation of his organization was received less than enthusiastically, even in the most liberal circles. *Magyar Jövő* wrote, "Rusztem Vámbéry has in the past twenty years not done anything, and now suddenly has political ambitions."[24] Referring to

Vámbéry as a "burnt out professor", it is clearly the reporter's view that Vámbéry's perspective on democracy did not embrace the concept of participation by the general public—a stance Vámbéry often ascribed to the Horthy regime.

The leadership of the Vámbéry organization was composed not just of Hungarians but also of other ethnic minorities that were potential members of a greater Danubian federation. There is no question that the organization was formed in order to neutralize Eckhardt and sabotage his work. As has been noted here previously, two months *before* Eckhardt arrived in the United States, Vámbéry wrote to Jan Masaryk in London to request Czech financial support for a proposed fortnightly publication espousing their point of view. In the letter, he attempts to frighten Masaryk into thinking that if Eckhardt were successful in the U.S., it would threaten the Czechoslovak cause. The letter first characterizes "the overwhelming majority of Hungarian-Americans as revisionists, the term being a convenient cloak for Nacism [*sic*] or Communists" and continues with the observation "that there is a thin stratum of intellectuals who being opposed to both are keeping aloof from political life in general."[25]

It is interesting that Vámbéry felt the need to discredit the support that he anticipated Eckhardt would receive from the Hungarian American community upon his arrival in the United States. The letter also reveals that Vámbéry realized that the majority of Hungarian Americans would be politically more in sync with Eckhardt's vision for Hungary's future than with his own. It does not seem to have entered into Vámbéry's analysis that the Hungarian Americans in question were long-term U.S. residents, the majority of them second generation, whose political decisions were quite free of any direct influence from the reactionary Horthy regime.

More than any other of his writings, Vámbéry's private and confidential letter to Masaryk reveals his fears.

> Our propaganda seems all the more important as the Hungarian government is making an effort through their emissary Dr. Eckhardt, using American revisionist organizations to establish a pseudo-exiled Hungarian government which would secure in case of an Allied victory the continuation of the post-war reactionary regime in Hungary. These efforts would find powerful support in the major part of the Magyar newspapers published in this country. It seems to us, therefore, of greatest importance to establish a literary foothold in support of our democratic, liberal and progressive movement.[26]

Vámbéry requested $1,000 a month from Masaryk to support the publication he had in mind and then closed with the sentiment that if Masaryk was kind enough to share his views, he would appreciate his taking up the matter with the

Czechoslovak Foreign Office and the Ministry of Propaganda. Subsequently, *Harc!*, "an anti-fascist paper", was funded and began publishing scathing criticisms of Eckhardt, the Free Hungary Movement and American support of it.

Vámbéry's private correspondence reveals a petty and vitriolic side to his character, which friends and supporters such as Oszkár Jászi chose to explain away by saying, "his passion and irony are natural results of his life as a fighter".[27] Vámbéry's writings for publication, on the other hand, "explained" the Hungarian situation to Western readers in prose that was erudite, scholarly, witty and convincing. Most objective scholars in the West recognized that his portrayal of Hungary's situation represented a convenient alteration of history to fit Vámbéry's personal arguments regarding that country's past and future. He did, however, become the darling of America's left-wing socialist and communist intellectual press.

Oszkár Jászi claimed that during the inter-war period Vámbéry was a "kind of ambassador for the oppressed people". He further asserted that "every distinguished and intelligent foreigner who tried to understand the situation of Hungary went into the Vámbéry home to hear the real story of the past, of the intricate machinations of the counter-revolution, and of its diplomatic repercussions."[28] This is certainly second hand knowledge, for Jászi chose to leave Hungary at the time of the Bolshevik takeover and did not return even for a short visit until after the Second World War. If being an "ambassador for the oppressed" is equivalent to undertaking unpopular activities such as the defense of Mátyás Rákosi at his trial for treason, then perhaps that accolade is apt. In the West, however, Vámbéry portrayed himself as a democrat and the spokesman for the oppressed Hungarian population as a whole, not as the supporter of special interests such as the legal defense of Communist Party activists.

Jászi's portrayal of Vámbéry as a sort of guru for uninformed Western visitors to Hungary is inaccurate. Some did indeed gravitate to Vámbéry, but the greater portion of diplomats and scholars held Pelényi and Eckhardt in far higher regard. Both the U.S. ministers who served in Hungary during the inter-war period were staunch Eckhardt supporters. When Vámbéry attempted to pick a very public fight in print with John Flournoy Montgomery regarding Montgomery's editorial support of Eckhardt, the former minister refused to take the bait, declining an ongoing dialogue.[29] Even Jászi admitted that Vámbéry had very little official support in America. He characterized Vámbéry's situation there as "[living] in noble poverty and unaided by the mighties of the land, who favor the Habsburgs and hidden exponents of the Horthy system."[30]

Vámbéry and his like-minded colleagues were motivated by their belief that the Hungarians could only be freed from oppression by their ruling classes by means of a dramatic break with the past and its leaders. They felt that in the future Hungary could survive only as a democratic nation that was part of a Danubian federation to which all the Successor States of the former Austro-Hungarian Empire would belong. Needless to say, using the Jászi model, the government would be free of any leaders from the Horthy years. Oszkár Jászi was viewed as the great champion of this vision, and it formed the basis of his and Vámbéry's collaboration over several decades.

The idea of Hungary's participation in a Danubian federation was hardly the exclusive property of Jászi and his group. The Revisionist League had proposed the idea in the late 1920s, when Eckhardt was the league's vice president, and it was also one of the points of the manifesto the Movement for Independent Hungary issued when it was formed in 1941. However, the political leaders of the Successor States were only too eager to endorse the Jászi concept, as their greatest fear was the success of the revisionist movement in Hungary (with Hungary regaining its lost territories) and/or the restoration of the Habsburg monarchy. If either or both cases succeeded, they knew they would be the political losers.

Vámbéry and his supporters had much in common with the political ideology espoused by the leadership of the Successor States, particularly with Czechoslovakia's Eduard Beneš. An adroit politician, Beneš straddled the political fence so cleverly that he was held in favor both at Whitehall and at the Kremlin. The Hungarian political establishment, in the person of Eckhardt and Pelényi, warned the United States that Beneš was, so to speak, "in Stalin's pocket". But as John F. Montgomery points out in *Hungary, the Unwilling Satellite,* their warnings were ignored. (The book gives Montgomery's account of his years as American minister in Hungary and his views on the Hungarian political situation. It was published after the Soviets closed their grip on Eastern Europe after World War II.) Interestingly, scholars now dealing with previously secret archival material from the former Soviet Union (the VENONA Archives) have become convinced that the long-held Hungarian belief that Beneš was a Soviet agent is true.[31] Throughout the war, the Czechoslovakian Government in Exile strongly supported Vámbéry's point of view—it even mailed out a newsletter, issued by the Czechoslovak Government Information Service's Carpathian–Russian desk, featuring an article by Vámbéry entitled "Fruits of the Berlin–Budapest Marriage 1944"! There is no question that Vámbéry threw in his lot with the Czechs in order to garner the post-war political changes he envisioned for Hungary.[32]

Vámbéry proposed his vision—a democratic Hungary in a Danubian or Balkan confederation with no leaders who had been involved in the Horthy government—to the U.S. State Department in a memo headed SECRET and dated 10 May 1944. In it he proposed that the committee Károlyi founded, the "Committee for a New Democratic Hungary", be utilized as the Hungarian advisory committee for the post-war governance of Hungary. This would, he said, avoid the involvement of "representatives of the ruling caste [who] are only too ready to conform to any foreign power which happens to be in charge of the country."[33] This memo outlines his committee's policy recommendations for post-war Hungary and states that their implementation should not be hindered, as "it seems probable that the Russian desire to have democratic, non-aggressive nations in her vicinity is meant seriously."[34]

Vámbéry is either being or appearing to be uncharacteristically naïve by not drawing an unavoidable conclusion in this memo. Since most Hungarian institutions, whether political, military, religious or educational, had been led by either pro-Horthy or Horthy-neutral individuals for over two decades, the only way for a leadership with few or no ties to Horthy could emerge after the war would be if the new leaders were either fascists or communists.

After Hungary's first post-war election, held in November 1945, Vámbéry sent the Department of State an undated memo in which he reveals that his committee had had to be dissolved and *Harc!* discontinued because Hungary had been recognized as "a truly democratic regime by the United States".[35] Nevertheless, he goes on, those who had carried on the hard struggle against reactionary Hungarian elements in the United States "feel it to be our duty to continue this struggle insofar it seems nevessary [*sic*]."[36] Revealingly, the memo continues in the same vein as during the war: "Hungarian-Americans in this country are still to a great extent supporting reactionary and anti-Semitic policy. Hungarian-American Communists are unfortunately no anti-dote to despoison [*sic*] because in persuance [*sic*] of their 'realistic' policy they were ready to co-operate with the archreactionary Hungarian-American Federation."[37] Then, after railing against the Hungarian American press for having stepped up its activities against his committee's point of view, Vámbéry gets to point six of his memo—"our request that you may kindly grant us the usual support for the next 6 months."[38]

While there is ample documentation that the Czechoslovakian Government in Exile provided financial support for Vámbéry's committee, this memo is the only primary document in which the U.S. State Department is directly identified as having been a source of funds for the Vámbéry organization. The Vámbéry papers contain a few references to financial support from Howard Travers, the same State Department official (head of the Visa Section) who provided secret financial support for the Committee of Ministers. Perhaps in its practice of political realism, the State Department was funding both exile groups.

In addition to his financial support from the U.S. State Department and the Czechoslovakian Government in Exile, circumstantial evidence also points to British support for, if not a financial connection with Vámbéry. This is evidenced by the British intelligence service's (SOE) establishment of the anti-Eckhardt/

Hungarian publication *Igazmondó*, using Ignac Schultz as their editor. Schultz's *Igazmondó* position was kept secret, yet he wrote openly each month for Vámbéry's publication *Harc!*.

Ironically, as a consequence of the plans that Bullitt shared with Pelényi in 1943, neither the mainstream Committee of Ministers, which had popular support at home and among émigré groups, nor the American Federation of Democratic Hungarians, which had little populist support but much clout on the Left and with the Successor States, ended up as the dominant force in Hungary's post-war government. Both groups dwindled and eventually halted their efforts. Individual members, however, kept up the effort to influence and assist post-war Hungary. It took the harsh political reality of the Cold War for the United States finally to approve and fund the creation of an émigré organization that could be effective both at home and abroad.[39]

Endnotes

1. János Pelényi to Count Pál Teleki, 28 November 1940, Papers of János Pelényi, Box 1, File: Letters Following My Resignation, Hoover Institution Archives. This letter followed his official resignation letter of 22 November 1940.
2. "A Link with Hungary", *New York Tribune*, 30 November 1940.
3. "The Hungarian Minister", *New York Times*, 2 December 1940.
4. János Pelényi to Tibor Eckhardt, 11 January 1941, Papers of János Pelényi, Box 1, Folder: Letters Following My Resignation, Hoover Institution Archives.
5. András Tamás to János Pelényi, 28 May 1943, Papers of János Pelényi, Box 1, Folder: Letters Following My Resignation, Hoover Institution Archives. András Tamás was the head of the Revisionist League office in Lisbon. Throughout the war, he served as a conduit for information that came through various underground networks. See: Tessa Stirling, Daria Nałęcz and Tadeusz Dubicki, eds. *Intelligence Co-operation Between Poland and Great Britain During World War II.* Volume 1: *The Report of the Anglo-Polish Historical Committee* (London and Portland, Oregon: Valentine Mitchell, 2005), p. 525.
6. "Short conversation with Bullitt", notes, 7 July 1943, Papers of János Pelényi, Box 1, Folder: Royall Tyler, Hoover Institution Archives.
7. Memorandum on the Mission and Composition of Members of the Committee of Ministers, 1944, Papers of György nagyalasonyi Barcza, Box 11, File: Committee of Ministers, Hoover Institution Archives.
8. Baron György Bakach-Bessenyey to János Pelényi, 2 May 1944, Papers of János Pelényi, Box 1, Hoover Institution Archives. (Letter is filed in a large envelope with miscellaneous papers.)
9. *New York Times*, 24 May 1944.

10. Memorandum on the Mission and Composition of Members of the Committee of Ministers, undated (probably 1944), Papers of György nagyalasonyi Barcza, Box 11, File: Committee of Ministers, Hoover Institution Archives. See the Appendix for the list of committee members.
11. Tibor Eckhardt to János Pelényi, undated note, Papers of János Pelényi, Box 1, Hoover Institution Archives. (Letter is filed in a large envelope with miscellaneous papers.)
12. While the Barcza-Pelényi "Committee of Ministers" was generally referred to by one of those two names, in any number of archival references the organization was also known as Követek Tanácsat, The Regency Council, Council of Ministers, United Free Hungarian Front, Követi Komité and most commonly Követi Bizottság.
13. János Pelényi, handwritten notes from a meeting with D. Howard Travers, Hanover, 19 May 1944, Papers of János Pelényi, Box 1, Envelope: My original and following memo and its transmission, Hoover Institution Archives. One name in Pelényi's notes (designated as [?] in this text) is somewhat illegible, it could be "Dulles".
14. Ibid.
15. Ibid.
16. Ibid.
17. Royal Hungarian Legation, Rome, to György Barcza, 19 September 1944, Papers of János Pelényi, Box 1, Hoover Institution Archives.
18. László Pathy, "Note on Hungarian Questions", memorandum, July 1944, SOE HS 4/97, Assessment of Situation Inside Hungary, National Archives of the United Kingdom. This memo deals with the formation of the Committee of Ministers. It shows that the British were well aware of the formation of the organization and notes that "there is no reason why it should not become the nucleus of all inclusive Organisation with the following objects [*sic*]". The memorandum then explores the possible functions that the Committee of Ministers (which it refers to as "United Free Hungarian Front" as a suggested organization name) could perform or achieve. The memorandum also mentions that the post-war propaganda campaign within Hungary was being formulated by the agent Mr. Howard (George Pálóczy-Horváth, who had originally been in the employ of Division D and the SOE and whom the Hungarian government regarded as a Soviet agent).
19. Papers of Rusztem Vámbéry, Box 3, Folder: Speeches and Writings, Hoover Institution Archives.
20. *Magyar Jövő* articles regarding the formation of the Vámbéry organization make negative statements regarding Vámbéry and highlight the lack of support for his political leadership. See endnote 95 in Chapter 2 and endnotes 23 and 24 below.
21. Charles Steinmetz to Prof. Wrong, 14 October 1940, Papers of Rusztem Vámbéry, Box 2, Folder: Charles Steinmetz, Hoover Institution Archives.
22. "Jöjjön, aminek jönni kell!, Kialtja Fényes, Vámbéry és Lelkesen Háboruba Indulnak", *Magyar Jövő*, 13 June 1941, Papers of Rusztem Vámbéry, Box 8, Folder: Demokratikus Magyarok Amerikai Szövetsége, Clippings 1941, Hoover Institution Archives.
23. Ibid. "Szánalmas 'gyûlés' volt, amin csak meghívottak vettek részt, nyilván el akarták kerülni, hogy 'nem oda való elemek' - értsd ezaatt a munkást, dolgozót, bekerüljenek." ("It was a pitiful meeting, with only invited attendees participating, [the organizers] wanted to avoid having those elements 'who did not belong', by that you should understand workers and laborers.")

24. Ibid. "Vámbéry Rusztem az elmúlt húsz év alatt nem tett semmit, most hirtelen poliltikai ambiciói vannak. Nem mintha egyetlen egy munkás is vágyakozna az elaggott professzor politikai mozgalmába, mert ottan amúgy sem hallott volna mást, mint háborús uszítást." ("For the past twenty years Rusztem Vámbéry has done nothing, now suddenly he has political ambitions. It isn't as if even one member of the working class is longing to participate in this burnt out professor's political movement, for there he would have heard nothing but warmongering.")
25. Rusztem Vámbéry to Jan Masaryk, 13 July 1941, Papers of Rusztem Vámbéry, Box 2, Folder: Jan Masaryk 1941, Hoover Institution Archives. The letter is marked "Confidential" and addressed to Masaryk in his capacity as Czechoslovak Minister of Foreign Affairs in London.
26. Ibid.
27. Oszkár Jászi, introduction to "The Hungarian Problem" by Rustem [*sic*] Vámbéry, *The Nation*, May 1942, p. 7.
28. Ibid.
29. Exchange of letters between Vámbéry and Montgomery, 9, 12, 14 February and 21 March 1942, Papers of Rusztem Vámbéry. Box 2, Folder: John Flournoy Montgomery 1942, Hoover Institution Archives.
30. Oscar Jászi, *The Nation*, May 1942.
31. Jacob Weisberg, "Cold War Without End", *New York Times Sunday Magazine*, 28 November 1999.
32. "Fruits of the Berlin Budapest Marriage 1944", newsletter, Czechoslovak Government Information Service, Carpathian–Russian Desk, New York, 1944, Papers of Rusztem Vámbéry, Box 4, Folder: Speeches and Writings, Hoover Institution Archives.
33. Rusztem Vámbéry to the U.S. State Department, Memorandum on Hungary, 10 May 1944, Papers of Rusztem Vámbéry, Box 4, Folder: Speeches and Writings, Hoover Institution Archives. This file contains a draft version with handwritten corrections and a typed original. Throughout this text, Vámbéry's organization is called the American Federation of Democratic Hungarians.
34. Ibid.
35. Rusztem Vámbéry, Memo on Hungarian Democracy, undated (probably late 1945/ early 1946), p. 1, Papers of Rusztem Vámbéry, Box 4, Folder: Speech and Writings, Hoover Institution Archives.
36. Ibid.
37. Ibid, p. 2.
38. Ibid.
39. György Barcza to Ministers Ambró, Apor, Pelényi, Wodianer and Bessenyey, November 1945, Papers of György nagyalasonyi Barcza, Box 11, File: Committee of Ministers, György Barcza, Hoover Institution Archives. This letter notifies the ministers of the decision to suspend the activities of the Committee of Ministers due to the 4 November free elections in Hungary. However, the letter closes with the caveat that should the need arise for further action to protect the interest of a democratic Hungary, the group would organize again.

CHAPTER 5

Hungarian American Leadership - Continued Fragmentation

At the end of World War II, the Hungarian communities in the United States were still under the leadership of individuals whose parents and grandparents had immigrated there during the Great Migration. Relatively few Hungarians emigrated to the United States during the inter-war period and World War II, and those who did, generally had not integrated into the existing émigré organizations or successfully formed new ones to represent them. Almost no Hungarian Americans who had arrived in the great wave of immigration that began around 1890 and continued through the years leading up to the start of World War I participated in the new organizations formed by the post World War II members of Hungary's social and educational elite. This was evident from the lack of success in gaining mass support for organizations such as the Movement for Independent Hungary, the Pelényi-Barcza Committee of Ministers and the American Federation of Democratic Hungarians. Admittedly, the primary objective of these three organizations was not to provide long term leadership for those who had settled permanently outside of Hungary but to prepare an organization of leaders who would assume primary roles in Hungary's government after the war. This was also the objective of the London-based Free

Hungary movement headed by the leftist Count Michael Károlyi, and of the two major émigré groups formed in Germany—the Magyar Szabadság Mozgalom (Hungarian Freedom Movement) and the Magyar Harcosok Bajtársi Közössége (MHBK, Fraternal Association of Hungarian Veterans).

Despite the fact that key leaders such as Tibor Eckhardt, János Pelényi, Oszkár Jászi and Rusztem Vámbéry all resided in the United States, no one could successfully unify the badly splintered Hungarian American community. Of the four, Tibor Eckhardt, the most recently arrived (1941), had the qualities that most closely matched the leadership needs of the broadest spectrum of Hungarians in America and the West, a great percentage of whom had conservative and very nationalistic political leanings. Although he had removed himself from the political arena after the failure of the Movement for Independent Hungary, at the end of the war Eckhardt was the only Hungarian émigré leader with any potential to build a populist base among both the recent arrivals and those who had arrived at the turn of the century and their descendants. Eckhardt's organization had been endorsed by the American Hungarian Federation, which put the clout of its constituency behind him, and he had had the support of the major Hungarian newspapers and national fraternities. However, his leadership potential had been destroyed by the smear campaign orchestrated by Rusztem Vámbéry, the Hungarian Left and its foreign supporters.

The Barcza-Pelényi Committee, also known as the Committee of Ministers (Magyar Követi Komité or Bizottság), had a brief life from April 1944 to November 1945. Its members were former diplomats who had no broad-based support in the United States, although many had superb political connections. The Vámbéry group, the American Federation of Democratic Hungarians, was very aggressive in its lobbying and attempts to sway public opinion but had very little public support even among those immigrants with left-wing political sympathies. Although supported heavily by the leftist press and by the Károlyi organization in London, the American Federation of Democratic Hungarians never sparked the popular imagination. The Károlyi organization itself had few proponents in the United States, principally individuals who supported a Danubian federation, as its socialist and very pro-communist stance did not reflect the political views of the greater émigré community.

Not these splinter groups but the American Hungarian Federation (AHF) provided the real leadership in the United States. It had served as the dominant organization for Hungarian Americans since the beginning of the twentieth century and continued to do so. "Of the nearly half a dozen organizations, councils and committees that tried to pass themselves off as the true representatives of the Hungarian-American community and of Hungary's national interests," writes historian Steven Béla Vardy, "only the American Hungarian Federation survived the war. The others failed to survive because they had very few followers among Hungarian-Americans."[1]

The vacuum of leadership and factionalism among the more recent arrivals to the West carried into the post-war years. It was a time where a unified front of all Hungarian American and Hungarian organizations could have served a valuable purpose in resettlement of refugees, repatriation and aid to a population in desperate need of shelter, clothing, food and medicine, but the new groups made little or no such contribution.[2] Meanwhile, the traditional organizations and fraternities that were part of the American Hungarian Federation marshaled their resources and responded to the needs of Hungarian refugees. Steven Béla Vardy characterizes the groups comprising the AHF as "the same organizations that were routinely and regularly labeled 'simple', 'backward', 'nationalistic' and even 'reactionary' by the various intellectual spokesmen of the rival organizations."[3] Yet these mainstream, old-line groups formed the only successful Hungarian American aid group working on behalf of war-torn Hungary.

The Aftermath of World War II: Hungarian Refugees in Western Europe

All of Europe was in chaos at the end of World War II. While war and tyranny have forced the movement of refugees since long before the beginning of written history, previous experience provided no parallel for the magnitude and complexity of the refugee problem of the Second World War. Some 60 million European civilians were forced to move—more than ten times the number of European refugees created by the First World War.[4]

Millions had been displaced from Central- and East Europe and were living in Western Europe, principally Germany. While their numbers were not even a fraction of those from Poland and the Soviet Union, nevertheless hundreds of thousands of Hungarian refugees were living in refugee camps or by their wits in the West, primarily in Germany and Austria and to a lesser degree in France.

As of September 1945, 235,000 Hungarian refugees had been in the care of or repatriated by SHAEF (Supreme Headquarters, Allied Expeditionary Forces), and another 50,000 had been in the care of or repatriated by the Soviet forces.[5] More than 100,000 additional refugees were not part of the official statistics because they received no maintenance from the military and little or none from the civilian authorities. Hungarian refugees fleeing the advancing Soviet armies continued to pour into Germany and Austria at an alarming rate at the end of the war. Most of the refugees were not Nazi sympathizers, in fact many were Hitler's victims, but they were people of strong nationalist and anti-communist views who feared the Soviet Union and its domination. It needs to be remembered that many of the immediate post-war refugees were not economic refugees like those of the Great Migration but political refugees with vivid memories of the brief but chaotic life of Béla Kun's Bolshevik government, which was only twenty-six years in the past. More than anything, it was the fear of Soviet occupation that prompted many Hungarians to emigrate who would otherwise not have left their homeland.

To relieve the refugee pressure in Germany and Austria, the Allies intended to repatriate as many people as possible. By October 1946, 223,787 Hungarians had been repatriated from western Germany and Austria, and an estimated 100,000 had repatriated themselves.[6] This left a core of some 120,000 Hungarian refugees in West Germany with "valid objections" to the so-called "reasonable" proposals for repatriation or resettlement. They came to be known as the Nyugatosok, "the Westerners", although in most scholarly references they are known collectively as the 1945 refugees, regardless of whether they left Hungary in 1944, 1945 or early 1946.

After June 1947, when the freely elected post-war Hungarian government was taken over by the communists, grim opposition to repatriation prevailed among the Displaced Persons (DPs) remaining in the refugee centers. Gyula Borbándi, the historian who writes most authoritatively on post World War II Hungarian emigration, observes that " even from the perspective of forty years, even the most critical would have to say that their fears [of repatriation] were not unfounded."[7] Repatriation of Hungarians slowed to a trickle, and between 1 July 1947 and 31 December 1951 only an additional 1,608 people returned to their homeland.[8]

Post-war Governments Topple, Creating a New Wave of Refugees

From the end of the war until 1947, the states of East-Central Europe were governed by fragile coalition governments, all of which fell under the control of their respective communist parties between 1947 and 1949 as the Soviet Union exerted more and more influence. The Sovietization of Central- and East Europe, coupled with the growing conflict between the Soviet Union and its former allies, grew into what would soon be referred to as the Cold War. Chilling indeed, because both the East and the West now possessed nuclear weapons. The newly formed ring of satellite states bordering the Soviet Union disappeared behind a physical and ideological Iron Curtain, the term aptly coined by Winston Churchill in his famous speech of 5 March 1946, given at Westminster College in Fulton, Missouri.

During this period of political turmoil and anticipation of a communist takeover, the people then referred to as neo-refugees began to emigrate. From 1946 until 1950, 40,000 Hungarians made it to the West.[9] Nowhere near the numbers of those who left Hungary during the waning days of the war, this group fleeing the post-war communist regime came to be known collectively as the 1947 refugees and joined the populations of Hungarian refugees who had preceded them.[10]

Post-War Hungarian Refugees—The 1945 and 1947 Groups

The first wave of Hungarian refugee movement to Austria and Germany (beginning in 1944) had included a large number of officials, military personnel and others with ties to the Hungarian government. Including their dependents, this group numbered over 100,000. Most were from one of two broad groups—one was comprised of the upper- and mid-level social and political elite, the professional officer corps of the Royal Hungarian Army or the Hungarian police; the other was comprised of former members of various rightist political parties. Many members of the latter group remained in Austria or Germany, although they did so for a variety of reasons. Some were involuntary refugees stranded by circumstance; others were afraid to return; still others were certain that the Western powers would liberate Hungary and wanted to wait until then to return. By the end of the decade, however, most realized that they should opt for emigration opportunities to various North- and South American countries and Australia, as liberation of their homeland did not seem imminent. A portion of the 1945 refugees stayed in Germany or Austria or emigrated to nearby countries. Approximately 16,000 of the 1945 refugees went to the United States, forming the core group of the post-war Hungarian immigrants, generally referred to as Displaced Persons or DPs. This group reflected the values, social structure and political ideology of prewar Hungary and closely mirrored the conservative social and political values of the Hungarians who had arrived in America during the Great Migration.

The 1945 DPs were joined by the 1947 refugees, who actually crossed the Atlantic almost simultaneously with the 1945 group. The 1945 group had been refugees in Europe until the Displaced Persons Acts of 1948 and 1950 finally made their entry into the United States possible. The same acts made it possible for the 1947 refugees to spend less time in limbo and get to the States with less delay. The greater portion of the "1947" refugees actually fled Hungary between 1947 and 1949, and the elite among them were political emigrants who had participated in Hungary's various post-war coalition governments but were gradually pushed out of power by their partners, the communists. This group included leaders and members of the Smallholders Party, the National Peasant Party, the Social Democratic

Party and a few smaller leftist groups. Unlike the 1945 refugees, the later group represented various shades of liberalism and socialism and many of its constituents were known as much for their opposition to the conservative and rightist regimes of pre-1945 Hungary as for their opposition to communism and Soviet control of Hungary. Either unwilling or unable to follow the Soviet line, they were pushed out of power and found themselves emigrant partners with their ideological opposites, the 1945 refugees! Conflicts between the two groups were inevitable.

After the political elite left Hungary, thousands of individuals who were not politically connected followed, having grown increasingly disenchanted with the repressive political regime that had imposed itself under Mátyás Rákosi's dictatorship. The 1947 refugees in the United States numbered only about 10,000, but they would come to have disproportionate control of the highly visible Hungarian immigrant leadership there. The two groups that entered the United States between World War II and the Hungarian Revolution of 1956 never successfully integrated with each other and continued as two distinct Hungarian immigrant factions.

Hungarians in America

Hungarians who comprised both the economic and political diaspora at the beginning of the Cold War fell into four rather distinct groups: those who emigrated (or whose forebears emigrated) at the beginning of the twentieth century, primarily seeking economic opportunity; the trickle of intellectuals and professionals who foresaw the war and emigrated in the 1930s and early '40s; political refugees who left Hungary toward the end of World War II; and political refugees who left Hungary shortly after the communists seized power in 1947.

The approximately three-quarters of a million Magyars who were turn of the century economic immigrants comprised by far the largest of these groups. They had formed mutual benefit societies, insurance companies, old-age homes, etc. to meet their needs in their new homeland. The inter-war group, which reflected a higher economic and educational status, was more quickly integrated into the greater American society and had little or no connection with Hungarian American society, even if remaining connected to the former homeland. The exceptions within this group were dissident Hungarian politicians such as János Pelényi and Tibor Eckhardt, both of whom were active in Hungarian American organizations and activities.

The next two groups were made up of 26,532 politically and socially diverse 1945 and 1947 DPs.[11] Among the many differences between them was the fact that the 1947 group, being refugees as a result of the Cold War, had received preferential treatment in Europe and upon arrival in the United States.

Establishment of the American Hungarian Relief Council

As the umbrella organization representing the vast majority of Americans of Hungarian descent in the United States, the American Hungarian Federation anticipated the disastrous conditions Hungarians would find themselves in at the end of the war and took action. On 23 September 1944 the AHF submitted an application to the War Relief Control Board in Washington, D.C., for recognition of the newly formed American Hungarian Relief Council (AHRC). The AHF detailed the Relief Council's purpose in the application:

> The plain people of Hungary have been plundered and exploited by the Nazi masters and the Quislings; they are completely helpless and hopeless, even without the most necessary and elemental essentials to sustain life. Their only hope and salvation lie in the United States and its ever-generous people, particularly those of Hungarian origin, who naturally carry the primary responsibility. We expect to be of substantial help to our government and its instrumentalities at home and abroad in the work of moral and material relief and rehabilitation. At present Hungary cannot even participate in the National War Fund. If and when the time arrives to make application in that direction, report will, of course, be made to the Board for instructions and approval. We will follow that course during the life of the project in every respect.[12]

The original incorporators of the organization had not included communists when organizing the AHRC, but "after being later advised by the President's War Control Advisory Board to include the HACD [Hungarian American Council for Democracy] as a member group, they were forced to admit the Communists into their organization."[13] Indeed, when the AHF submitted its application to the War Relief Control Board, the HACD had already applied on behalf of its proposed relief organization, American-Hungarian Relief, Inc. The War Control Advisory Board stated that it would only sanction one agency per nationality and insisted that the two organizations join forces in their relief efforts.[14] The HACD, whose president was the well-known Hungarian American actor Béla Lugosi, presented itself to the public as a left-leaning socialist workers' group. In truth, the leadership included key communist figures whose intention was to use propaganda to influence mainstream Hungarian Americans and smooth the way for the Soviet-dominated Communist Party in Hungary. A confidential Federal Bureau of Investigation (FBI) memo dated 4 May 1945 detailing the AHRC's activities states that "informants indicate six out of thirty individuals who compose directorate of the American-Hungarian Relief, Inc. are Communists."[15]

The complexity of the political dynamic among the various groups jostling for a power base in post-war Hungary and among the émigré groups in the West was astonishing. At a time when aid to the political refugees and to war-devastated Hungary was most vital, efforts in the United States to organize such aid through the centrist AHF were hindered by the political machinations of the small but aggressive, left-wing American-Hungarian Relief, Inc.

Although left-wing groups, including those with ties to the Communist Party and communist-related organizations, operated at will in the United States, the American intelligence community was alert to the subversive intent of their political agenda. FBI Director J. Edgar Hoover instructed his organization to monitor anyone or any group with a suspected tie to the Communist Party. Even during the time the Soviet Union was allied with the Western powers, communists in the United States had been closely monitored. Thus, while the FBI was interested in the activities of all the émigré groups, no matter their size or orientation, there was particular focus on those with communist connections.

It should be noted that the founding members of the AHRC directorate included the leaders of the most respected mainstream Hungarian American organizations: John Bencze, president of the Verhovay Fraternal Insurance Association based in Pittsburgh, Pennsylvania; Rev. George Borshy, chairman of the executive committee of the Hungarian Reformed Federation of America based in Washington, D.C.; Dr. Tibor Kerekes, Professor of History at Georgetown University and coordinator of the AHRC; Paul Nadanyi, editor of the *Amerikai Magyar Népszava*, published in New York; and Emery Kiraly, treasurer of the Washington, D.C.-based AHF. John Flournoy Montgomery, former U.S. minister to Hungary, was approached about serving as AHRC's president, but he refused, saying he did "not want to be associated with any Hungarian Communists".[16]

AHRC activities were made difficult from the onset by the communists they were forced to include in their leadership, including their associate secretary, Mátyás Török of Los Angeles. Also known as Mathew Török and Alfred A. Neuwald (the Neuwald family name was also used by his wife and brother), the FBI identified Török as active in a number of communist front organizations and as directing "practically all of the radical-political activities of the Hungarians".[17] Török was not a registered member of the Communist Party of America (CPA) "because of the part he is playing in the Hungarian field",[18] but he was said to be working under the direction of Dr. John Gyetvai, a key figure in communist activities and editor of *Magyar Jövő*, the decidedly left-wing/communist

Hungarian-language newspaper. Török publicly acknowledged his friendship and ongoing contact with Mátyás Rákosi, then (1945) a member of Parliament in the Hungarian Provisional Government at Debrecen and former secretary of the Third International (Comintern) in Moscow. Török also acknowledged his ties to an alleged communist front organization in Mexico, Hungaria Libre de México, headed by Guillermo Weinstock.[19] In August 1944 Weinstock resolved to suggest to the Hungarian Council in London and to the HACD in Los Angeles and New York that they get in touch with the Hungarians residing in the Soviet Union, for "it is our opinion that in the near future there will be the opportunity and the possibility to work with them."[20]

If there were any doubt as to the international nature of this coalition of the Left and its political agenda for the future of Hungary, one need only look to *Magyar Jövő* of 28 March 1945. That issue reprinted an article originally published in Debrecen, Hungary, on 2 March of that year entitled "Proposals Made at Monster Rally of the Hungarian Communist Party", referring to a rally held on 25 February in Budapest. The article contained the statement: "We are in agreement with the speech of Matyas Rakosi which he delivered in Budapest last Sunday".[21]

Magyar Jövő editor John Gyetvai had a long history of communist involvement, having been press chief of the Red Army in the days of Béla Kun. According to one of the FBI's confidential informants, Gyetvai (or Gyetvay) originally came to the United States in 1923 on an illegal passport under the name John Kiss and later returned to Europe and spent considerable time in the USSR. For that trip he used the citizenship papers and passport of Joseph Mihalka, later known as Joseph Magyari, who was active in communist circles in Los Angeles. In the 1930s, in order to obtain American citizenship, Gyetvai married a U.S. citizen active in the Communist Party of America.

Count Michael Károlyi, honorary president of the HACD, was instrumental in obtaining a visa for John Gyetvai (in the name of Dr. Jan Gyetvay) to attend meetings in London in October 1944 regarding Russian Hungarian activities. On 4 October 1944 the *Manchester Guardian* reported that "when Russian troops reach Budapest, Moscow will ask Hungary to set up a democratic system and order land reform like the program of the 1918 government."[22] Informants in the USSR also reported to the FBI that "the Communist Party in Moscow has designated Count Michael Károlyi for honorary position only in post-war Hungary (providing the Károlyi movement is successful) and the real head will be Mátyás Rákosi, then residing in Moscow. ... He is the so-called 'top man' from Stalin's viewpoint."[23]

The HACD was also connected to Count Károlyi through its secretary, Mózes Simon. According to FBI sources, Simon had been military commissar in the Berehovo (Beregszász in Hungarian) region of the Carpatho-Ukraine. "He was one of those Communists who were rounded up by the English during the Russo-German Peace pact and as a result spent ten weeks in jail in London, England in the summer of 1940. He was released through the intercession of Eduard Beneš, Premier of Czechoslovakia, who in turn was asked to use his influence by Count Michael Károlyi."[24] Simon made his way to the United States, where he edited the "Hungarian Information Bulletin" in addition to serving as secretary of the HACD. However, although he attended AHAC's early organizing meetings, he was not permitted to join actively, as he was not a U.S. citizen.

The Communist Party of America made it a major priority to increase its influence and control over the American Hungarian Relief Council, as revealed in an internal report submitted on 4 February 1946 to Steve Nelson, chairman of the Nationality Group Commission of the American Communist Party, by John Lautner of the International Workers Organization (IWO).[25] Reporting on his work among the Hungarians, Lautner outlines the Communists' view of the AHRC and its work and details their attempt to control the AHRC and derail the schemes of the more moderate faction. As an example, at the AHRC board meeting in Pittsburgh in November 1945, the CPA faction sabotaged the directors' plans to extend AHRC aid to Hungarian refugees in Austria and Bavaria—plans the directors had already approved by a vote of twenty-four to six. The HACD faction accounted for the six dissenting votes. The CPA faction wanted the aid to flow directly to Hungary rather than to refugees in the West, most of whom were there because they were anti-communist and feared the Soviets or had been associated with the fascists. However, as Lautner states in his report, "We raised this question [of direct aid] with the War Relief Board reasoning this would disrupt the relief movement. The War Relief Board prevented the initiation of this action."[26]

The unusual shared power arrangement between the AHF and HACD did not become more successful as time went by. The squabbling continued and the anti-communist members made a determined and successful effort to oust their opponents. In March 1946, the executive board terminated Mátyás Török's contract and at a 2 April 1946 meeting in Washington, D.C., made a clean sweep of almost all communist forces. Only two communists, Alexander Stone and Imre Komlós, were allowed to retaining their positions, and that only because the terms of its charter compelled the organization to recognize their privilege to be on the board. John Gyetvai, Lajos Weinstock, Imre Lusztig and János Launtner were ousted.[27] Though the shared power arrangement had not worked out, it should be noted that during the time the communists were part of the AHRC, they were very successful fundraisers and some of the most active workers. There was some concern that their removal and departure would seriously weaken the organization.

Within a few months, Gyetvai returned to Hungary, where it was reported to the FBI that he was "known to be giving a misleading picture regarding actual conditions in America, and he has stated the President of the United States is surrounded by a capitalist clique which was influencing the foreign policy of the United States."[28]

The AHRC served as a clearinghouse for collecting aid for Hungary and was successful in raising funds and material aid. The funds were used primarily to purchase desperately needed medicine and medical supplies.[29] It also shipped other donations such as clothing and food to Hungary. At first, distribution of supplies was handled through the Allied Control Commission (Szövetséges Ellenőrző Bizottság), but in 1946 that commission asked the AHRC to assume distribution responsibility. This was surprising, as the Soviets held the chairmanship of the Allied Control Commission in Hungary and completely dominated all affairs, whether internal or external.[30] At the time it was taking over responsibility for distribution, the directorate decided to send Arthur Dobozy, the group's secretary, to Hungary to set up an office and staff to supervise the distribution, a process anticipated to take six months to a year. It was also arranged that three directors, Dr. Francis Ujlaki, Alajos C. Falussy and Imre Komlós, would also travel to Hungary to make certain that aid distribution was being handled correctly. Although these events transpired in April 1946, more than a year prior to the coup d'état, the Communists' influence was so strong in Hungary that it was decided that none of the four individuals would leave New York until they had been assured of entry permits into Hungary. If any of the four attempted to travel without entry permits, only Imre Komlós, known to be a communist sympathizer, would be assured of entry.[31]

Once the AHRC purged the HACD from its ranks, the former continued to provide valuable assistance to Hungary and its people through a most difficult time in their history. In the course of its half decade of existence, it sent about US $3 million worth of food, medicine, clothing and even agricultural machinery to Europe. Initially, the committee's HACD members were able to ensure that most of the aid went to Hungary, but later, particularly after the intensification of the Cold War in 1947, aid was also sent to various refugee camps in Germany and Austria.[32]

Groups Formed by the New Hungarian Refugees

While the AHRC provided what assistance it could to Hungary, the refugees that remained in Western Europe began to form their own organizations in hopeful expectation of their return to Hungary. The uniformly anti-communist and anti-Soviet 1945 group represented every (non-communist) political stripe and educational and social level, and spawned several groups of some size, which became international organizations as the refugees spread from Western Europe to new homelands.

One of the larger groups was the Magyar Szabadság Mozgalom (Hungarian Freedom Movement), founded in Germany in June 1946 by General Ferenc kisbarnaki Farkas, who the following year would be elected as Hungary's new "Regent" by the Hungarian Parliament in exile in Altötting, Germany.[33] This action was precipitated by the fact that Admiral Horthy had fallen out of favor with kisbarnaki Farkas and other professional army officers because of his decision to throw his support behind Otto von Habsburg and the Legitimists and his subsequent efforts to steer the organization into the archduke's camp. Needless to say, the creation of what was intended to be a Hungarian government in exile in Germany's American-occupied zone was of great interest to U.S. intelligence. The group's formation was detailed in a report stamped "Top Secret" and sent to U.S. Secretary of State George C. Marshall. It notes that Zoltan Koltai [*sic*], known in Hungarian circles as the apostolic delegate of the Vatican, was one of the scheme's principal architects and that the officials of the new organization "travel on Vatican passports and hold Vatican diplomatic credentials". It also notes that due to the Western powers' vigorous reaction to the Communist coup in Hungary, it was expected that the United States would approach the new government in exile to "solicit all support short of recognition".[34]

Unknown at that time to American intelligence, General Farkas had made several visits to the U.S. consul general in Munich to present his plans to form the government in exile and had set forth the details of the organization's activities and its basis of legitimacy. The Altötting meeting on 20 August 1947 was to have ninety-four members of the former Hungarian Parliament in attendance, with the intention that they would legally vote the sitting Hungarian government out of existence. General Farkas maintained that the prewar Hungarian constitution was legally still in effect, since the post-war constitution and government of Hungary were formed as a result of Soviet pressure and hence did not represent the Hungarian people. It was further pointed out that under the old constitution, any fifty Parliament members constituted a quorum and could function as a legal government. Subsequently, General Farkas also revealed the details of his plans to the American CIC (Counter Intelligence Corps). His general intention was to secure State Department support for the Magyar Szabadság Mozgalom before a rival group being formed by Gusztáv Hennyey could organize.[35]

Not only was General Farkas's group refused State Department support, on 3 September, just a few weeks after the Altötting meeting, the general and two members of his committee were called to a conference at the American consulate in Munich, where representatives of the Military Government informed them categorically that they must cease all attempts to form a government in exile.

An agreement was signed by all present, including Vice Consul Delmar R. Carlson, Lieutenant Colonel Paul Burns, representing the Military Government of Bavaria, and S. Wahrhaftig of the Civil Administration Division. The agreement listed the following conditions: "a. No government-in-exile, open or secret, will be tolerated in the U.S. Zone of Occupation; b. Political activities of refugee and DP groups are subject to existing Military Government regulations; c. Criticism by organized refugee and DP groups of any one of the Allied nations, or of their governmental leaders, will not be tolerated; d. All attempts to form governments-in-exile must cease immediately."[36]

Although the Farkas organization was thwarted in its attempt to establish a government in exile, it persevered and did succeed in building a political organization, the Magyar Szabadság Mozgalom, which was active in émigré affairs for several years, representing the rightist elements among the refugees. It eventually claimed 21,268 members organized into 108 local chapters in thirty-two countries. However, as the membership dispersed through emigration, it lost its potential for political effectiveness and essentially functioned as a social group.[37]

The Magyar Harcosok Bajtársi Közössége (MHBK, Fraternal Association of Hungarian Veterans), was more successful than General Farkas's group. In 1947, independent veterans' groups that had been started in various locations in Germany and Austria by former Hungarian professional military officers were consolidated under the leadership of General András Zákó. The MHBK was primarily intended to serve as the central association of professional Hungarian military officers, although for a period of time the Zákó organization did attempt to dabble in the market for intelligence and tried to peddle information to any and all interested parties. However, once emigration spread it to other continents, the MHBK, like the Magyar Szabadság Mozgalom, increasingly became a social organization. At its height it had 15,000 to 20,000 members, who with their extended families accounted for 60,000 to 80,000 émigrés and represented some of the most influential refugees in several dozen countries.

The only other military-based organization with some broad-based support was the Magyar Királyi Csendőr Bajtársi Közösség (MKCsBK, Royal Hungarian Gendarmerie Benevolent Association). The MKCsBK and its Cleveland, Ohio-based affiliate, Magyar Csendőrők Családi Közössége (MCsCsK, Familial Association of Hungarian Gendarmerie) never rivaled the MHBK in terms of influence, as many of its members also were members of the MHBK.[38]

The central leadership of the MHBK remained in Germany even after the mass emigration of the late 1940s and early 1950s, but its influence and financial base was increasingly centered in the United States. Regardless of its fairly broad-based membership and its popularity, the MHBK never received the official U.S. government support and recognition later accorded to the 1947 refugees' far less broadly based political organizations. This was primarily because the MHBK's military leadership was never free of the fascist label the Hungarian Left continued to attach to it.[39]

A number of smaller refugee groups were also formed, most of them with unrealistic and virtually unattainable political goals. Among them were the Magyar Vitézi Rend (Hungarian Order of Knights), the Cleveland, Ohio-based Felszabadító Bizottság (Committee for Liberation) and the Magyar Társaság (Hungarian Association). In addition, various revisionist organizations were formed that focused on the former Hungarian territories in Romania, present-day Slovakia, present-day Serbia, and Croatia and the Soviet Union. Over the years, the thrust of these groups changed from a focus on the restoration of former Hungarian territory to the human rights of the Hungarian minorities in those countries.

It should be noted that while still in Europe, the extreme Right also formed its own organizations, carrying on the cult of executed Arrow Cross leader Ferenc Szálasi. These groups were referred to as the Hungarista Mozgalom (the Hungarianist Movement, or as it is sometimes referred to, the Hungarian Nativist Movement) and operated under the leadership of Árpád Henney. However, very few individuals on the far right qualified for entry into the United States, and most of them emigrated to Argentina and Australia, taking their fringe organizations with them.

Gyula Borbándi aptly summed up the Hungarian émigrés' political plight in writing of the reasons why the Hungarian communities remained fragmented in Europe and America:

> In the Freedom Movement's publications, and in the publications of other émigré organizations, they regularly urged the formation of a central leadership body. This never happened primarily because of divisive viewpoints and the personal rivalries among their various leaders. As an example, in Germany a rivalry broke out between three former high-ranking military officers who were very politically ambitious. Gusztáv Hennyey, Ferenc Farkas and András Zákó's personal rivalries and power struggles for years absorbed the energies of the politically interested refugees. The first had the Hungarian Office in Munich as his base of power and then later played a leadership role

> in the Hungarian National Committee, the second had the leadership of the Hungarian Freedom Movement as his base and third the influential MHBK behind him. Their attitudes and views and divergent ambitions prevented the formation of a strong central organization.[40]

Originally founded with specific if divergent political goals in mind, eventually all of these groups increasingly became social and cultural organizations. Because they fulfilled that function for the most recently arrived immigrants, the new arrivals did not join the Hungarian American organizations already in place in the United States, thus preventing the formation of a unified Hungarian American society.[41]

The Hungarian National Council ... a Unifying Force?

The refugees of 1945 had little credibility with the Western powers, due in part to their association with the defeated Germany and her allies and in part to their own constant infighting and political agitation. In contrast, the leadership of the 1947 refugee group was comprised of elected Hungarian officials who had been forced out of their positions and into exile—men who were generally characterized as liberals and as advocates of a Western-type democracy in their homeland. With the escalation of the Cold War, the 1947 group was received with enthusiasm by the West and for the next decade enjoyed the political and financial support of the West's governments, including the United States—support that had been denied the earlier, more numerous immigrants.

Most of the 1947 refugees emigrated to the United States, with the U.S. government supporting them in the hope that a democratically elected leadership could be restored in Hungary. Ignoring the fact that the Hungarian emigration was represented by more than just the 1947 arrivals, the U.S. government treated them as the true representatives of the people of Hungary and of the Hungarian Americans. As a result, the only officially sanctioned Hungarian political organziation in exile, the Magyar Nemzeti Bizottmány (officially, the Hungarian National Council, but also known as the Hungarian National Committee), was organized in 1947 and launched in the summer of 1948 under the auspices of the U.S. government. Throughout the 1950s and well into the 1960s, this organization's leaders were accepted in America as the most prominent spokesmen for the greater Hungarian American community—despite the fact that their relationship to that community was negligible.

Endnotes

1. Steven Béla Vardy, *The Hungarian-Americans*, p. 113.
2. During its brief existence, only the Követi Bizottság assisted the AHF efforts. Principally, it purchased over US $250,000 worth of much-needed medical supplies in Switzerland on behalf of the AHRC and arranged through American auspices to have them flown into Budapest. György Barcza, memorandum, Követi Bizottság #134, Papers of György nagyalasonyi Barcza, Box 11, Folder: Committee of Ministers, Hoover Institute Archives.
3. Steven Béla Vardy, *The Hungarian-Americans*, p. 113.
4. Malcolm J. Proudfoot, *European Refugees: 1939–1952, A Study in Forced Population Movement* (Evanston, Illinois: Northwestern University Press, 1956), p. 21.
5. Ibid., pp. 158–159.
6. Ibid., pp. 285–287.
7. Gyula Borbándi, *A magyar emigráció életrajza: 1945–1985* (Bern: Európai Protestáns Magyar Szabadegyetem, 1985), p. 13.
8. Malcolm Proudfoot, *European Refugees*, pp. 285–287.
9. Ibid.
10. "Hungarian Political Emigration as of July 1, 1949", Embassy of the United States of America, Paris, 25 October 1949, Secret Memorandum #934, NARA/CP, RG: 59, File: 864.00 10.2549. The memorandum estimated the number of Hungarian refugees in the West as of July 1949 as follows: Germany: 30,000; France: 10,000; Austria 18,000. Refugee counts vary in the various sources consulted for this research, such as Julianna Puskás's books on Hungarian immigration and the official counts referenced in Proudfoot's book. I have used those sources that provide an actual count of numbers of refugees, with estimates used for supplemental, undocumented refugee populations.
11. Steven Béla Vardy, *The Hungarian-Americans*, p. 118.
12. William Ward, FBI Report, 4 May 1945, FBI File # 100-74681 MJG, Subject: American-Hungarian Relief, Inc., Character of Case: Internal Security, p. 8, NARA/CP, RG: 59, File: 864.48/8-1445, National Archives and Records Administration, College Park, Maryland.
13. John Edgar Hoover, Director, Federal Bureau of Investigation to Frederick B. Lyon, Chief, Division of Foreign Activity Correlation, State Department, 14 August 1945, "American-Hungarian Relief, Inc. Confidential Synopsis of Reports dating from November 14, 1944 to April 23, 1945", NARA/CP, RG: 59, File: 864.48/8-1445.
14. Fern C. Stukenbroeker, Special Agent, Cleveland, Ohio, FBI Report, 4 June 1946, Subject: American Hungarian Relief Inc., copy forwarded by J. Edgar Hoover to Frederick B. Lyon, State Department, NARA/CP, RG:59, File: 864.48/6-2546, pp. 1–2.
15. William Ward, FBI Report, 4 May 1945, pp. 10–12.
16. Ibid., p. 1.
17. Török's brother, Jenő (Eugene) Neuwald, was the former editor of *Új Előre*, the Hungarian communist daily that later became known as *Magyar Jövő*. During this period Eugene Neuwald acted as Béla Lugosi's secretary. According to the Ward FBI report, "Eugene Newald [*sic*] is acting as secretary to Bela Lugosi and that Newald has a long record of Communist activity in the United States and abroad. Newald is the brother of Matyas Torok and was the former editor of 'Uj Elore' alleged Hungarian

Communist daily which later became known as the 'Magyar Jovo'. The informant is of the opinion that in the capacity as secretary to Lugosi, Newald does the propaganda work particularly in connection with his activities as president of the Hungarian American Council for Democracy." Ward, FBI report, 4 May 1945, p.18.

18. Ibid., p. 12.
19. Ibid.
20. Ibid., p. 13.
21. Ibid., p. 15.
22. Ibid., p. 16.
23. Ibid., p. 15.
24. Ibid., p. 19.
25. The FBI memos refer to the IWO (International Workers Organization), but its accurate name is IWA, International Workers Association. Both names were often used interchangeably. All of the FBI reports refer to the organization as the IWO, as does this work. The IWA was founded in 1922 as an anarchist labor movement.
26. James F. Bland, Special Agent, FBI Report, 14 June 1946, FBI file #100-74681, Subject: American Hungarian Relief, Inc., Character of case: Internal Security, NARA/CP, RG:59, File: 864:48/7-146, pp. 11–13.
27. Fern Stukenbroeker, FBI Memo, 4 June 1946, pp. 1–2.
28. John Edgar Hoover to Frederick B. Lyon, Chief, Division of Foreign Activity Correlation, State Department, memorandum, 1 July 1946, Subject: American Hungarian Relief, Inc., NARA/CP, RG: 59, File: 864.48 /7-146.
29. James F. Bland, FBI report, 14 June 1946, p. 12.
30. Selden Chapin, U.S. minister in Hungary, to the Secretary of State, Budapest, 22 July 1947, Secret Report #3284, *Foreign Relations*, Vol. IV, 1947, pp. 340–349.
31. James F. Bland, FBI Report, 14 June 1946, p. 8.
32. Steven Béla Vardy, *The Hungarian-Americans*, p. 114.
33. Gyula Borbándi, *A magyar emigráció életrajza*, pp. 34–44. The precursor to this group was founded as the Antibolsevista Nemzetek Blokkja (ANB; in English, Anti-Bolshevist Block of Nations or ABN) on 23 November 1943 with eight nations participating. The ABN was founded by Ukrainian groups that were anti-Soviet.
34. Carmel Offie, Political Officer, Frankfurt, to the Secretary of State, 22 July 1947, Top Secret Report #287, Subject: Formation of Hungarian Government in Exile, NARA/CP, RG: 59, File: 864.00/ 7-2247.
35. James R. Wilkinson. American Consul General, Munich, to the Secretary of State, 19 August 1947, Top Secret Despatch #787, Subject: Plan for Formal Organization of Hungarian Government in Exile, NARA/CP, RG: 59, File: 864.00/8-1947.
36. Robert Murphy, United States Political Adviser for Germany, to the Secretary of State, 10 September 1947, Top Secret Memorandum, Subject: Dissolution of the So-Called Hungarian Government-In-Exile in the U.S. Zone of Germany, NARA/CP, RG: 59, File: 864.00/9-1047.
37. Steven Béla Vardy, *The Hungarian-Americans*, p. 123.
38. Gyula Borbándi, *A magyar emigráció életrajza*, pp. 42–49.
39. Embassy of the United States of America, Secret Despatch #934, "Hungarian Political Emigration as of July 1, 1949", NARA/CP.
40. Gyula Borbándi, *A magyar emigráció életrajza*, pp. 51–52.
41. Ibid., pp. 42–49.

CHAPTER 6

Eckhardt in the Post-war Years

Lingering Charges against Tibor Eckhardt

Although the slanderous personal attacks against him continued to have repercussions for decades after the war ended, Tibor Eckhardt stuck to his policy of not striking back at his attackers. He spent the years after his resignation from the Movement for Independent Hungary working in close collaboration with the U.S. State Department and continued to play a behind the scenes role within the Hungarian American community. He applied for and received a permanent U.S. residency permit and lived in New York City and in Washington, D.C., from 1942 to 1945.

The post-war scenario in Central- and East Europe played itself out as Eckhardt had predicted and warned against—the Soviet Union finally folded Hungary and her neighbors into its "sphere of influence". In the preface to his 1947 book, John F. Montgomery notes that his "regular post of observation in those critical years was Budapest (1933–1941)". He goes on to observe that it "was a unique post because the Magyars, neither Teuton nor Slav, were always aware of being between the two fires of German and Russian imperialism. During those years, most of us saw only one fire, the German one. Hungary's vision was far ahead of ours. Had we listened to Hungarian statesmen, we should perhaps have been able to limit Stalin's triumph in the hour of Hitler's fall."[1]

The Hungarian government's confidential plan for a government in exile involved only John Pelényi and was aborted in 1940. How it became integrated into the disinformation propaganda about Eckhardt remains to be researched more fully. A recent examination of the British SOE files, however, provided ample evidence that the story of Eckhardt's supposed embezzlement of Hungarian funds was covered in at least three confidential SOE ciphers. Since the stated goal of the SOE propagandists was to discredit Eckhardt and ruin him politically, it is not beyond the bounds of reason to assume that the British circulated the story of Eckhardt's embezzlement, and his enemies kept it alive. Nevertheless, regardless of its origin, the anti-Eckhardt propaganda was extremely successful and the damning information regarding his supposed involvement in the plan taints historical studies to this day. For example, accusations of financial impropriety, although unfounded, continue to surface. John Pelényi's 1964 disclosure that the officially funded Hungarian government plan never involved Eckhardt, either in the planning stages or in the financial transaction, cleared Eckhardt of charges that he made improper use of Hungarian government funds. Yet although that information was published in a widely-circulated journal, scholars have sometimes ignored it. As to his finances, Eckhardt's personal records show that prior to leaving Hungary in 1941 he requested permission to convert funds in the amount of US $15,000 for the purposes of his trip. This request was granted, and half of the money was transmitted to Washington, D.C., to be held for him until his arrival. As it turned out, he had great difficulty obtaining those funds, even though they were his personal assets, and it took him several months to finally do so.[2]

The charge against Eckhardt of having fascist sympathies also lingers. Even recently, some journals and political writers persistently refer to Eckhardt and other Hungarian leaders as fascists. The charge does not square with historical fact. For example, on 10 April 1943 the German ambassador to Budapest, Dietrich von Jagow, denounced the Hungarian diplomat György Barcza, former Hungarian ambassador to England and Italy, as a "European Tibor Eckhardt".[3] In addition, on 4 December 1944 Eckhardt was sentenced to death, in absentia, by the Arrow Cross Peoples' Tribunal.[4] Clearly the fascists themselves did not regard Eckhardt or his compatriots as "one of their own" or even as fascist sympathizers.[5]

After the war, the communist journalist Dr. John Gyetvai continued to sow disinformation with the intention of destabilizing the émigré leadership, even though FBI documents clearly show that that agency was aware of his activities and knew his background as a communist loyalist. Although Gyetvai's actions were tracked, the FBI took no action against him,[6] and he continued his campaign against Eckhardt—as, for example, in the 22 March 1946 issue of *Szabad Nép,* where he again attacked Eckhardt and his activities in the United States.[7]

While charges of financial impropriety were being leveled against Eckhardt, it was clear from the way that he lived that he had very modest financial means. Eckhardt certainly was never a wealthy man, nor did he have large financial resources at his disposal. After his wife, Ellen, and their two children joined him in the United States in 1946, he was able to sustain the family through his lectures and writing and with the generous help of several friends. When difficulties arose in their relationship just six months after the family was reunited, Eckhardt and Ellen agreed that their marriage was irretrievably broken. Eckhardt first installed his family in an apartment at 92nd St. and Park Ave., then later at 1060 Park Ave and eventually on Madison Ave. Tibor Eckhardt Jr. remembers the latter as a "very fancy place". This gave the family the impression that Tibor Sr. was well off, which they were to learn was not the case. Tibor Jr. recalls that during the immediate post-war years and until he married Judy Dwyer in 1957, his father lived alone in exceedingly austere circumstances and had very limited financial resources. One of his father's studio apartments was so small one had to thread a pathway through the books and papers that took up almost the entire room, and Tibor Sr. once had to borrow money from his son in order to have enough funds to change apartments.

When the end of World War II was in sight and immediately thereafter, Eckhardt was occupied with the post-war issues that Hungary was facing. There is evidence from his correspondence with the members of the Smallholders Party and with public figures inside and outside Hungary that he was a very active participant in the dialogue among members of the political leadership. Among his surviving correspondence is a severely critical letter to the Smallholders Party leadership dated 13 August 1945.[8] In *Recollections of Tibor Eckhardt: Regicide at Marseille*, it is stated that in preventing Eckhardt's return to his homeland that same year, the Hungarian government was bowing to the personal demands of Soviet Foreign Minister Molotov.[9]

His family situation, his inability to return to Hungary and the continuation of the bitter attacks against him all made Eckhardt's life extremely difficult. This was compounded by the fact that at a time when the euphoria of the Allied victories was still in the air and the Cold War was not yet a reality, in some circles in both Hungary and the United States he was perceived as a negative, out of touch politician with an anti-Communist mania. His inability to return to Hungary to lead the Smallholders Party, which won the 1945 post-war election by a sizeable majority and had a clear mandate, had to be the lowest point of Eckhardt's career. Instead of the end of the war providing relief from the strain of the attacks against him, he faced post-war prospects that were bleak indeed.

During this immediate post-war period, Eckhardt regularly shuttled back and forth between New York and Washington, D.C. In early 1946 he accepted a position as adjunct lecturer at the Graduate School of Arts and Sciences at Georgetown University. He presented a series of talks there entitled "Political Disintegration of Europe: A Survey of Current World Politics", which was given under the auspices of the Department of Political Science.[10] From the end of January 1946 throughout that year's spring semester, he spent a great deal of time in Washington, D.C., in order to deliver the lectures.

Communist agents operating in the émigré community in the United States continued to monitor Eckhardt's activities closely, and Dr. John Gyetvai continued to attempt to discredit him. On 29 January 1946, just two days before Eckhardt's first Georgetown lecture, Gyetvai, in his role as editor of New York City's (communist) Hungarian-language newspaper, *Magyar Jövő*, sent a letter to Dean Hunter Guthrie, S.J., of Georgetown University demanding that the invitation extended to Eckhardt be withdrawn.[11]

Two days later (31 January), Georges Faludy, one of Gyetvai's fellow travelers, also wrote Dean Guthrie a scathing letter. Showing a remarkable ignorance of the fundamentals of the English language, Faludy wrote:

> There is no doubt that Mr. Eckhardt is one of the toughest political gangsters of my native country. He started his carreer [*sic*] as leader of the "Ébredő Magyarok" a Fascist gang credited with some 20,000 murders. He became in the early 20's Chief of Press and had to resign because he was bribed by Jewish bankers. He became member of the Extreme Right anew and visited Hitler in 1923 imploring funds from him. Having enormous debts ("his Paraclete is the Diamond Ace"), he left the Right and became member of the Small-Landowners Party, advocating an agrarian reform. Later, he became head of this Party. Just before the elections in 1937, on a confidential meeting, he told his collaborators he wont tolarate [*sic*] an agrarian reform. Everybody deserted him and his Party took a terrific beating. To pay for his gambling debts, Mr. Eckhardt visited in February, 1939, Mr. Samuel Stern, president of the Jewish community in Budapest, imploring for Pengő 250,000 ($50,000) and promising to vote against the Nuernberg Laws. He got the money and voted for the law.

In conclusion, Faludy asserts, "... besides of political ore religious considerations and beyond his filthy past Mr. Eckhardt happens to be an ignoramus, utterly unfit to lecture for the American youth."[12]

Dean Guthrie was not swayed, and Eckhardt went on to great success with his lecture series. After the final lecture, delivered in May 1946, Dean Guthrie wrote to Eckhardt, "It is my pleasant duty to thank you for the outstanding contributions you have made to the Department of Political Science. The reports which have come to this Office have been warm and enthusiastic in their appreciation of your work. And I wish to express my personal gratitude that a man of your singular talents and background should be so generous of your time and interest in our behalf."[13]

Eckhardt lectured widely in the period from 1945 to 1947. On 12 April 1947 he delivered a lecture entitled "The War of the Twentieth Century" as the keynote speech at the annual Burke Society dinner, given in the Marble Room of Keating Hall at Fordham University in New York. In appreciation of the lecture, which was published in the September 1947 issue of *Thought*, the Fordham University Quarterly, Eckhardt was awarded permanent honorary membership in the Burke Society.[14]

By 1946 things were not going all well in the Grand Alliance between Great Britain, the United States and the USSR. Winston Churchill made his seminal "Iron Curtain" speech in Fulton, Missouri in what one historian has referred to it as that "year of uneasy tranquility".[15] Even those who did not want to believe in the USSR's territorial ambitions had to face the stark reality of its intent.

Immediately following the war and for at least a decade thereafter, Eckhardt continued his active involvement with the American intelligence community. Tibor Eckhardt Jr. thinks that his father continued that collaboration until the end of his life. Eckhardt's wartime affiliation was with the Department of the Army Military Intelligence Service (MIS).[16] He and Archduke Otto von Habsburg were also offered the opportunity to work with the OSS, but they knew that there were many left-leaning individuals and Communist plants in that organization and were leery of lending it their cooperation. Eckhardt clearly states in his memoirs that he chose to assist the MIS rather than the OSS for that reason.[17] As documented in the State Department and War Department correspondence cited in Chapter 3, Eckhardt worked with military intelligence virtually full time from shortly after his arrival in the United States until the mid 1950s.[18]

John V. Grombach was Eckhardt's contact person at MIS; at the State Department it was usually Howard Travers. The Hungarian diplomats and politicians all knew Travers, as he had been the U.S. charge d'affairs in Budapest and only left that city after Pearl Harbor was attacked. Travers's title at the Department of State during the war was Chief of the Visa Division. However, as soon as the Allies gained a foothold in Europe, the State Department planned to send him there to attempt to stabilize the situation in Central Europe.[19] In fact, Travers asked Eckhardt to accompany him on that mission (there was even talk of parachuting Travers in), and Eckhardt had agreed, but the plan was never implemented. Travers seems to have been a point person for all things related to Hungary at the State Department, as he was in regular contact with Eckhardt and Pelényi regarding not just political issues but also social issues related to Hungarians or Hungarian communities in the West. For example, in Pelényi's collected papers there is a letter from Travers dated 2 November 1944 that deals with the problems of destitute Hungarian students living in Western Europe and references Eckhardt's request for his assistance in the matter.[20] As mentioned in Chapter 4, Travers was also in contact with the Hungarian émigré group headed by Rusztem Vámbéry and the Károlyi followers, and evidence points to State Department support, including financial assistance, for several of the émigré groups representing the whole Hungarian political spectrum.

Eckhardt's network during the war and after included John Pelényi, György Barcza and other important Hungarians, particularly the leadership of the Smallholders Party. It also included Count István Bethlen, with whom Eckhardt's correspondence was intense and detailed until the end of the war, when Bethlen, who was certain the Russians would not harm him, was lured out of hiding and sent into exile in the USSR. He died there in 1946.

Having spent the war years away from his family, in the immediate post-war years, despite his busy and challenging schedule, Eckhardt made an effort to spend time with his children. During the summer of 1948 he wrote to John Pelényi, "I have more to do than I can perform in the three or four days which I now spend in New York. I am taking somewhat of a rest by spending long weekends on Fire Island with my children, where I enjoy most of all the lack of telephones and motor cars."[21]

Vámbéry, the Czechs and Beneš—
"Failure of a Mission and a Mission of Failure"

In the euphoria of the immediate post-war years, the Czech and Hungarian left-wing and liberals, Beneš, Vámbéry, Károlyi, felt that their goal was in sight—Central Europe, including Hungary, would be within their sphere of influence. Many of the right-wing and conservative groups of the region had been eliminated or lost their leaders. In Czechoslovakia, the Slovak nationalist leader, Milan Hodža died a mysterious death in 1944. Members of the intra-war and wartime Hungarian establishment had been murdered (Bethlen, Bajcsy-Zsilinszky) or discredited (Eckhardt, Horthy), and many of the diplomats had fled or not returned to their homelands. Austria first admitted Archduke Otto and his family, but shortly after their return Otto and his brothers were exiled from that country, thus preventing the Habsburgs from building a power base or assisting in the restoration of the nation.[22] The conditions were thus optimal for major changes in the political landscape of Central Europe favoring socialists and left-wing politicians.

Hungary's first free elections were held in 1945. The following year, Vámbéry wrote *Hungary—To Be or Not to Be*, a book outlining his views on the country's future. In it he defended Eduard Beneš and his alignment with the Soviet Union and continued to savage the Hungarian leadership and what he saw as the power elite, including respected Hungarian historians such as Domokos Kosáry.[23] "He [Beneš] and the wicked, 'imperialistic' Czechs were supposed to be the spearhead of Soviet Russia", Vámbéry wrote, failing to recognize that that was indeed the case.[24] When he wrote the book, there seemed to be no fear of what domination by Soviet Russia would bring, and Vámbéry went on to say dismissively, "Journalists not familiar with the Hungarian background are predicting either complete economic ruin or the ultimate communization of Hungary. Political forecasts are always risky, and this one borders on utter nonsense."[25] He does go on to say, however, "Regardless of the orientation of other neighbors, the influence of Russia, the greatest power bordering on Hungary, will be predominant. ... Anyone not living in a fools paradise must admit that Hungary's foreign policy and its army are de facto going to be controlled by the Soviet Union. Other members of the Allied Control Commission, as was made clear at the conference of the Foreign Secretaries held in Moscow in December, 1945, have only an advisory role."[26]

After Ferenc Nagy relinquished his position as premier on 31 May 1947 and left Hungary, Vámbéry agreed to accept the position of Hungarian ambassador to the United States, continuing to believe in the benign and non-interfering nature of Soviet policy toward Hungary. His tenure was brief and ineffectual. Appointed on 6 September 1947, he was frustrated at every turn in attempting to do his job, and when he eventually realized that his underlings, Communist Party members, were dictating policy to him, he understood that he was being used as window dressing. He resigned on 19 May 1948, after just nine months in the post, and then wrote an unpublished seven-page memorandum entitled "Failure of a Mission and a Mission of Failure", which outlines his experience in vivid detail.[27]

Unfortunately, even after his awakening to the USSR's real intent in Hungary, Vámbéry continued to consider the Hungarian leaders and even the Hungarian peasants (because of what he viewed as their ignorant conservatism) as the enemy. Rusztem Vámbéry died in 1948, still an avowed foe of the Hungarian establishment but also a bitter and disenchanted man, cut adrift by Károlyi and his followers, estranged from Jászi, and still not admitting to what he had helped bring about in Soviet-dominated Hungary.[28]

The Hungarian National Council is Formed

As the Communists consolidated their power in Hungary, the trickle of emigrating Hungarian political figures became a flood. Ferenc Nagy, Msgr. Béla Varga, Zoltán Pfeiffer and many others left their homeland. They joined the politicians who had already gone to the West as part of the 1945 emigration. By 1947 the balance of world power had changed dramatically and the Cold War was in full force. The United States, reluctant in the past publicly to endorse or financially support political groups, now felt that the time was right to support the efforts of exiles from Soviet satellite countries, and it had to find some means of occupying the energies and time of the émigré politicians—as well as provide them with some form of "employment". Finally the reality of the Cold War and the descent of the Iron Curtain in Europe made the conditions right for an organization that would represent the interests of all Hungarians abroad.

The Hungarian National Council was born in 1947. It was to be the longest-lived organization of Hungarian political exiles in America.[29]

The first organizational meeting of what was to become the Hungarian National Council (Magyar Nemzeti Bizottmány or HNC) was held in Chicago, Illinois, in November 1947. On November 18 the principals involved—Tibor Eckhardt, Ferenc Nagy, Zoltán Pfeiffer, Dezső Sulyok and Béla Varga—issued a proclamation entitled "Appeal to the Hungarian People".[30] It stated, in part, "... the Hungarian people must survive this darkest period in their history. Resistance at this point in time is futile and purposeless unless the western powers choose to step into the situation. Because of this we are calling upon you; remove yourselves from public life; don't work together with your oppressors; don't listen to those that would deceive you; remain in your homes, but support the passive resistance."[31] The declaration went on to say, "the problems and direction of the resistance will be accepted as the responsibility of the Hungarian leadership living abroad. We abandon all party politics and divisions and create in the free world a living Hungarian national organization, from whom only the fascists and Communists who intended to deliver Hungary to the foreign powers are excluded." The authors concluded by vowing that the "1000 year old Hungarian nation will rise again."[32]

By 1948 the new organization had been launched in New York. Composed of key Hungarian leaders, almost all of whom had recently fled the communist takeover in Hungary, the Hungarian National Council was regarded by many as a virtual government in exile, and its executive committee functioned as such, with its president in the role of "prime minister". Tibor Eckhardt was one of the council's founders and served on its executive committee as chairman of the military committee. Msgr. Béla Varga, speaker of the Hungarian Parliament until 31 May 1947, headed the council. The executive committee was composed entirely of Hungarian citizens, most of whom intended to return to Hungary after its liberation from Soviet occupation. The HNC was sponsored and generously funded by the U.S. government through the National Committee for a Free Europe (later renamed the Free Europe Committee). The HNC's goal was to "represent the nations muted [by Soviet occupation] as well as to care for and to supply spiritual and political guidance to the dispersed Hungarians."[33]

By 1954 the HNC leadership had seventy-six members and included virtually all of the political figures who had left Hungary after 1947, including two former prime ministers, several ministers and the former leaders of all the political parties purged between 1947 and 1949.[34] The group was somewhat resistant to including *every* former official, however, and was selective about its choices. This lack of inclusiveness was specifically directed toward the pre-1947 émigrés, a situation that troubled Eckhardt and was later to become a larger issue. Initial funding was obtained for offices in both New York and Washington, D.C., and satellite offices were opened in some twenty countries outside the United States.[35]

Almost immediately after its establishment, the HNC became a center of political controversy among Hungarian Americans. Whether conservative, right-wing or radical Left, they all accused the HNC of evil intent. The conservatives and the Right radicals regarded the participants as pseudo communists and possible agents of the Soviet system in Hungary; the Left regarded them as traitors and "agents of United States Imperialism". The most valid criticism was that the HNC did not represent the Hungarian American community. The spokesmen for most of the Hungarian American organizations viewed the HNC's members as recently arrived, appointed agents of certain American political interest groups who were on the U.S. government payroll. In the immigrant community it was thought that the HNC had been granted the U.S. government's official recognition and financial support in exchange for representing the interests of U.S. foreign policy with regard to Hungary and the world during the Cold War.

The primary difference between the newly arrived political leaders and Tibor Eckhardt was that Eckhardt had strong ties to all of the Hungarian American organizations. He had established and cultivated these relationships over two decades, beginning when he was in the United States on his Carnegie Endowment lecture tour in 1930. Eckhardt was particularly close to and well regarded by the most prominent of these organizations, the American Hungarian Federation, a hugely influential force that served as the umbrella organization for over 300 American Hungarian groups in the United States. Its president was Tibor Kerekes, a Georgetown University professor who was well connected and well regarded in Washington, D.C. The AHF's unequivocal support of Eckhardt's

Movement for Independent Hungary had provided him with exposure to many émigré communities and organizations and made him a much sought-after speaker among émigré groups.

The recently arrived Hungarian leaders were basically unknown to Hungarian America. The most prominent among them, Ferenc Nagy, had the prestige of the prime minister's position behind him, and, like Eckhardt, he was invited to give many lectures and make personal appearances—a fact amply illustrated by the fourteen file boxes in his archived papers that contain his lecture correspondence. Although there can be no doubt that he was in demand as a speaker, virtually none of the institutions represented in the archived correspondence appear to be Hungarian American civic groups, churches or fraternal organizations, which emphasizes his lack of connection with the Hungarian American community at large.[36] When he arrived, Nagy was simply not well known to Hungarian America, and he remained very selective in his contacts. For example, Gabriella Mauthner, who has served as a volunteer at Magyar Ház since its inception, remembers that he never once visited that cultural and political heart of the New York City Hungarian community. The remaining political émigrés were also basically unknown to the Hungarian American community, accounting for the fact that that community viewed them with suspicion and mistrust.

The U.S. government granted the HNC what Eckhardt and the Movement for Independent Hungary had been denied—official endorsement and financial support. Six years had passed since Eckhardt resigned from the Movement's chairmanship, and the political changes in Hungary that he predicted and feared had come about. But even with U.S. government support and the participation of so many key Hungarian émigré politicians and leaders, the HNC was ultimately just as ineffective as the Movement for Independent Hungary had been. As years passed, the West realized that the Soviets' control over their satellites was to be permanent. Slowly relinquishing the dream of returning to a democratic Hungary, the HNC leadership increasingly put down roots in the United States and other countries in the West—particularly after the failed Hungarian Revolution of 1956.

The intent of the communists' slanderous campaign against Eckhardt in exile became clear in the light of post-war events. The Soviets wanted to neutralize anyone who had the potential to be a strong post-war political leader, particularly one with close ties to the Habsburgs and to the Roman Catholic Church. The Czechs, Slovaks, Yugoslavs and Romanians wanted to silence the cause of Hungarian revisionism and its advocates, thus ensuring the existence of their countries and their borders. The clever disinformation and the considerable financial resources utilized in their campaign indicate the importance they attached to the prize—control of Central- and East Europe.

Not only was the Hungarian National Council viewed with great skepticism by the Hungarian American community, its work was internally fractious from the onset. Eckhardt was not inclined to compromise with the far Left and what he regarded as increasingly leftist elements in the HNC, and on 4 October 1950 he provoked HNC President Varga to issue a statement of incompatibility directed against him within the executive committee. The convoluted details of the problems Eckhardt encountered in the executive committee are beyond the purview of this research. Suffice it to say that the ongoing tension between the Ferenc Nagy camp and the Eckhardt camp escalated rapidly after the organization was formed. However, the ostensible cause of the incompatibility statement was that as the chair of the military committee Eckhardt had joined the Magyar Harcosok Bajtársi Közössége, an organization that had been labeled pro-fascist. A long-time friend of Eckhardt, Varga was determined to be diplomatic and include Nagy in all of his decisions and in the process. He also deferred to Nagy as a former prime minister. Varga also attempted to placate and please the Eckhardt faction. In the end, he pleased no one, as the extensive correspondence in both the Eckhardt and Nagy papers reveals.[37] Eckhardt viewed the struggle within the executive committee as a matter of the rightists versus the leftists and felt that in terms of committee composition, the scale was tipping heavily to the left as a result of Varga's weak leadership.

It was not until 4 September 1951 that Eckhardt responded to Msgr. Varga regarding the statement of incompatibility, explaining the delay and reiterating the reasons the HNC was formed.

> Since October 4, 1950, when you Mr. Chairman, had submitted a statement of incompatibility directed against me to the Executive Committee, I have never referred publicly to this accusation, to the smear campaign directed against me or to the injurious decisions taken by that sub-committee. By doing so, I wished to respect the public interest …
>
> In November 1947, in our Chicago proclamation, we have agreed to set aside "all party politics" and to create "the national unity of all Hungarians living in free lands." It is on this foundation, that in the summer of 1948 the Executive Committee of the Hungarian National Council was established from all the leaders of Hungarian political groups who "form a part of the general political picture of our country." At that time, in the composition of the Executive Committee, a certain balance was achieved between the pre-war and post-war, Rightist and Leftist political tendencies and it is a real national interest that that balance be maintained continuously.[38]

Eckhardt went on to state his objections to the lack of political balance in the executive committee:

> Contrary to all democratic and reasonable evolution the insistence of the Hungarian extreme Leftist group has put through in recent months an extension to the Left in the composition of the Executive Committee. The original balance does not exist any more and if the Executive Committee wishes to remain true to its fundamental national program, it has to complete its ranks from the Right in the same proportion as the Left. In its present composition, the Executive Committee is no more the organ of national policy but is rather a representation of the Peasant-Marxist classes and their class-warfare with an extreme Leftist predominance. What results may be expected from this change I did experience during the action taken by the Sub-Committee on Incompatibility dealing with my case when the extreme leftist members forming a majority of the sub-committee, pushed aside the fundamental requirements of all legal action and brought an incriminating verdict without hearing or even informing the accused.[39]

The sad truth was that most of the émigré politicians had so little to occupy their time that the Committee on Incompatibility's report regarding Eckhardt runs to fully fifty pages.

These issues roiled within the HNC for several years, with bitter accusations on all sides. Finally, Eckhardt reluctantly concluded that the HNC Executive Committee's policies were not going to change and his efforts on Hungary's behalf would be better utilized outside that forum than within it. He submitted his resignation on 14 April 1954.[40] Since the HNC Executive Committee was composed of foreign nationals, his resignation freed Eckhardt to apply for U.S. citizenship, which he did that same year. With his resignation he also voluntarily relinquished his only regular source of income, the $300 per month stipend that he, Ferenc Nagy, Béla Varga, Béla Fábián, Zoltán Pfeiffer and József H. Közi earned on the Hungarian National Council.[41]

On 1 June 1954, Eckhardt wrote a realistic and analytical letter to Archduke Otto von Habsburg, who had written Eckhardt to advise him to meet with the HNC to try to find "some satisfactory solution". Eckhardt replied:

> We had that meeting last week where we frankly exchanged our views without, however, having made any progress. In fact, no concrete change for the better has been proposed and therefore no change in my position could even be considered. The reason for this evasive attitude of my three guests was obviously the fact that Ferenc Nagy, although just returned from Japan has not yet been consulted. The decision on the part of Msgr. Varga not to attempt

anything that has not been previously agreed upon with Ferenc Nagy. It is this approach by B.V. which has been the main cause of the gradual but constant switch to the Left, and had I further accepted the situation, the continued swing to the Left could not be halted. I do not believe that my demand for the restoration of the original equilibrium of the Executive Committee is anything that could be qualified as extreme. The Hungarian Executive Committee was organized in the darkest days of the Truman-Acheson period and represented that minimum which, from the Hungarian point of view, could still be accepted as useful. While American internal policies have been gradually moving toward the Right, the Executive Committee has been pursuing the opposite direction, which is obvious in the changes which have occurred in its composition. Sulyok and Pfeiffer were accepted in the Executive Committee as representing national bourgeois, that is Right political views. Sulyok has committed hara-kiri and had to be eliminated.[42] Pfeiffer for material reasons has gone over to the other side and may be considered now as the most obnoxious representative of subversive Leftist tendencies. It also was expected that Msgr. Közi will represent the views of Cardinal Mindszenty. Unfortunately, when he arrived in New York years ago, he openly admitted having joined the coalition of the "People's Front". Then as a representative of Catholic policy Mr. Barankovics was admitted into the Executive Committee—a Trojan horse—and in my opinion the most dangerous member of that outfit. I do not have to characterize Mr. Auer, again a new member of the Executive Committee. The original balance of the Executive Committee has thus been utterly changed. One Rightist member was eliminated. Two passed over to the opposite side. And two new Leftist were added to the original setup. Therefore, even if Mr. Kállay would give us his firm support with Bessenyey and Fábián, we are only four against six members belonging to the people's front. As a result, instead of fulfilling its patriotic duty, Leftist members of the Executive committee have become guilty of participating in and encouraging smear campaigns against the good name of the Hungarian nation in the same vein as has been done previously by the agents of Mr. Beneš ... [T]he only man who could be used as militant against this aggressive Leftist coalition is a little Jewish member, Béla Fábián. No wonder the 95 percent of the Hungarian emigration has turned its back on this outfit which rightly they consider dangerous to national interests. ... I am determined not only to stop the Leftist trend, but also to prevent the Hungarian emigration from going to any extreme toward the Right.

The impressions which I have gained in this respect since my resignation are very encouraging. It has also become necessary to criticize certain activities of the Free Europe Committee, which I can only do if, having restored my complete independence, I assume for that criticism the personal responsibility without the Executive Committee participating in it. …

I feel very much flattered by Your Majesty's insistence on my continued participation in the Executive Committee, but feel certain that in view of the above-said, Your Majesty will also understand the motives for my resignation. Therefore I beg to state that, on certain conditions, to be previously fulfilled (and not only promised) by the Executive Committee, I would accept again to be elected as a member of the Executive Committee in charge of military affairs.

a. The original equilibrium of the Executive Committee has to be restored, which can be done if, besides myself, two new members representing the national point of view are elected as members of the Executive Committee. …

b. Preceding the new election the basis of the National Committee has to be extended by inclusion of all those former legislators who have not been guilty of having promoted either the Nazi or the Communist dominations for Hungary. The absurd delaying of this indispensable broadening of the basis has perhaps caused more harm than anything else to the prestige on the Committee and is considered as an insult by all those who have been unduly kept outside.

c. Since the National Council and its Executive Committee are not representing the Hungarian State but the Hungarian nation, the Hungarian population detached from present day Hungary, must gain representation in the Executive committee. The Czechoslovak National Committee has included a member from Ruthenia with much less justification than we could. The danger also exists that a sudden deterioration of the international situation might lead to the recognition of the present Executive Committee as a kind of official representation of Hungary. In that event the inclusion of the representatives of the detached Hungarians would become most difficult if not an impossible problem. There results an unbearable responsibility from these undue delays.

I do not believe that there is anything extreme or personal in these objective demands, which should appear justified and overdue. I do not believe that the present Executive Committee, which has so easily given way to American Leftist influences, can ever gather strength and moral fortitude sufficient to carry out these changes. I have made almost desperate efforts from within to no avail, and I

> wish to continue now the same efforts from outside. … I have not acted on momentary impulses, but have been pondering for months, in fact for years, over this problem.[43]

Once leaked to the general public by HNC members, the details of these intra-organizational struggles were dissected and chewed over in the Hungarian émigré press worldwide. The political battles went on for years, while the HNC's credibility, never robust in the eyes of Hungarian Americans, quickly eroded—for as the HNC leaned farther to the left, Hungarian American sentiments, always conservative, were moving farther to the right.

In a conversation with this author, Dr. Otto von Habsburg attributed some of the problems between Nagy and Eckhardt to the strong influence of Steven Swift (birth name, Schlesinger), Nagy's Hungarian-born CIA handler. Swift was, the archduke said, "the CIA man in Austria, he was based in Salzburg and he was very close to Ferenc Nagy. He was assigned to him and traveled with him everywhere. He was a former Hungarian expatriate, a brilliantly intelligent man … He was not a friend of Eckhardt that was very clear. He was very cynical about him."[44] Swift moved to the United States with Nagy and served as his translator until Nagy learned English. Swift also translated Nagy's autobiography from Hungarian into English and was instrumental in getting it published in the United States, handling negotiations with the publishing houses on Nagy's behalf.[45] After his work with Nagy ended, the U.S. government sent Swift back to Austria to be posted in Salzburg. The friendship between Nagy and Swift endured for the rest of their lives, as their warm and personal correspondence attests.[46]

Observers of the day who were familiar with Eckhardt's temperament ascribed much of the dissention within the HNC to his intractable views and fiery temper. They also saw the dissent among the HNC Executive Committee members as being split between those who had been in power before 1947 and those after. Certainly, the individuals who left Hungary after 1947 felt that they, rather than the earlier arrivals, held the Hungarian people's current mandate. On the whole, they were also individuals with a more liberal and socialistic outlook, who had not recoiled from collaboration with the Soviet Union. In truth, however, it was not ideological issues but the constant infighting and pettiness among the HNC Executive Committee members that created the most severe problems within the organization. The HNC functioned in spite of rather than because of its leadership.

It is probably true that Ferenc Nagy leaned to the left; witness his affinity for the world's agricultural workers and peasants as demonstrated by his trips to Asia (particularly India, Japan and Taiwan) and shift of attention toward the problems of the developing world's peasants. It is also true that even when fighting for universal franchise, the secret ballot and the rights of the Hungarian small landowner, Eckhardt was a statesman with a global, educated and urbane viewpoint. He was also personally religious, devout and a conservative. One can imagine that although Nagy wrote generously about Eckhardt and his years in Hungary prior to World War II, the two of them would clash when they came into competition in the very small world of post-war émigré power politics. Clash they did, and Nagy's HNC correspondence is full of political positioning and strategizing against Eckhardt.

For his part, Eckhardt seems to have gone it alone, and when he could no longer deal with what he felt was a strong drift to the left and an imbalance in the HNC, he resigned his position. The following letter from C.D. Jackson to Msgr. Varga dated 10 March 1952 is indicative of the situation. Jackson was president and American administrator of the Free Europe Committee, which completely underwrote the entire HNC operation and provided it with all of its resources. In reviewing his year at the helm of the HNC's parent organization, Jackson does not mention Eckhardt at all but singles out Ferenc Nagy and Zoltán Pfeiffer as troublemakers, adding that the "NCFE does not intend to be hampered or sabotaged by exile political maneuvering".[47]

This recently uncovered letter provides an insider's objective perspective on the HNC that cannot be ascribed to someone with a "hidden agenda". The entire text is reproduced here, for it gives a first hand view of the intrigues and personal agendas that seem to have dominated the HNC and sucked the life blood out of its effectiveness.

> Dear Monsignor Varga:
>
> As I wind up my year with the National Committee for a Free Europe, I thought it appropriate to send you a letter–not a letter of farewell, but rather some thoughts on the Hungarian National Council as I have observed it during the year.
>
> In the first place, I would like to congratulate you and your associates on having done an extraordinary job of holding a very volatile situation together. In fact, it was a unique job, and one whose value we may never fully appreciate because so many of the benefits are intangible.
>
> I hope, therefore, that you will continue to work with undiminished will to hold the Council together, as it would present a very serious problem to Admiral Miller if the Hungarian group were to fall apart.[48]
>
> I would also like to congratulate you on the effective work the representatives of the Hungarian National Council have done abroad, particularly in France and Germany. You know how important I consider this work. It seems to me that the real task and duty of a National Council is to help the exiles, and the front lines of this work are in Europe.

Aside from the obvious necessities of food, clothing, shelter, the most important aspect of the work is what I would call a "consular" service, as these people do not know where and how to turn. In this consular-type work, I think that General Hennyey and Mr. Auer have been doing an excellent job, and personal feelings in this matter are completely confirmed by reactions I have received from the International Refugee Organization and the official foreign and American administrations in these countries.

To my way of thinking, exile political matters in New York and Washington should take a definitely second place to helping human beings in distress, and although there are some who do not agree with this order of priority, I am delighted and grateful that the work of the Hungarian National Council indicates that you share these ideas.

***

Since this is an honest letter, and not just pro-forma appreciation by a retiring President, I must also, unfortunately, include some observations that are not so pleasant.

I remember very early in my work with NCFE, that you taught me the political meaning of the word "polarization", and since then I have had ample opportunity in the Hungarian National Council to see polarization at work.

NCFE has grown in the past year into a large organization engaged in serious work, and frequently proving its effectiveness behind the Iron Curtain. To put it another way, during the past year NCFE has evolved from just a hope into a professional weapon in the war against the enemy. <u>Therefore, activities which a year ago were deplorable but pardonable, are today inexcusable and intolerable.</u>

Admiral Miller agrees with me completely on this point, and intends to take such action from time to time as may be necessary to counter such activities when they occur.

However, I recognize that it is not enough for NCFE to take unilateral action. We must be assisted by you and those of your associates who understand who the real enemy is, and are willing to subordinate fratricidal strife, polarizing attempts, and disloyal activities.

***

I fully realize that these are nothing but big words unless I can illustrate them more specifically.

I have in my possession enough illustrations to fill a volume, but would like to select three in particular to mention in this letter, not because I have any particular desire to single out the individuals for censure, but rather because what they have done not only illustrates the point I am trying to make, but also reveals an attitude of mind which is practically incomprehensible to an American working for a great cause.

The first case that I have in mind is that of Mr. Ferenc Nagy.

Last February, Mr. Nagy wrote a letter to Mr. Frank S. Land of Kansas City, Missouri, complaining bitterly about the National Committee for a Free Europe, accusing it of "supporting outmoded and old-fashioned reactionary political ideologies," and asking Mr. Land to advise him as to how this situation could be brought to the attention of President Truman in order to have him do something about it. As a result of that letter, Mr. Land wrote to the White House, and in the normal course this full correspondence came to me.

I asked Mr. Nagy to come to the office, and tried to explain to him that what he had done was not only bad, but a very silly thing. It was bad in the sense that he had violated our hospitality by secretly attempting to conspire against the organization which was supporting him. It was silly in assuming that he could carry on this kind of intrigue without my knowing about it—in fact, without having the White House check with NCFE, an American organization, as to what action should be taken.

Mr. Nagy seemed to understand what I tried to explain to him, and with what I considered complete honesty and sincerity expressed his regrets and said that it would not happen again. In return for this frank understanding on his part, we shook hands, and I promised that the correspondence would be put away in our files and never referred to again. And as you know, I have never even mentioned it to you.

Mr. Nagy has once again written to President Truman—this time directly. And once again the White House has sent me the memorandum.

I consider that Mr. Nagy has broken his pledge, and therefore I am free to tell you about the incident.

This time, although the words of Mr. Nagy are more temperate, the melody is the same—dissatisfaction with what NCFE has done; dissatisfaction with the Hungarian National Council. Let me quote a passage: "The existing National Committees are not in themselves suitable for this task, partly because of the general intra-Committee controversies between Democrats and reactionaries, and partly because these Committees are not considered by the peoples behind the Iron Curtain international guarantee that promises would be carried out."

I cannot help commenting at this point that in the Hungarian National Council there is probably no one who has contributed more to "intra-Committee controversies" than Mr. Nagy himself. Furthermore, an analysis of Mr. Nagy's definition of "Democrats and reactionaries" would be extremely interesting. It might have been more accurate had he said "people who supported my Government in 1947 and everybody else."

As to the matter of <u>any</u> exile committee, whether the Hungarian National Council or Mr. Nagy's Central Eastern European Committee, being able to "guarantee" to the people behind the Iron Curtain that promises would be carried out, Mr. Nagy's statement is either frivolous or preposterous.

Mr. Nagy winds up with a request that the President give his blessing to Mr. Nagy's proposed super-committee—the Central Eastern European Committee—which represents "a total majority of 70 to 80% of the entire population of Central Eastern Europe."

I am frankly fascinated by the processes of Mr. Nagy's mind. I cannot believe that all he thinks about is the promotion of Leftish Hungarian politicians in exile. I cannot believe that as a human being he does not feel some sense of responsibility toward NCFE and the Hungarian National Council, who have month after month helped him. I do not wish to sound dramatic, I do not ask for thanks, and I am not suggesting that in return for our help we impose an obligation of a quid pro quo. I <u>do</u> say that the question of loyalty does arise, and the question of responsibility is very real.

Furthermore, Mr. Nagy has been in this country long enough now to understand that this kind of intriguing is a distressing irritation to everyone, including the White House.

***

My second illustration also concerns Mr. Nagy. Mr. Nagy recently sent a telegram to Mr. Dessewffy, of which the following is a translation. I have the original Hungarian if you care to see it:

"YOU HAVE SUBMITTED TO THE BOARD OF THE NEW YORK RADIO FREE EUROPE NAMES NEW STAFF MEMBERS: HEAD: ANDREW GELLÉRT, STAFF: KÁROLY ANDRÁS, LAJOS HALÁSZ, DEZSŐ SALY, PÉTER STEPHAICS, MRS. L. VARGA. STOP. CONSIDERING THE FACT THAT THIS RADIO STATION BROADCASTS IN THE NAME OF THE DEMOCRATIC HUNGARIAN EXILES, I AS THE PRESIDENT OF THE PEASANT FEDERATION CALL THE MEMBERS OF THE POLITICAL COMMITTEE TO IMMEDIATELY VOTE WHETHER THIS SOLUTION IS ACCEPTABLE TO US."

Again, I would like to know what is going through Mr. Nagy's mind.

NCFE, an American organization, hired Mr. Dessewffy to be the responsible head of its Hungarian Desk in Munich. Mr. Dessewffy was a very careful choice after weeks of consultation on both sides of the Atlantic. His specific instructions were that the Munich Desk should be staffed by people <u>selected for functional competence</u>, excluding, of course, Communists and Fascists.

At the same time, it was felt that the NCFE had permitted political affiliation to overshadow functional competence in the New York Hungarian Desk, and the New York Desk simply wasn't any good. Therefore, the New York Desk and the Munich Desk had to be brought into alignment. So Mr. Dessewffy was sent to America and given the responsibility of hiring the necessary personnel—and in New York was instructed to apply the same yardstick that he applied in Munich.

When Mr. Dessewffy had fulfilled his New York task, again after the most serious consideration of all the angles involved in each one of his choices, Mr. Nagy sent him the telegram quoted above as though Mr. Nagy were in the position to control, or at least to veto, the membership of the Desk.

Does Mr. Nagy really believe that he is in that position? Or is this pure polarization. As we all know, this is a move directed against Mr. Gellert, who does not have the same political coloration as Mr. Nagy. In a recent conversation with Mr. Nagy, I asked him if the telegram would have been sent if Mr. Gellert had not been selected, and he admitted that it would not have been sent.

There is an additional interesting element in this, in that Mr. Nagy calls for a vote as the President of the Hungarian Peasant Union. Doesn't Mr. Nagy know that the Hungarian Peasant Union does not exist as a viable political party; it only exists in the individual persons in exile who happen formerly to have been members of the Hungarian Peasant Union. Mr. Nagy is not a member of a government-in-exile, or even of a parliament-in-exile, so that action of his is totally unreal, indicating unwillingness to recognize the world as it exists.

Doesn't Mr. Nagy realize that the only way that exile politicians can achieve political reality is through national and international unity in order to bring about the liberation of their countries, and therefore the day when they can once again start legitimate and real party rivalry to appeal to a free electorate?

***

The third case I would like to mention concerns Mr. Zoltan Pfeiffer.

After Mr. Dessewffy made his selections for the New York Desk, Mr. Pfeiffer got in touch with him to protest against the fact that in selecting Mr. Gellert, Mr. Dessewffy had been unfaithful to the Smallholders Party, which because Mr. Dessewffy had formerly been a member of that party, expected a clean sweep of the New York Desk, irrespective of functional competence. Mr. Pfeiffer further stated—and this the really important point—that because of the appointment of Mr. Gellert, Mr. Pfeiffer would have to "attack" Mr. Dessewffy from now on, wherever and whenever possible; in short, a declaration of war.

Again, I would like to understand Mr. Pfeiffer's mental processes. Who does he think he is? Where does he think he is? This is a very serious world, and not a Rufolf [*sic*] Friml operetta. Mr. Pfeiffer is not in Budapest conducting a political campaign against a wayward member of a Left-wing party. Mr. Pfeiffer is in New York, an associate of NCFE, with every opportunity to has his opinion heard and his influence felt. But after a decision has been made, in good faith and after long consideration, to employ a man because of his competence to do a job, it is Mr. Pfeiffer's responsibility as an associate of the same organization to help that man do his work, and not to indulge in declarations of war in order to disrupt the operation.

***

I am sorry to have had to go into this unpleasant detail, but after a year of patiently observing and listening, I feel that I have earned the right to speak plainly.

I hope that somehow or other, it will be possible for you to explain to your membership that NCFE does not intend to be hampered or sabotaged by exile political maneuvering.

I also hope that you will be able to persuade your compatriots that insofar as NCFE can interpret U.S. policy it believes that the Government of the United States, looking forward to the eventual liberation of Hungary, will not permit any political group or individual in exile, to set up a monopoly for himself, his group, or his party.

With renewed thanks for your highly successful work in the past, and the fervent hope that you will be equally successful in the future, I am

Sincerely yours,

C.D. Jackson"[49]

This eye-opening letter clearly illustrates how disruptive and counter-productive Nagy and Pfeiffer's actions were within the Hungarian National Council. Jackson clearly states that "no one … has contributed more to 'intra-Committee controversies' than Mr. Nagy himself." The letter also illustrates how thoroughly Ferenc Nagy misunderstood his own position and that of the other political émigrés in relationship to the NCFE leadership, whose direction he clearly disregarded after his first incident in contacting President Truman. Was it naiveté on his part that he felt comfortable in attacking the very U.S. agency that had spirited him and his family out of Hungary, reestablished them in the United States and provided the financial means that they lived on? Could it be ascribed to the fact that Mr. Nagy did not understand English very well and misunderstood the language (although by 1952 that surely was no longer the case)?

It is interesting to note that while Eckhardt is not mentioned in Jackson's letter, Jackson's point of view regarding both Nagy and Pfeiffer is in concert with Eckhardt's own perspective. Given that the letter was written within nine months of Eckhardt's censure by the committee on incompatibility, one might think Jackson would cite the Eckhardt issue rather than the examples he chose. Unless, of course, we are to believe that the censure was simply a power play by Eckhardt's opponents and had nothing to do with the HNC's functioning.

Perhaps more than anything else, Nagy and Eckhardt were characterized by opposing political beliefs and styles. Nagy was an honest, self-made man and a patriot, but he was intimidated by Eckhardt and constantly attempted to contrive against his rival in large and small ways. Eckhardt was above the pettiness of day-in-day-out sniping, as his personal correspondence readily attests. He seldom made personal comments about anyone therein, though he became less flexible and accommodating as time went on. How far left Ferenc Nagy became or how far right Tibor Eckhardt was is not the issue. They were simply men whose viewpoints were dramatically different. If one understands their respective backgrounds, there is no mystery as to why they did not see eye to eye.

Dr. Otto von Habsburg has called Eckhardt the "towering giant of Hungarian politics, a real statesman". He asserts that Eckhardt was the target of so much sniping because the other politicians, "especially Ferenc Nagy, were jealous of him … these so-called little politicians hate the ones that are capable as statesmen and are towering mentally over them. That is why the relations with Varga and Eckhardt remained good. Varga was a humble man and he didn't have these enormous ambitions. Those little people like Ferenc Nagy and the others, they of course went with Eckhardt as long as he could give them a free ride. Then with emigration, this is when they certainly became something and they came to hate him. His ability with languages, his intellect, they all served to fuel the animosity of the little politicians, who could never measure up to him."[50]

Endnotes

1. John Flournoy Montgomery, *Hungary, the Unwilling Satellite*, p. 11.
2. *Tibor Eckhardt In his Own Words*, pp. 100–101.
3. For contemporary references to Eckhardt's 'fascist' background see: Christopher Simpson, *Blowback* (New York: Weidenfeld & Nicolson, 1988), p. 234.
4. Peoples Tribunal/nyilas Népbíróság.
5. Ferenc Virágh, *Makótól New Yorkig*, p. 27.
6. William Ward, FBI Report, 4 May 1945, p. 15.
7. Ferenc Virágh, *Makótól New Yorkig*, p. 27.
8. Ibid.
9. Tibor Eckhardt, *Recollections of Tibor Eckhardt: Regicide at Marseille*, biographical information on flyleaf.
10. Tibor Eckhardt, "Political Disintegration of Europe: A Survey of Current World Politics", Georgetown University course outline, Varia Collection, Box 6, Folder #494 ECK–ECO, Lavinger Library Archives, Georgetown University, Washington, D.C.
11. John Gyetvai to Hunter Guthrie, 29 January 1946, Varia Collection, Box 6, Folder #494 ECK–ECO, Lavinger Library Archives.
12. Georges Faludy to Hunter Guthrie, 31 January 1946, Varia Collection, Box 6, Folder #494 ECK–ECO, Lavinger Library Archives.
13. Hunter Guthrie to Tibor Eckhardt, 23 May 1946, Varia Collection, Box 6, Folder #494 ECK–ECO, Lavinger Library Archives.
14. Tibor Eckhardt Papers, Box 1, Lectures, American Hungarian Library and Historical Society.
15. Stanley M. Max, *The United States, Great Britain and the Sovietization of Hungary 1945–1948* (Boulder, New York: East European Monographs, Columbia University Press, 1985), p. 76.
16. His MIS work is described in detail in Chapter 3 and in *Tibor Eckhardt in His Own Words*, pp. 442–447.
17. Ibid.
18. John V. Grombach to Robert C. Alexander, 11 August 1954, Tibor Eckhardt Papers, Box 1, File: Extension of Stay in the United States. Citizenship Application, Hoover Institution Archives. See the Appendix for a copy of this letter.
19. *Tibor Eckhardt in His Own Words*, p. 466.
20. Correspondence among Eckhardt, Travers and Pelényi, 18 August 1943, 2 November 1944, 13 November 1944, 23 July 1948, and undated, John Pelényi Papers, Box 1, untitled folder, Hoover Institution Archives.
21. Ibid, 23 July 1948.
22. Gordon Brook-Shepherd, *Uncrowned Emperor: The Life and Times of Otto von Habsburg*, p. 176.
23. Rustem [*sic*] Vámbéry, *Hungary—To Be or Not to Be* (New York: Frederick Ungar Publishing Co., 1946), p. 37.
24. Ibid., p. 139.

25. Ibid., p. 183.
26. Ibid., p. 171.
27. Rusztem Vámbéry, "Failure of a Mission", Rusztem Vámbéry Papers, Box 3, Folder: Speeches and Writings—1948, Hoover Institution Archives.
28. In a very revealing letter chastising Vámbéry for not playing by the rules, Michael Károlyi, then Hungarian ambassador to France, wrote: "Ebben az esetben megkérdezem tőled, hogy vajjon miért vállaltad el a követi állást? Mint régi politikus, tisztában voltál azzal, hogy Magyarország politikája milyen irányt vett és Neked, mint Rákosi Mátyás védőjének, nem lehetett meglepetés, hogy Magyarország nem egy nyugati, formális, hanem egy újtipusú népi demokrácia van kialakulóban. Ha ezzel nem értettél egyet, akkor, ismétlem, nem lett volna szabad ezt az országot Washingtonban képviselned." ("In this case I ask you, why did you agree to accept the position of Ambassador? As an old time politician, you were perfectly clear on the direction that Hungary's political orientation was taking, and you, as the defender of Rákosi, should not have been surprised that Hungary was not going to have a western, formal [democracy] but a new type of peoples democracy which will evolve. If you did not agree with this, then, I repeat, you should not have agreed to serve as this country's representative in Washington.") Károlyi also criticizes Vámbéry for replying to the question of why Hungary was not participating in the Marshall Plan by saying, "I don't know, ask Stalin." Michael Károlyi to Rusztem Vámbéry, 7 July 1948, Rusztem Vámbéry Papers, Box 1, Folder: Correspondence Mihály Károlyi, Hoover Institution Archives.
29. The Hungarian National Council was also known as the Hungarian National Committee, as the word Bizottmány was translated differently by various participants. The official name was the Hungarian National Council, which was printed on the English-language stationary. Eckhardt in some of his correspondence referred to the organization as the Hungarian National Committee, and the Hoover Institution file headings therefore reflect his usage of that name.
30. Proclamation, 18 November 1947, Ferenc Nagy Papers, Box 69, File: Émigré Organization/Hungarian National Council/Appeals, Columbia University Archives. See the Appendix for a photocopy of the original appeal.
31. Ibid.
32. Ibid.
33. Steven Béla Vardy, *The Hungarian-Americans*, pp. 127–128.
34. Tibor Eckhardt Papers, Box 15, File: Magyar Bizottság Membership List, Hoover Institution Archives.
35. Ferenc Nagy Papers, Box 71, File: Hungarian National Council – Financial, Columbia University Archives.
36. Ferenc Nagy Papers, Index of Collection, Columbia University Archives.
37. Tibor Eckhardt to Msgr. Béla Varga, Chairman of the HNC, 4 September 1951, Tibor Eckhardt Papers, Box 1, File: Bizottmány, Hoover Institution Archives.
38. Ibid.
39. Ibid.
40. Msgr. Béla Varga to Tibor Eckhardt, 9 June 1954, Tibor Eckhardt Papers, Box. 1, File: Bizottmány, Hoover Institution Archives.
41. Ferenc Nagy Papers, Box 71, File: Hungarian National Council – Financial, Financial Ledgers of HNC, Columbia University Archives. Others who earned the top directors'

fee of $300 per month also included some of the directors of the HNC's foreign offices, including Apor in Rome, Auer in Paris.

42. Gyula Borbándi, *A magyar emigráció életrajza: 1945–1985*, p. 188. This comment refers to Sulyok's 1954 book *A Magyar tragédia*. To quote Gyula Borbándi, in *A Magyar tragédia* Sulyok "... amelyben minden rosszat elmondott bizottmányi végrehajtó bizottsági társairól és azok pártjairól". ("... said everything bad about the HNC Executive Committee members and their political parties".)

43. Tibor Eckhardt to His Highness, the Duke de Bar (Otto von Habsburg), 1 June 1954, Tibor Eckhardt Papers, Box 2, File: Correspondence – Otto von Habsburg, Hoover Institution Archives.

44. Otto von Habsburg, interview by author, 28 October 2003.

45. Ferenc Nagy, trans. Stephen K. Swift, *The Struggle Behind the Iron Curtain.*

46. Ferenc Nagy Papers, Box: 14, Folder: Correspondence – Steven Swift, Columbia University Archives.

47. C.D. (Charles Douglas) Jackson was a guiding figure at Time, Inc. for over 33 years, holding positions as general manager of *Life Magazine*, vice president of Time, Inc., publisher of *Fortune* and finally senior vice president of Time, Inc. He was a confidant of President Dwight D. Eisenhower, serving as his special White House assistant on the Cold War from 1952–1954. Throughout his career, Jackson took frequent leaves of absence for military, political and diplomatic assignments. One of them was to head the psychological warfare division of General Eisenhower's headquarters in 1944, leading a campaign for support of D-Day in Europe. As a successful publisher, he was knowledgeable about media and was given the assignment to set up Radio Free Europe. He served as the president and American administrator of the Free Europe Committee (or National Committee for a Free Europe, as it was later known), the organizing body and funder of the various national committees of liberation, including the Hungarian National Council. After 1954 he served as a delegate to the United Nations. Jackson was a politically savvy and worldly individual, and his assessment of the goings-on at the Hungarian National Council is that of a man who was impatient with the self-destructive nature of some of the Hungarian leadership. It is clear that those Hungarian leaders who crossed Jackson had no idea of his importance and connections, otherwise they would never have disregarded his counsel in such a cavalier manner. "CD Jackson Dies, Time Inc. Official: Adviser to Eisenhower had been Publisher of Fortune", *New York Times*, 20 September 1964, p. 88.

48. Rear Admiral Harold Blaine Miller was an Annapolis graduate who retired from the military in 1946. His last post was as director of public information for the Navy. He was a Navy pilot who served in World War II and was an aide to Admiral Chester Nimitz. He headed the Free Europe Committee in 1951 then went on to a career in aviation at Pan American Airways and in education.

49. C.D. Jackson to Msgr. Béla Varga, 10 March 1952, Ferenc Nagy Papers, Box 69, File: Correspondence 4, Columbia University Archives. Asterisks, underlines and capitalization are all in the original letter.

50. Otto von Habsburg, interview by author, 28 October 2003.

CHAPTER 7

Eckhardt's Continued Efforts on the Hungarians' Behalf

Eckhardt's explanation of his resignation from the HNC makes it clear that he found it a difficult decision to make; and it should be noted that although he resigned his leadership role on the executive committee, he remained an active member of the organization. His position on the executive committee was taken over by former Hungarian Prime Minister Nicholas Kállay. The HNC was disbanded in 1972, and for the reasons previously discussed, it never became an effective force. Also, as is clear from C.D. Jackson's letter to Msgr. Varga, the HNC's chronic infighting had stretched the NCFE's patience and tolerance to the limit. In 1952, five years after the founding of the HNC, the NCFE (also known as the Free Europe Committee) tightened the purse strings and asked the HNC to close its Washington, D.C., office and discontinue publication of the *Hungarian Observer*.[1] The organization's irrelevance became more apparent with each passing year, although it continued to soldier on with Msgr. Varga at the helm. It did receive an infusion of new leadership after the 1956 Hungarian Revolution, which revitalized it somewhat. However, as the realization sank in that the political climate in Central- and East Europe was not going to be altered in the immediate future, most of the political émigrés put down roots in their new homeland, as Eckhardt did when he became an American citizen.

Eckhardt and the Assembly of Captive European Nations

After resigning from the HNC Executive Committee, Eckhardt became involved in forming a new organization, the Assembly of Captive European Nations (ACEN), which was also funded by the Free Europe Committee.[2] In fact, he headed the delegation to the ACEN that represented the Hungarian National Council, having been appointed to that post by the executive committee from which he had recently resigned. Founded on 20 September 1954, the ACEN was established to "symbolize in one name both the plight and the aims" of the Central- and East European nations that, because they were under Soviet domination, were either unrepresented or misrepresented in the United Nations.[3] A coalition of former government and cultural leaders representing Albania, Bulgaria, Czechoslovakia, Estonia, Hungary, Latvia, Lithuania, Poland and Romania, the ACEN was intended to operate as a UN-type organization and voice for the exiled leadership of those nine nations whose role in the United Nations was controlled by the Soviet Union. The ACEN's founding clearly indicated that while U.S. financial support for the various émigré national committees may have been on the wane, American intelligence (the CIA, as funder of the Free Europe Committee) was willing to fund the creation of another organizational format within which the various national groups from the captive nations could operate and collaborate on common problems.

The organization's mission was to "work together to give power to their individual voices, and have their representatives become the authorized source of information about conditions behind the Iron Curtain and become the forum through which views and actions could be put forth and discussed." In the words of the founding members, the goals were "to provide liberation from communist dictatorship by peaceful means, to educate public opinion on the actual situation behind the Iron Curtain, and to enlist the cooperation and assistance of governmental and non-governmental institutions."[4]

Generously funded by the NCFE, the ACEN established a main office in New York as well as offices in Paris, Bonn and London and delegations throughout the world. It sponsored symposia and exhibitions and mailed thousands of letters and reports to government officials. ACEN-published materials were distributed throughout the United States and abroad and were provided free of charge to libraries, schools and institutions.

Membership was restricted to national committees and councils whose political purpose, character, structure and by-laws were consistent with ACEN policy. Those same national committees and councils were also funded by the NCFE. The ACEN structure provided for the nine member-country councils to select sixteen delegates each to participate in the organization's executive functioning.

The Hungarian National Council represented Hungarian interests on the ACEN, with Eckhardt as chairman of the delegation. In this capacity he served as rapporteur in the United Nations on the fate of Hungarian prisoners of war. Eckhardt initiated a resolution on the "Forcible Repatriation to the Iron Curtain Countries of Certain Prisoners of War in Violation of the Geneva Agreement on Truce in Indochina" that was adopted by the ACEN Assembly in December 1954.[5] It dealt with French Foreign Legion veterans from countries that had fallen under communist power, specifically legionnaires who had been captured by the communist Viet Minh forces and were being repatriated to their country of origin against their will. Another Eckhardt-originated report relating to the same topic has survived. Entitled "Treatment of the Captured and Discharged Veterans of the French Foreign Legion", it deals with the condition of some 1,000 legionnaires in France who were of Hungarian descent.[6] Eckhardt and his fellow members of the ACEN ad hoc committee on forced labor strove to publicize and to have the United Nations condemn forced labor practices on two counts. The first objection was "forced labour for the purpose of political coercion, especially as such measures may be applied by decision of the administrative authorities without the intervention of a court of law." The second was that "the restrictions placed on freedom of employment, if rigorously enforced, might constitute the basis of a system of forced and compulsory labour imposed with a view to carrying out the economic plan of the state."[7]

Also on behalf of the ACEN, Eckhardt researched and presented addresses and reports with the following titles: "Admission of Albania, Bulgaria and Hungary to the U.N." (22 October 1954); "Violation of Military Clauses of the 1947 Peace Treaty" (22 October 1954); "Forced displacement of the population of the so-called Moldavian Republic to the Russian provinces of Astrakhan, Rostov and Pavlodar region of Kazakhstan" (14 April 1955). The latter was a move designed to change the predominantly Romanian structure of the provinces of Bessarabia and Northern Bukovina, which had been forcibly annexed by the USSR. Delivered at the 14th Plenary Meeting of the ACEN, at which Eckhardt presided as president, this speech also addressed the continual deportations, undertaken for similar reasons, from Estonia, Latvia and Lithuania.[8]

Eckhardt also led a successful campaign in protest of and to publicize among the United Nations delegations Cardinal Mindszenty's arrest and conviction by Hungary's Communist government. However, the Eckhardt-organized protest, among many others around the world, did not sway the Hungarian Communist judiciary. The Cardinal had been accused of treason and plotting with Archduke Otto von Habsburg to overthrow the Hungarian government and restore Hungary's monarchy. He was convicted of the trumped-up charges and imprisoned until 1955, remaining under house arrest until the 1956 revolution.[9] During the years leading up to the revolution, Eckhardt toured the United States extensively as a speaker on topics related to the conditions in Communist Hungary and others matters of interest to Hungarian Americans, such as the Mindszenty case.[10] He was active in the ACEN from its inception in 1954 until 16 May 1955, the day after he became an American citizen and was no longer eligible to be an ACEN delegate.[11]

Though Eckhardt had long-since resigned from the ACEN, it is interesting to note that the Ferenc Nagy Papers show that Eckhardt was present at an HNC Executive Committee meeting on 26 March 1958 at which the Hungarian ACEN delegation was to be chosen. These thorough records include rather unflattering profiles of most of the candidates for the delegation and indicate that the infighting among the Hungarian émigrés had escalated! The political figures who arrived in the United States after the 1956 Hungarian Revolution, among them Anna Kéthly and Béla Király, had brought with them a new and completely different political agenda, thus creating an even more complex and fragmented situation in the world of the Hungarian immigrants.[12]

One small example of this intra-Hungarian conflict occurred when the International Rescue Committee (IRC) took the lead and, with the assistance of the American Friends of the Captive European Nations and the Conference of Americans of Central-European Descent, organized a protest rally to be held at Madison Square Garden in New York City. Originally scheduled for 20 November 1956, after the Soviets' treacherous attack on Hungary, the rally was moved up to 8 November. Suggested by Christopher T. Emmet, chairman of the ACEN, and designed as a huge public protest of the situation in Hungary, the rally's theme was "Stop the Massacre". The theme, Emmet said, "indicated the purpose was not so much to collect funds as to dramatize a great political protest."[13] With such luminaries as Eleanor Roosevelt helping on the organizing committee, the organizers were expecting huge attendance from all the émigré groups.

As the featured speaker the IRC chose Anna Kéthly, leader of the Social Democrats in Hungary, who had arrived in the United States after the start of the Hungarian insurrection. It was assumed that as leader of the Hungarian community in the United States HNC President Béla Varga would also speak, but the organizers were told that Ms. Kéthly would not agree to share the stage with him. The IRC organizers then made the ill-advised decision to remove Msgr. Varga from the speakers lineup. The mostly conservative crowd that gathered at Madison Square Garden was not pleased to be faced with a speaker they considered to be a "left-wing Socialist and whom many in the audience believed to be a Trotskyite, and not bring on a Hungarian Catholic Priest who was President of the

Hungarian Parliament and is Chairman of the Hungarian National Council."[14] Ms. Kéthly further enraging the audience by "giving the Communist closed fist salute" at the close of her talk.[15] Two Polish singers who were known left-wing sympathizers then took to the stage (for far too long according to Emmet), and "after the schedule of the meeting was virtually in shambles, Kiepura and his wife [the singers] were permitted to sing repeated numbers, some in bad taste for the occasion." The political resolutions that were to be presented for approval were "repeatedly skipped over and finally omitted altogether",[16] and when Msgr. Varga finally had a chance to speak, the house was already half empty.

In a post-rally memo, Emmet, a member of the IRC Executive Committee, raised a central question: "Why were the spokesmen of the captive nations and the Chairman of the Assembly of Captive European Nations omitted from the program altogether, until I secured a last minute extension of time by appealing to the police so that some of them could speak to a virtually empty house? These were the spokesmen of the organizations that had brought thousands of people to the rally and had gone to great expense and difficulty in doing it. Moreover, since they were all strongly anti-Communist their militant speeches would have been the best antidote for the unruly section of the audience next to a speech by Monsignor Varga."[17] Both Msgr. Varga and Dr. Fábián of the HNC had been reluctant to go to the rally until Unitarian Bishop Alexander Szent-Iványi prevailed upon them to represent the Hungarians. As a result of this debacle, "a renewed insult was given to [Msgr. Varga] and his Hungarian Catholic followers. This insult must have appeared to be deliberate."[18]

This unpleasant incident amply illustrates the power of the lobby of American leftists supported by the Communists. Despite the support of many Americans of stature, the rally's intended purpose—to pass resolutions condemning the Soviet Union's actions in Hungary—was subordinated to that of the leftist lobby. Not only were the resolutions not passed, they were not even presented. This powerful lobby was not without funds, operatives and some strong allies among the Americans, including, perhaps unwittingly, Mrs. Eleanor Roosevelt.

Small wonder that C.D. Jackson referred to the constant infighting and intrigue within and among the émigré communities as the stuff of comic opera—although situations such as that described above seem more akin to opera seria.

Eckhardt's Years as a U.S. Citizen

After Eckhardt became a naturalized U.S. citizen in April 1955, he was no longer stateless and could travel on a U.S. passport. He returned to Europe in September that year and spent the month observing the situation of Hungarian refugees in Austria, a country that still housed 37,257 war refugees. Over 270,000 refugees from behind the Iron Curtain had already become Austrian citizens and thus ceased to be the responsibility of any Western or international organization; the 37,000 plus individuals living in Austria were the remaining refugees from that post-war diaspora. The occupying Allied forces had finally withdrawn from Austria the previous July, having been there since 1945. Although he was no longer on the ACEN board, Eckhardt traveled to Austria on assignment from the ACEN and sent it a nine page report detailing the conditions faced by the over 8,000 Hungarians of refugee status in Austria, over 1,500 of whom were still living in refugee camps, some since the end of the war. In the cover letter to his comprehensive report, Eckhardt asks Vilis Masens, chairman of the ACEN, for that organization's assistance in publicizing the Hungarian refugees' plight. "I feel that right now, following the restauration [*sic*] of Austrian sovereignty, the Assembly of Captive European Nations could perform a highly meritorious work in calling attention of the respective national and international authorities to the existing painful problems, in outlining their proper solution and in lending its aid in the performance of further, more effective measures."[19]

A few months later, in December 1955, Eckhardt followed up his report with a "Very Confidential" memorandum regarding "Re-defections Engineered by the Communists". This outlined the campaign begun in 1954 to encourage Hungarian émigrés who still had family in Hungary to return "home". Based on refugees' personal accounts, Eckhardt reveals the extent to which the Communist-led Hungarian government was willing to go to bring émigrés home. One particularly interesting paragraph in the report deals with attempts within the immigrant community to destabilize the committee politically: "... spreading <u>political subversion</u> in the U.S. among the groups of alien descent. The process consists of: infiltration of their non-communist organizations; then polarization into two or more hostile groups, often using extreme Rightist elements for this purpose; finally disintegration of all organized resistance against Communist actions and endeavors. Isolated and intimidated, even leading figures of the emigration may then be induced to relinquish their anti-Communist stand and accept neutralism or the revived concept of 'popular front governments'."[20]

Eckhardt continued to write analytical works on current political situations for the ACEN board. Two of the reports, written in 1955 and early 1956, addressed the issue of "Soviet Colonialism and Its Political Aspects" and were sent to the chair of the ACEN political committee, Brutus Costas, for his personal information. Béla Varga, president of the Hungarian delegation, wrote to George Dimitrov, acting president of the ACEN, on 3 June 1955 confirming that he had "decided to keep Dr. Tibor Eckhardt in charge of the study of Russian Colonialism". Vilis Masens's earlier correspondence with Msgr. Varga indicates his approval of Varga retaining Eckhardt: "I am confident that the contribution of Dr. Eckhardt to the Assembly will be as valuable as his contribution as the chairman of the Hungarian delegations has been in the past."[21] This assignment indicates that while not necessarily always in step with the HNC, Eckhardt was on good terms with the ACEN leadership and clearly had its ear when it came to political analysis. Eckhardt was also regularly quoted in Radio Free Europe press releases reporting on Hungarian National Council activities. For example, in a four-page report on the exile community's response to Mátyás Rákosi's May 1956 speech to the Budapest party organization, a full page was devoted to Eckhardt's analysis of the situation.[22]

The American Hungarian Library and Historical Society

After he relinquished his role as a Hungarian delegate to the ACEN, Eckhardt became involved with a new organization that was to be an important focus of his efforts for the rest of his life. The first meeting to establish the American Hungarian Library and Historical Society was held on 11 April 1955 in the large meeting room of the Baltic Freedom House at 70th Street and Lexington Avenue in Manhattan.[23] Eckhardt had spearheaded the idea of establishing a "Magyar Ház", and with the cooperation of the leadership of the New York Hungarian community, it became a reality. A portion of this building now houses the American Hungarian Library and Historical Society, which contains some of Eckhardt's papers. Eckhardt's commitment to the library and his fundraising on its behalf (he convinced Countess Széchenyi to provide the bulk of the funds to purchase the Magyar Ház building) spanned the next seventeen years of his life.

First Aid for Hungary (Elsősegély Magyarországnak) - 29 October 1956–1 May 1957

Ten years after the end of World War II, émigré leadership in the Hungarian communities abroad had settled into a structure that somewhat mirrored the structure that had existed in their homeland. The Hungarian Left had its organizations and leadership, the centrist groups and the Right had theirs, the Hungarian Scout movement continued to flourish, as did the Hungarian social, religious and civic organizations. Most prominent among the numerous organizations operating in the United States were the Hungarian National Council and the Assembly of Captive European Nations, which provided the structure for the émigrés to continue to work toward an independent and democratic Hungary—a dim prospect, but one into which many threw their energies and resources.

Having already extensively evaluated the refugee situation in Austria in 1955, when the Hungarian Revolution broke out on 23 October 1956, Eckhardt immediately took the lead in responding to the needs of the 15,000 new Hungarian refugees who had made their way into Austria by the end of October. Since there were no adequate medical or relief facilities in the border area for this unexpectedly large and destitute group, an urgent appeal for aid reached the United States from both Hungary and Austria. According to papers in the First Aid for Hungary archives, "On October 29, 1956, Dr. Tibor Eckhardt called a mass meeting of several prominent Americans of Hungarian descent to form an American corporation which would offer whatever help official and private organizations could not provide in the emergency. Dr. Eckhardt proposed that the new corporation should be charitable, non-political, non-denominational and, that, established on a temporary basis, it serve as a stop-gap organization, adapting its work day by day to the situation in Hungary and on the border, and to the needs of refugees who reached the West."[24]

The meeting's attendees received these proposals favorably and resolved that First Aid for Hungary be set up in the United States, with a field office in Vienna under General Béla Lengyel, an Austrian citizen who was in good standing with the Austrian government and had experience in relief work.[25] First Aid's activities began on 1 November, just three days after its formation, when three of its members flew to Vienna with funds for General Lengyel to establish aid stations on the Austrian border and with the first shipment of medicines for hospitals in Hungary. The Knights of Malta successfully delivered the medicines to Hungary.[26]

First Aid for Hungary, Inc. was officially incorporated in New York State on 5 November 1956, and at the urging of Frederick Dolbeare, then president of the National Committee for a Free Europe, former president Herbert Hoover agreed to become its honorary chairman.[27] Although President Hoover's position was technically "honorary", he kept himself well informed and up to date on all the organization's activities. He made certain that both Perrin C. Galpin, head of the Belgian American Education Foundation, and Tracy Voorhees, whom President Dwight Eisenhower later in December 1956 appointed to head the President's Committee for Hungarian Refugee Relief, communicated to him personally the details of Hungarian refugee aid and the work of First Aid for Hungary. Both men turned to President Hoover, whom they called "the Chief", for advice in matters related to refugee relief as they had worked with him closely when President Hoover had headed the post World War II Famine Emergency Commission. At that time,

Galpin was honorary chairman of President Truman's Famine Emergency Committee in 1946, and Voorhees was the War Department's Food Administrator for Occupied Areas.[28] Hoover asked Galpin to serve as advisor to First Aid for Hungary, and at Hoover's request Galpin was also placed on the First Aid board.[29] Both Tibor Eckhardt, the president of First Aid, and Tibor Jahoda, the treasurer, communicated with Galpin regularly, and Jahoda also submitted First Aid's financial reports to him. In his "honorary" capacity as chairman, President Hoover took the time to send a personal letter of acknowledgement to every donor who sent First Aid for Hungary a donation check that was addressed to his attention. Hoover's office was kept busy mailing thousands of thank you letters for donations that ranged from two to many thousands of dollars.[30]

Mrs. John Chambers Hughes, wife of the former U.S. ambassador to the North Atlantic Treaty Organization (NATO), was Tibor Eckhardt's de facto co-chair on the First Aid board of directors. The high-powered "Sponsors Committee" included, among others, Mrs. Vincent Astor, Ferenc Chorin, the Honorable Frederick R. Dolbeare (of the NCFE), Mr. and Mrs. Walter Hoving, Mr. and Mrs. Archibald Roosevelt, Mr. Elihu Root Jr., Mr. George Stinson, Countess Antal Szapáry and Mr. Károly Széchenyi as well as Countess László Széchenyi.[31] Countess Széchenyi, nee Gladys Vanderbilt, was very supportive of Hungarian causes and a close friend of Tibor Eckhardt. She contributed generously to the fundraising efforts, as did her daughter, Countess Antal Szapáry, who was also married to a Hungarian nobleman.[32]

The board's treasurer, Tibor Jahoda, was a banker whose employer, the J. Henry Schroder Banking Corporation, had lent his services to the First Aid for Hungary Committee.[33] He served in that position for the life of the organization. In January 1957, at the request of the board, he undertook a fact-finding trip to Austria to make certain that First Aid's European organization was distributing the funds and aid properly. He reported back to Tibor Eckhardt and to Perrin C. Galpin, who then forwarded Jahoda's report to Herbert Hoover.[34]

The First Aid for Hungary Committee was primarily East Coast-based and was very active. Walter Hoving, then president of both the New York department store Bonwit Teller and the Fifth Avenue Merchants Association, provided funding for a full page advertisement promoting the campaign and soliciting funds and donations of clothing. The ad appeared in the 17 December 1956 *New York Times*. Five days later, the Lord & Taylor department store underwrote a similar ad in the *New York Herald Tribune*. As a result of both ads, retailers and manufacturers donated major amounts of clothing. First Aid for Hungary sponsored fundraising dinners, luncheons, fashion shows, etc., all of which roused New York society to support the cause of the Hungarian refugees. The Washington, D.C., committee, chaired by Mrs. Jouett Shouse, staged a fundraiser in Constitution Hall on 30 December that capped a month of aggressive efforts that raised

$182,000.[35] During the holiday season, First Aid volunteers sent out postcards encouraging people to donate to its fund in lieu of purchasing Christmas gifts. Acting on a suggestion from Tibor Eckhardt's stepson, Douglas Graham, on 7 January 1957 the president of the Investment Association of New York sent an appeal to all of its members asking them to contribute to First Aid.[36]

In addition to the New York organization, First Aid sponsored a parallel organization, Ungarische Soforthilfe, in Vienna, Austria. This organization was recognized by the Austrian National Committee for Hungarian Aid, Austria's official coordinating agency for Hungarian charities, headed by Archbishop Koenig of Vienna.

In its organizing and mission statement and in its subsequent communications with its sponsors and donors, First Aid pledged to keep expenses at a minimum and to rely primarily on volunteers who would receive no compensation for their work. Far from being just an organization of socially prominent individuals, First Aid had a large contingent of volunteers, many of Hungarian origin, who labored long and hard at the York Avenue location receiving and organizing donations, assembling aid packages and helping Hungarian Americans send packages to Hungary. The organization was able to honor its pledge and keep its overhead at just 2.1 percent of total contributions received.[37] Miss Gabriella Mauthner, long active in Hungarian affairs in the United States, was a member of the volunteer steering committee from First Aid for Hungary's first day to its last. She remarked to this author in a personal interview that not only did none of the volunteers receive compensation, there was also an amazing feeling of collegiality and unity of purpose among them throughout the organization's existence.[38]

Flooded with refugees, Austria had begged for "non-bureaucratic" help. First Aid was formed with exactly that in mind—to provide relief as quickly as possible.[39] It was specifically a stopgap organization and, according to its archived papers, "was the only foreign charity working on the Hungarian border during the hectic first half of November, 1956.[40] Gen. Lengyel set up a total of nine refugee centers on the border and later, in other provinces of Austria. Later when the large permanent aid organizations and their staffs came into the area, General Lengyel's field workers were assisting in 17 first aid stations and at the Austrian Refugee Collection points, as well as handling four field kitchens and three mobile pharmacies."[41] First Aid also transferred funds to other charities if it was felt that they could more quickly and effectively render some particular form of relief to the refugees.[42]

As long as the border with Austria remained open (until 20 November), First Aid was able to reach hospitals within Hungary that were desperate for medical supplies. Donated supplies were flown to Vienna and transported into Hungary by the Red Cross and the Knights of Malta. After the Soviets sealed the border, only the International Red Cross was allowed into Hungary, and First Aid worked in collaboration with them to supply hospitals until April 1957. (First Aid volunteers at one of the border stations actually found a way to deliver large quantities of medicines directly to four hospitals in Hungary in February of 1957.[43])

By January 1957, over 170,000 recently arrived refugees were living in overcrowded situations, and First Aid provided them with assistance in the form of clothing, funds and supplies. It also underwrote the cost of cables, stamps and stationary for communication with families and friends still in Hungary. Those who were departing for overseas were given travel kits containing some of the essential items many had been forced to leave behind in their haste to flee Hungary.

Until 1 March 1957, food packages were admitted free of duty into Hungary. First Aid sent about 10,000 food packages from a donation center in a former school building at 1532 York Avenue on Manhattan's East Side. The Center, which was staffed entirely by volunteers, also packaged and financed the mailing of parcels of donated clothing. Over 12,356 refugee children in Austria received clothing packages through First Aid during its time of operation.

In the United States, First Aid provided refugee assistance beyond what was available from the government. At Camp Kilmer in New Jersey, for example, First Aid provided recently arrived refugees with interpreters and Hungarian–English dictionaries. It donated clothing as well, until the AHF and the new Coordinated Hungarian Relief, Inc. took over that task in January 1957. First Aid for Hungary also organized transport to the United States for the Hungarian Olympic athletes who defected at the Melbourne games in December 1956.[44]

By January 1957, thanks to the help of President Hoover and the success of the Washington benefit chaired by Mrs. Shouse, First Aid had collected a substantial amount of money for the refugees. The major aid organizations by then having established themselves in providing aid to the Hungarian refugees, the First Aid board recognized that in order for their efforts to benefit the Hungarians in Austria effectively, they needed to channel the funds toward a specific pressing need. On 18 February 1957, Tracy R. Voorhees, the president's Representative for Hungarian Refugee Relief and Resettlement Matters, wrote to Dr. Eckhardt about the acute problem of higher education for refugee students with unusual qualifications.[45] Since federal funds could not be used for this purpose, Voorhees suggested that First Aid's board "consider the existing need for education in the US of deserving Hungarian refugees at the college and university level." With the wholehearted recommendation of President Hoover, the board provided $76,000 to the International Rescue Committee, as Voorhees recommended.[46]

Additionally, at its board meeting of 19 February 1957, the board "unanimously resolved to deal with the emergency created by interruption of studies, particularly of high school age children, since other organizations were not paying attention to this problem."[47] When the First Aid for Hungary organization's charter was granted, this need had not been anticipated, and therefore the funds were provided to other organizations to assist in filling it. The need was urgent, as there were over 8.000 young people in Austria who fell into this category, and most spoke not a word of German and thus could not be mainstreamed into Austrian schools. While funds for university scholarships in the United States were given through the International Rescue Committee, they subsequently were administered through the Institute of International Education (IIE). For its part, Coordinated Hungarian Relief administered the funds donated by First Aid for the care and shelter of Hungarian students in the United States and abroad. Coordinated Hungarian Relief utilized the funds as specified by First Aid for programs in Austria, Belgium, Germany and the United States. In March 1957, Tibor Eckhardt personally traveled to Austria and Germany to oversee the expansion of a school for Hungarian students in Innsbruck from twenty-five to 300 students. First Aid also provided books and sporting equipment and a portion of the seed money required to build a dormitory to house 100 students. By the summer of 1957, 746 new refugee students had passed their examinations in the Hungarian high schools in Austria, 411 in the Tyrol. In Belgium, the University of Louvain granted scholarships to 100 Hungarian students at the end of 1956 and provided them with a dormitory building, for which First Aid supplied the funds for much-needed restoration. In Germany, First Aid provided $25,000 in assistance to an existing Hungarian-language high school so that it could expand its housing capacity from forty students to 200.

First Aid's final audited financial statement shows that over its lifetime, 31 October 1956–1 May 1957, it dispersed a total of $1,052,444.86—$556,555.98 in cash and $495,888.88 in in-kind contributions. Total receipts were $1,143,055.43, with administrative expenses having been held to 2.1 percent and fundraising expenses to 4.4 percent of the total revenue generated.[48]

As had been agreed when the organization was founded, First Aid would provide such stopgap, emergency aid as was needed in the Hungarian refugee crisis. Thus, when the established aid agencies had geared up to work with the Hungarian situation, First Aid prepared to wrap up its mission. When it was agreed that the point had been reached when First Aid had fulfilled its mission, the organization was disbanded and First Aid transferred its remaining funds to other charitable organizations working with Hungarian refugees. On 26 April 1957, Dr. Eckhardt presented a check from First Aid for Hungary in the amount of $116,000 to Rev. George E.K. Borshy, vice president of Coordinated Hungarian Relief, to further aid Hungarian refugees in Europe and the United States.[49]

Dr. Eckhardt and Mrs. Hughes resigned their positions as of First Aid's final board meeting, held after Eckhardt returned from Europe. No better testimonial to the positive nature of First Aid's work exists than a letter to Mrs. Hughes from Kenneth Holland, president of the Institute of International Education. Dated 15

May 1957, it details how First Aid's $76,600 grant to his organization was used to assist Hungarian students. "This entire grant has been designated as a scholarship fund for Hungarian refugee students and none of it is used for any other purpose. ... I cannot stress too much how important these supplementary funds are, and you may be sure that we will make them go as far as possible. I should like to repeat that the grant is being used only to fill out scholarships and to make it possible for students to attend colleges and universities, in most cases in which it would not otherwise be possible. ... We have already placed approximately 300 on scholarships..."[50]

Anticipating the approaching disbanding of First Aid, for it was felt in official circles that its mission had been fulfilled, President Hoover wrote to Tibor Eckhardt on 12 February 1957 to thank him for organizing and leading First Aid to Hungary's emergency service in the Hungarian crisis. He closed by saying, "I do wish to express my admiration for you and your colleagues for the magnificent service you have given."[51] It is indicative of Tibor Eckhardt's respected status with the National Committee for a Free Europe and with the administration, that the president of the United States had not only urged support for Eckhardt and the First Aid committee but also urged former president Herbert Hoover to lend his support and prestige to the First Aid committee's effort. This would not have been the case had Tibor Eckhardt not been highly regarded in official circles in Washington, D.C.

A great deal of literature addresses the history of the Hungarian American community in the United States and its unwillingness or inability to unite under one banner and one cause. Certainly there are ample illustrations of that in this book. Nevertheless, it can be said that in its 1956 response to the Hungarian refugee crisis, the Hungarian American community rose to the occasion and worked together to aid their fellow Hungarians through their support for First Aid for Hungary. The results that First Aid was able to achieve speak for themselves.

Eckhardt's Last Years

In June 1957, shortly after wrapping up his efforts on behalf of First Aid for Hungary, Eckhardt married Judy Dwyer and started a new phase of his life as a newly married man at the age of sixty-eight. As previously mentioned, this marriage brought him great joy after the many reverses he had suffered and was a true blessing in his life.

Although he continued to have myriad interests within the Hungarian community, at this point Eckhardt's activities on behalf of the American Hungarian Library and Historical Society moved to the forefront. He found time, however, to write *Regicide at Marseille*, his account of the 1934 League of Nations affair in which he had played such a pivotal role; it was published by the American Hungarian Library and Historical Society in 1964. He also served as honorary president of the Hungarian Scouts in America, as president of the Republican Party's Hungarian Division, and as president of the Alumni Board of the Piarist Fathers Schools, where he continued his work to secure scholarships for Hungarian refugee children and establish English-language schools in America for Hungarian refugee students. He also served on the board of the Conference of American Citizens of Central and Eastern European Descent, the American Hungarian Federation, and the Hungarian Catholic League of America. In addition, he was an editor of the *Free World Review* and a member of various scientific societies in Europe. He earned several decorations in his lifetime, among them a Grand Cross from both the Order pour la Merite of Hungary and the Order of the Knights of Malta.[52]

Tibor Eckhardt spent a happy nine years lecturing and writing on issues related to Hungary before the untimely death of his young wife on 30 October 1966, which plunged him into a deep depression.[53] At the time of her death, he had already begun to write his memoirs, which remained in unedited typescript, some of it virtually illegible, at the time of his own death—although portions had been transcribed by his long-time secretary, Dr. Magda Barany. These memoirs were at last published in June 2005 by East European Monographs and distributed by Columbia University Press. New archival material that has been uncovered since the memoirs were completed over thirty-four years ago, makes some of their material out of date and/or no longer relevant. A portion, however, remains of great interest, particularly that which focuses on the war years and details the events and actions that positioned Hungary to become a Soviet satellite after the war.

Although Eckhardt recognized that the Hungarian situation had changed and Soviet control over Hungary and its affairs appeared to be permanent, virtually to his last breath he continued to make his voice heard on subjects he felt were important to Hungarians and remained an active participant in matters related to Hungary. One of the last major issues of concern with which he was involved was the dialogue between the United States government and the communist-led government of Hungary regarding the latter's request for return of the Crown of St. Stephen and the Crown Regalia. At the end of World War II the regalia had been turned over to the U.S. military for safekeeping by the Hungarian Crown Guard, who had taken them out of Hungary. After being stored in Germany by the Americans for several years, the Crown and the Crown Regalia made their way to the United States where they were stored at Fort Knox. The communist-led Hungarian government had unsuccessfully pressured each successive American administration for their return, which was opposed by a great percentage of Hungarians living abroad, including Eckhardt, who was very much opposed. When the thaw in relations between Hungary and the United States began in the late 1960s, the request was renewed. When Cardinal Mindszenty wrote a letter to President Richard Nixon protesting the return, he wanted it delivered to the White House in person. He requested that Eckhardt make the delivery in his role as a member of the board of the Coordinating Committee of Hungarian Organizations in North America. In response to the letter delivered by Eckhardt on Cardinal Mindszenty's behalf, Presidential Advisor Harry S. Dent stated in a 1971 letter that in the Nixon White House "there are no plans for giving up the Holy Crown. It is understood that any such eventual action must serve the general goodwill, instead of sowing disagreement."[54] The Hungarian government continued to press the issue; and in a rather dramatic policy about face, President Jimmy Carter returned the Holy Crown and Regalia to Hungary in 1977, the first year of his administration. The return was carried out over the objections of the great majority of Hungarian Americans living in the United States, who vehemently opposed entrusting the Holy Crown of St. Stephen—not only the historic symbol of Hungarian nationhood but also the symbol of its Christianity—to an atheist government in communist Hungary.[55] Mail received by the White House ran ninety-nine percent against the return of the Crown and Crown Regalia to one percent in favor of the return.[56]

On the twenty-fifth anniversary of Hungary's occupation by Soviet forces, Eckhardt organized some of his fellow Hungarian émigrés and issued a resolution from the Coordinating Committee of American-Hungarian Organizations, which he chaired.[57] This resolution of 4 April 1970 states in part that the Hungarians would not recognize as valid the "Potemkin"-style celebrations of the tragic occupation, that they still mourned the Treaty of Trianon on its fiftieth anniversary, and that the Hungarian people would never accept the finality of either decision.[58]

The next year, Eckhardt and the Coordinating Committee issued a second declaration protesting the Soviet occupation. This time it was in response to Leonid Brezhnev's speech at the USSR's 24th Party Congress demanding that the world powers accept the status quo as permanent and "proceed from the final recognition of the territorial changes which took place in Europe as a result of the Second World War." Prepared on 26 September 1971, the declaration specifically protested German chancellor Willy Brandt's offer to the USSR on behalf of Europe to stabilize the situation in Europe. (Brandt's offer, prompted by Brezhnev's demand, meant recognizing as permanent the borders drawn and the spheres of influence established at the end of World War II.)[59]

The original text of the Coordinating Committee declaration survives, both in Eckhardt's handwriting and in printed form, and reads in part:

1. We cannot accept as final Hungary's exclusion from the Free World to where she inseparably belongs!

> 2. We cannot acquiesce in the Soviet Union's dictatorial rule, preparing Hungary's absorption as a member-state!
>
> 3. We insist unalterably on the Hungarian people's right of self-determination due to every nation in the entire world and will never accept the present evil order in the Carpathian Basin as the final solution of our destiny!
>
> As a peace loving people we address a single demand to all peace-loving peoples and their governments: don't try to stabilize the present intolerable European status-quo.
>
> The European Security Conference shall be held, when after elimination of the present double standard every nation in Europe will have its right of self-determination restored. The free will of independent nations will then arrive at valid decisions on the future common fate of Europe.[60]

The Coordinating Committee adopted the resolution unanimously. Most of the group's leadership was composed of representatives of the new emigration—Eckhardt, the chairman, was one of the exceptions. In passing the resolution and calling attention to the USSR's attempt to legitimize its twenty-five year occupation by making it permanent, the Coordinating Committee stated that it "was convinced that we are expressing the attitude of the entire Hungarian people—of those living in the Free World as well as of all the oppressed Hungarians in our homeland and in Soviet dominated foreign lands ..."[61]

Rather than live in quiet retirement, Tibor Eckhardt continued to be involved in Hungarian causes and issues until well past his eightieth birthday. Indeed, on the occasion of his eightieth birthday, 26 October 1968, the American Hungarian Library and Historical Society honored Eckhardt with a grand celebration of his life. His old friends and colleagues Bishop Sándor Szent-Iványi, András Frey and László Acsay spoke and lauded him with great affection. László Acsay said, "We have come together to ask the Lord's blessing for the 'Great Old Man' of the Hungarian community on the occasion of his eightieth birthday. In the New York Hungarian House, the idea for which is due to Tibor Eckhardt's vision, its existence is due to his efforts, and without his fifteen years of efforts on behalf of its existence, this building would not stand here in the Hungarian neighborhood of this world class city."[62]

Despite advancing age, Eckhardt's handwriting did not waver, nor did his mind, as attested to by the monograph "Scanning the Horizon: World Politics and Central Europe", written in 1970 for inclusion in Francis S. Wagner's anthology *Toward a New Central Europe: A Symposium on the Problems of the Danubian Nations*.[63] His original handwritten papers from this period show the same vigor and clarity of thought as the monograph, but as is also the case in his memoirs, he continued to focus repetitively on the same themes. These writings are clearly oriented toward explaining his activities and decisions with a view toward establishing his place in history.

Tibor Eckhardt made his final trip to Europe in 1971, having been asked to give an address in Lucerne, Switzerland. Eckhardt's grandniece, Mrs. Andor (Maria) Hertelendy, the granddaughter of his older sister Marika, lived in Switzerland with her family at the time. She was able to make arrangements for her grandmother to travel there from Romania, where she had lived since before the war.[64] Eckhardt had not seen Marika since he left Hungary in 1941, and both of them knew that this reunion was probably their last. Maria Hertelendy recounted poignantly that upon parting, the Eckhardt siblings said to one another, "See you in the other world." Both siblings passed away the following year, without having seen one another again.[65]

Tibor Eckhardt passed away suddenly of a heart attack on 3 September 1972. The American Hungarian Library and Historical Society honored him with a memorial, photos of which show the main room of the Magyar Ház awash with flowers and two Hungarian Scouts, a young man and a young woman, standing at attention by the flag-draped coffin. Tibor Eckhardt is at rest in Saint Raymond's Cemetery in the Bronx, New York, alongside his wife Judy.

Endnotes

1. Ferenc Nagy Papers, Box 69, File: Emigré Organizations–HNC Appeals, Columbia University Archives.
2. The NCFE, often referred to as the Free Europe Committee, was covertly funded by the CIA. NCFE sponsored the organization and funding of various national committees such as the Hungarian National Council, Radio Free Europe, Radio Liberty and the ACEN as well as other organizations that spearheaded the public relations support for the Cold War domestically in the United States, for example, the Crusade for Freedom.
3. Assembly of Captive European Nations Papers (hereafter ACEN Papers), 1953–1972, Collection #136, Historical Sketch, p. 1, Immigration History Research Center (hereafter IHRC), University of Minnesota.
4. Ibid.
5. ACEN document #21, Tibor Eckhardt Papers, Box 1, Folder: Speeches and Reports, American Hungarian Library and Historical Society.
6. Report, 9 February 1955, Tibor Eckhardt Papers, Box 1, Folder: Speeches and Reports, American Hungarian Library and Historical Society.
7. ACEN Papers, Box 38, Folder: 5, IHRC.

8. Tibor Eckhardt to Elco Van Kleffens, President United Nations General Assembly, and Dag Hammerskjöld, Secretary General of the United Nations, 14 April 1955, ACEN Papers, Box 38, Folder: 5, IHRC.
9. For an interesting book published in English on the various complaints of the Hungarian People's Republic about the activities of the United States government see: Information Department of the Ministry for Foreign Affairs of the Hungarian People's Republic, *Documents on the Hostile Activity of the United States Government Against the Hungarian People's Republic* (Budapest: Hungarian State Publishing House, 1951). The book also includes the text of portions of the Mindszenty trial.
10. Tibor Eckhardt Papers, Box 1, Folder: Biographical Materials, American Hungarian Library and Historical Society.
11. Vilis Masens to Tibor Eckhardt, 16 May 1955, ACEN Papers, Box 38, Folder: 5, IHRC.
12. Ferenc Nagy Papers, Box 65, File: ACEN, Columbia University Archives.
13. International Rescue Committee Papers, Christopher T. Emmet Papers, Box 1, File: Help Free Hungary Rally, American Friends of the Assembly of Captive European Nations, p. 1, Hoover Institution Archives.
14. Ibid., p. 4.
15. Ibid.
16. Ibid.
17. Ibid.
18. Ibid., p. 5.
19. Tibor Eckhardt to Vilis Masens, "Problem of Refugees and Escapees in Austria", October 1955, Tibor Eckhardt Papers, American Hungarian Library and Historical Society.
20. Tibor Eckhardt, "Very Confidential Memorandum on Redefections Engineered by the Communists", p. 5, ACEN Papers, Box 38, Folder: 5, IHRC.
21. Vilis Masens to Msgr. Béla Varga, 3 June 1955, and Msgr. Béla Varga to George Dimitrov, 20 June 1955, ACEN Papers, Box 38, Folder: 2, IHRC.
22. RFE Hungarian National Council Activities, 19 May 1956, ACEN Papers, Box 38, Folder: 2, IHRC.
23. Amerikai Magyar Könyvtár és Közgyűjtemény Egyesület. Jegyzőkönyv, 11 April 1955, Tibor Eckhardt Papers, Box 2, Folder: Library, American Hungarian Library and Historical Society.
24. First Aid for Hungary Papers, Box 2, Files: 2–5, General Correspondence, Hoover Institution Archives.
25. Gyula Borbándi, *Magyar politikai pályaképek 1938–1948*, pp. 277–278. General Lengyel also served on the boards of both of the Austrian agencies involved with Hungarian Relief, the *Österreichisches Nationalkomitee für Ungarnhilfe* and the *Ungarischer Hilfsdienst* headed by Archbishop Koenig of Vienna. First Aid for Hungary Papers, Box 2, Folder: General Correspondence 6 November 1956–1 March 1957, Hoover Institution Archives.
26. Report on First Aid for Hungary 1956–1958, Appendix I, p. 10, 15 March 1958, First Aid for Hungary Papers, Box 2, File: 2, Hoover Institution Archives. First Aid's Board of Directors is listed here as: Dr. Tibor Eckhardt, President. Mrs. John Cham-

bers Hughes, Mr. Alajos Falussy, Mr. Lajos Jáger, Dr. László Acsay, Vice-President, Dr. Jenő Végh, Secretary, Mr. Tibor Jahoda, Treasurer, Dr. György Dumtsa, Assistant Secretary, Mr. István Ráth, Assistant Secretary.

27. First Aid for Hungary Papers, Box 2, Files: 2–4, General Correspondence, Hoover Institution Archives. President Hoover was urged to accept the honorary position by Frederick R. Dolbeare (the President of the National Committee for a Free Europe) and also by the White House: "November 7, Mr. Dolbeare telephoned asking HH to take the honorary Chairmanship of First Aid for Hungary—said that 'on high' wanted it …"
28. T. Voorhees to H. Hoover, First Aid for Hungary Papers, Box 3, Folders: 3–28, Correspondence, Hoover Institution Archives.
29. First Aid for Hungary Papers, Box 2, Folders: 2–5, General Correspondence, Hoover Institution Archives.
30. First Aid for Hungary Papers, Box 1, Folders: 1–3, Contribution Files and Donor Acknowledgement, Hoover Institution Archives.
31. Mrs. John Chambers Hughes (Margaret) was later made an honorary citizen (díszpolgár) of Balatonboglár, Hungary, in appreciation for her continued support of Hungarian causes. Gabriella Mauthner, interview by author, 10 April 2006.
32. Countess László Széchenyi, formerly Gladys Moore Vanderbilt (27 August 1886–29 January 1965), was the seventh and youngest child of Cornelius Vanderbilt II, president and chairman of the New York Central Railroad.
33. Perrin C. Galpin to Herbert Hoover, 28 December 1956, First Aid for Hungary Papers, Box 2, Folders: 2–4, Correspondence 6 November 1956 to 1 March 1957, Hoover Institution Archives.
34. Perrin C. Galpin to Tibor Jahoda, Report of January 1957 Austrian Trip, 8 February 1957, First Aid for Hungary Papers, Box 3, Folders: 3–5, Correspondence, Hoover Institution Archives.
35. Bess Furman, "Drive Gets $150,000 In Month to Assist Hungarian Refugees", *New York Times*, 6 January 1957, p.7.
36. Tibor Eckhardt Papers, Oversize scrapbook, First Aid for Hungary, American Hungarian Library and Historical Society.
37. Report on First Aid for Hungary, Financial Statement, p. 15, First Aid for Hungary Papers, Box 2, Folder: 2, Hoover Institution Archives.
38. Miss Gabriella Mauthner, interview by author, 10 April 2006.
39. Max Frankel, "Austria Flooded with Refugees, Pleads for Help", *New York Times*, 23 November 1956, p. 1.
40. The International Red Cross, for example, did not begin its campaign in New York to raise funds for Hungarian refugees until 28 November 1956. See: "Kilmer Defended on Refugee Work", *New York Times*, 29 November 1956, p. 21.
41. Report on First Aid for Hungary, pp. 4–5, First Aid for Hungary Papers, Box 2, Folder: 2, Hoover Institution Archives.
42. Ibid., p. 5.
43. Ibid.
44. "Lag Is Reported In Refugee Help, Funds for Hungarians Below Needs, Five Groups Say—Olympic Team Coming", *New York Times*, 22 December 1956, p. 6.

45. First Aid for Hungary Papers, Box 2, Folder: 2–4, Hoover Institution Archives. Voorhees had served former President Hoover during his leadership of relief efforts in post World War II Europe and had been urged to take the position by President Hoover. W. Hallam Tuck also worked with Hoover in relief efforts and was cajoled into returning to serve as a member of the Voorhees team. Tuck was the "high American official" who wrote a first-hand field report for Perrin Galpin and President Hoover on the First Aid efforts in Austria (dated 24 December 1956). His assessment was positive, and of General Lengyel and his volunteers he said, "They are as fine a little group as you could find—gentle people—(ex-Prisoners in Hungary in some cases) completely tireless and devoted. I can't express my admiration too fully."
46. Report on First Aid for Hungary, p. 8, First Aid for Hungary Papers, Box 2, Folder: 2, Hoover Institution Archives.
47. Ibid., p. 6.
48. Ibid., pp. 12–15.
49. "Hungarian Relief Gets $116,000", *Washington Post*, 26 April 1957, p. A 11.
50. Kenneth Holland to Mrs. John Chambers Hughes, 15 May 1957, First Aid for Hungary Papers, Box 2, File 2, Hoover Institution Archives.
51. First Aid for Hungary Papers, Box 2, File: Tibor Eckhardt Correspondence with Herbert Hoover, 12 February 1957, Hoover Institution Archives.
52. Tibor Eckhardt, *Államférfi a száműzetésben*, p. 23 and Tibor Eckhardt Biography, p. 3, both in Box 1, File: Personal Papers, American Hungarian Library and Historical Society.
53. Obituary, Judy Dwyer Eckhardt, *New York Times*, 1 November 1966.
54. Attila L. Simontsits, *The Last Battle for St. Stephen's Crown* (Cleveland: Weller Publishing Co. Ltd., 1983), pp. 789–790. Although the date of the Dent letter is not known, the letter itself was made public by Senator Robert Dole and Congressman Lawrence Hogan on 2 December 1971.
55. Katalin Kádár Lynn, "Return of the Crown of St. Stephen and its Subsequent Impact on the Carter Administration", *East European Quarterly*, Vol. 34, No. 2, 2000, pp. 185, 193–95, 201–202.
56. Ibid., p. 202.
57. The leadership of this group was composed of the leadership of the various Hungarian organizations in North America (US and Canada). They were: Amerikai Magyar Szövetség, Egyesült Magyar Alap, Erdélyi Bizottság, Kanadai Magyar Szövetség, Külföldi Magyar Képzőművészek, Magyar Bizottság, Magyar Cserkészszövetség, Magyar Felszabadító Bizottság, Magyar Harcsosok Bajtársi Közössége, Magyar Iskola Alapítvány, Magyar Szabadságharcosok Világszövetsége, Szabad Magyar Jogászok Szövetsége és a Magyar Diákszövetség.
58. *Az Északamerikai magyarság nyilatkozata a szovjet katonai megszállás 25. évfordulóján*, Tibor Eckhardt Papers, Box 17, File: Coordinating Committee of Hungarian Organizations, Hoover Institution Archives.
59. James Reston, "Brezhnev States Program" and "Brezhnev's World View", *New York Times*, 31 March 1971, pp. 1 and 45. Recapping Brezhnev's six-hour speech opening the 24th Communist Party Congress in Moscow, Reston wrote: "He wants 'final recognition' of the territorial changes that took place in Europe after the Second World War—that is, general acceptance of the division of Germany and Europe as a permanent condition of the European states. He wants the annulment of the Warsaw

and NATO military alliances and the 'dismantling of foreign bases'—that is, he wants the Americans to go home, leaving the Red Army as the sole dominant military force on the threshold of Europe."

60. *Az Északamerikai magyarság nyilatkozata a szovjet katonai megszállás 25. évfordulóján*, Tibor Eckhardt Papers, Box 17, File: Coordinating Committee of Hungarian Organizations, Hoover Institution Archives.
61. Ibid.
62. Tibor Eckhardt, *Államférfi a száműzetésben* (New York: American Hungarian Library and Historical Society, 1971), p. 9.
63. Tibor Eckhardt, "Scanning the Horizon: World Politics and Central Europe" in Francis S. Wagner, ed., *Toward a New Central Europe: A Symposium on the Problems of the Danubian Nations* (Astor Park, Florida: Danubian Press, 1970), pp. 73–78.
64. Sándor Betégh, personal interview by author, Budapest, 18 December 2004.
65. Maria Hertelendy, email to the author, 23 May 2005.

CHAPTER 8

Tibor Eckhardt's Legacy

Tibor Eckhardt has been largely forgotten since his death in New York City in 1972, save by Hungarians of a certain age and by those who had the opportunity to know him personally. He is still revered at Magyar Ház on 82nd Street in Manhattan, where his portrait hangs in the American Hungarian Library and Historical Society/The Tibor Eckhardt Library.

Eckhardt's post-war reputation in Hungary was largely formed by the propaganda machine that specialized in character assassination of prewar politicians, particularly those with a nationalist or conservative bent. It was convenient to label Eckhardt fascist or neo-Nazi due to his early involvement in the ÉME and his alleged participation in the White Terror following World War I. In 1944 the Arrow Cross, which he was and still is accused of abetting, had him sentenced to death in absentia, but that fact lies forgotten in the dust of history. Surely supporters or followers of the Fascist cause were not accorded such sentences.[1]

Contemporary historians should be asking what lay behind all the disinformation targeting Eckhardt. Why is his legacy much more murky and unsavory than that of political figures who managed their own legacy more carefully—Ferenc Nagy, for example. The Soviet and Czech and British propaganda machines' consistent and voluminous output of anti-Eckhardt material made it easy to stereotype him. We do not have the archival material from the Soviet and Czech campaigns, although we know that they are linked and we have proof that they funded anti-Eckhardt propaganda on a major scale. The records of the British SOE, however, are accessible, and they prove that the disinformation campaign against Eckhardt was international in scope, heavily supported and absolutely relentless. Eckhardt himself aided and abetted the problem because although he suffered fools badly he chose not to retaliate in kind when he became a target. As Dr. Otto von Habsburg observed, "They continued [to vilify him] because he was towering over them! He was the towering giant of Hungarian politics. There was a tremendous envy against him, which was especially the case with Ferenc Nagy."[2]

The crude character assassination in Georges Faludy's letter to Georgetown University (see Chapter 6) typifies the verbiage and tactics of the anti-Eckhardt faction. János Gyetvai, editor of *Magyar Jövő* and another writer of letters vilifying Eckhardt, had a verifiable affiliation with the Communist Party, as documented by the FBI. Gyetvai and others who were either Communist Party members or were compromised in some way by their affiliation with it were charged with the task of discrediting Eckhardt. For the better part of a decade they applied many resources to this mission. The mission statement from the November 1941 meetings of the Central Bureau of the Third International provided a template for political action (see Chapter 3) that appears to have been followed. The FBI kept records on the activities of the Hungarian American Council for Democracy as well as on the Communist Party members and their operatives who participated in the American Hungarian Federation-sponsored Hungarian American Relief Council at the end of World War II. These records provide a small window on how the supporters of Hungarian communism functioned in the United States and the extensive nature of their resources and network (see Chapter 5). Proof of their concerted action plan against Eckhardt is evident in key sources documented in this work: the British funding of *Igazmondó*, the Gyetvai and Faludy correspondence, the letters denouncing Eckhardt written to the editors of major publications, the Czechs' funding of Vámbéry's efforts to discredit Eckhardt and his supporters, and the Czech–Moscow connection in relationship to Eckhardt as revealed in the VENONA documents, to name just a few. It is unfortunate that to this day the success of their efforts remains visible in scholarship regarding Eckhardt.

Another factor that serves to cloud Eckhardt's legacy is the fact that during World War II he saw the political situation in Great Britain with great clarity, although he had no idea of the extent of the British SOE campaign against him. During the war, it was his opinion that Britain had not just turned pro-Soviet but, with the exception of Churchill, its establishment was willing to sell all of Central- and East Europe down the river in exchange for the USSR's participation on the Allied side. Eckhardt saw this early on and warned against it, which made him a rather unpopular, Cassandra-like figure who was regarded with suspicion, especially during the World War II era of intense Anglo-American friendship and collaboration. He also felt that the communists had compromised the British Foreign Office while the war was still on. He was right on all counts. Donald Maclean, first secretary at the British embassy in Washington, D.C., during World War II, was later revealed to have been a Soviet spy since the 1930s. Kim Philby, perhaps the most famous British intelligence officer in the service of the NKVD (the Soviet spy agency), was chief of Britain's Secret Intelligence Service (SIS) in Washington, D.C., beginning in 1949 at the height of the Cold War.[3] How these communists influenced policy in the foreign office is beyond the scope of this book, but certain telling details stand out with reference to the Eckhardt campaign. Major (later Sir) Basil Davidson was agent DH 18 who advised and directed a good portion of the campaign against Eckhardt in the SOE. Davidson may have been only "left oriented",[4] but his second in command in SOE was James Klugmann, whom Davidson seems to have admired, as evidenced by the portrayal of Klugmann in his book *Special Operations Europe*.[5] A friend and contemporary of Maclean, Klugmann had joined the Communist Party in 1933 during his days at Cambridge and was the Party's post-war historian in England. Klugmann was later accused of having used his position to manipulate British operations and policy in the interests of the communists and was identified by Anthony Blunt as a long-time Soviet agent.[6]

Eckhardt's views on the compromised nature of the British Foreign Office were compounded by the fact that Great Britain was a great supporter of Eduard Beneš and the Czechoslovakian Government in Exile. Remembering those times, Dr. Otto von Habsburg observed, "One man who hated Eckhardt more than anybody else was Beneš. Beneš was the man who in my opinion would have been the man who most likely would demand that Eckhardt be eliminated from the Central European scene. When you examine the records of the Beneš administration, it becomes evident how close Molotov and Beneš were to each other."[7] One can deduce that Eckhardt's anti-Beneš stand combined with his reservations about the wisdom of the British Foreign Office's deference to Soviet demands made him rather unpopular in political circles—certainly it made him a target for destruction by the SOE.

This is not to say that Eckhardt was not respected in the West, particularly by the members of the organizations that comprised the American Hungarian Federation, which tended to have a conservative bent. However, as the Cold War ended, bringing a growing thaw to the Central European political scene, the causes Eckhardt espoused became largely irrelevant in the minds of many. After all, it was "goulash communism" that prevailed in Hungary, not old-line Bolshevism. However, Eckhardt realized that the apparent thawing of Soviet policy toward its satellites was superficial at best. To illustrate this point, in writing in 1970 on the situation of the Soviet satellites, Eckhardt quotes *New York Times* columnist Max Frankel as saying, "Hungary is the best example of how far de-Stalinization can proceed without much significant desatellization."[8] In 1970 Hungary's state apparatus was still tightly under Soviet control. Only in the years after his death were some of the positions from which Eckhardt never veered found to be true. Yes, the Soviet Union had always had an agenda to destabilize the West, even when it was ostensibly an ally. Yes, the Soviet Union ran agents and fellow travelers in the West, agents who had infiltrated and influenced the highest levels of government.

Former CIA Director Richard Helms wrote in his 2003 autobiography that the Soviet Union had intensified its espionage efforts against the United States during the Second World War. "It was in Washington when we were putting our postwar house in order that we fully grasped the fact that throughout the war, the intelligence services of our co-belligerent, the USSR, had actually intensified espionage against the United States. In the Western world, the widespread respect for the Red Army's resistance to the Nazi invasion, the tremendous sacrifices of the civilian population reinforced the motives of Communist Party members and their fellow travelers, and created an optimum operational atmosphere for Soviet espionage."[9] Who in the American diplomatic world would have suspected that Alger Hiss, who stood behind Roosevelt in photos at the Yalta conference, had been compromised by the USSR?[10]

In the immediate post-war era, Eckhardt was regarded as an alarmist and a political has-been, and his views were disregarded. He had warned against the Communist danger, as only someone who had intimately lived through the Hungarian Red Terror and its repercussions could. He continued to warn against it until the end of his life. History has proven him to be more correct in his assessments than many other respected observers of the political scene.

The U.S. State Department had initially (1941) welcomed Eckhardt's counsel, but, influenced by the British and the pro-Soviet establishment, it cooled on Eckhardt and his efforts. Although Eckhardt did continue to work with the State Department along with Archduke Otto throughout the war years, it rather soon came to exercise caution regarding his views.[11] He did not regain credence in those circles until the Cold War became reality. In 1947 "unofficial" Washington turned to him to organize the establishment of the Hungarian National Council and later asked him to serve as the first Hungarian delegate to the Assembly of Captive European Nations. Further government recognition came in 1956 when Eckhardt founded First Aid for Hungary to respond to that year's Hungarian refugee crisis. That organization not only received official government support, but at the urging of a sitting president of the United States it found itself blessed with an honorary chair who had also been a U.S. president. Eckhardt's co-chair in the First Aid effort was the wife of a former U. S. ambassador to NATO. Greater validation of Eckhardt's value to the United States would be hard to find. Eckhardt was always well regarded within the secret world of military intelligence, as the letters to him in the Appendix attest; but his long association with the MIS Division of the War Department remained a closely guarded secret within government, and the details were kept even from his family until after his death.

Tibor Eckhardt was almost eighty-four years of age when he died. The wave of immigrants who came to the United States after the 1956 revolution and those who trickled in afterwards barely knew who he was. Imbued with their own views of the Hungarian issues and causes that emerged after World War II, few would have thought they had much to learn from the man who led the opposition party in Hungary in the inter-war period. Yet Eckhardt is remembered today as an extremely influential figure in the life of Hungarian youth due to his activities as head of the Piarist School Foundation and as honorary chair of the Hungarian Scouts. Dr. László Hámos, who amassed the newspaper record of the 1956 Revolution for the American Hungarian Library and Historical Society under Eckhardt's supervision, recalls that Eckhardt gave generously of his time to young people at the Hungarian House and was always there to instruct and inform.

Eckhardt's legacy is also at a disadvantage because he did not publish a great deal or teach full time, as did many of his contemporaries, and therefore did not build an image in American scholarly circles. Oszkár Jászi and Rusztem Vámbéry both used publication in the world press much more effectively than did Eckhardt. Until the recent publication of *Tibor Eckhardt in His Own Words*, only two Eckhardt works were somewhat readily available in English—*Regicide at Marseille*, the one book he published in the West in his lifetime, and a chapter in a book on Transylvania edited by Louis C. Cornish. Both works are now out of print. The chapter in Cornish's book is a reprint of a speech Eckhardt gave at the League of Nations in September 1934 entitled "Roumanian Treatment of Hungarian Minorities".[12] Many of his shorter writings and speeches given in the United States are also available, particularly in the editorial- and news pages of Hungarian émigré newspapers. For a greater body of his work, however, one must go to his writings and speeches published in Hungary during the inter-war period.

Eckhardt had completed his memoirs by the time of his death, except for the story of the history of his work with American intelligence, but the text had vanished from his apartment by the time his son arrived there immediately after his death. For many years, Tibor Jr. assumed that the manuscript had been purloined by his father's friend in the intelligence community, who had told him that he would arrange to have it published.[13] The original copy is probably in the archives of U.S. intelligence or perhaps among the papers of John V. Grombach. It is not clear whether it was Grombach who removed it from Eckhardt's apartment after his death or whether he was given the manuscript by the American Hungarian Library and Historical Society leadership to attempt to have it published. What is clear is that at some point soon after Eckhardt's death it came into Grombach's possession. John Edwin Bakeless, a prominent and well-respected author, literary editor and scholar, had offered to help Grombach find a publisher for Eckhardt's book, but neither man succeeded in doing so, and the manuscript was then forgotten.[14] In 2003 this author discovered a photocopy of the unpublished manuscript in the archives of the American Hungarian Library and Historical Society in New York City and brought it to the attention of Dr. Eckhardt's son in 2005. Thirty-two years after his passing and with the approval of his son and the American Hungarian Library and Historical Society, the book Tibor Eckhardt referred to as his "only legacy" was published by East European Monographs and distributed by the Columbia University Press. Dr. Ottó Hámos, president of the library and Eckhardt's personal friend, wrote the introduction to the book, which is fitting, given Eckhardt's role as a founder of the library and a major source of its collections.[15]

Eckhardt's sole goal after coming to the United States in 1941 was freedom for Hungary and the establishment of democracy there. For better or worse, he chose to put all of his energies and resources into the cause of Hungarian freedom from Soviet domination. His overarching wish was that the Soviet monolith would fall, that Soviet troops would be pulled out of Hungary and the Hungarian nation would be freed from the yoke of occupation. When he died in 1972, there was little prospect of his dream being fulfilled. However, his faith in the indomitable spirit of the thousand-year-old Hungarian nation was not misplaced, as events fifteen years later were to demonstrate amply.

Since the regime change in Hungary, the renewed Smallholders Party has taken up Eckhardt's cause, though that party today is a far cry from its namesake of the 1930s and '40s. The reorganized Smallholders Party has named its political institute for Eckhardt and has arranged lecture series and organized seminars in his name, but however well intentioned in so doing, it represents him in name only.

A few individuals remember Tibor Eckhardt for his contributions to his nation and people. His birth city of Makó has placed a commemorative plaque on the home in which he was born on Szép (now Teleki) Street. The person who placed the plaque was none other than his old friend Archduke Otto von Habsburg, who still regards Eckhardt as the "giant of Hungarian politics".[16] The American Hungarian community of New York has as his legacy the Hungarian House and the American Hungarian Library and Historical Society, which Eckhardt spearheaded establishing and for which he helped obtain the funding. The Hungarian Scouts honor his memory to this day by placing memorial wreaths at his grave in Saint Raymond's Cemetery in the Bronx, New York.

For scholars of Central Europe's history, the Second World War and the Cold War, it is worth revisiting Tibor Eckhardt's contribution to the cause of Hungarian life and independence. Whatever his shortcomings, his legacy deserves to be clarified once and for all. His efforts on behalf of an independent, democratic and free Hungary need to be separated from the fiction of disinformation that clouds his memory to this day.

Endnotes

1. Ferenc Virágh, *Makótól New Yorkig*, p. 27.
2. Otto von Habsburg, interview by author, Pöcking, Germany, 28 October 2003.
3. Richard Helms with William Wood, *A Look over my Shoulder, A Life in the Central Intelligence Agency* (New York: Random House, 2003), pp. 158–159.
4. Nigel West, *Secret War: The Story of SOE, Britain's Wartime Sabotage Organization*, p. 78.
5. Basil Davidson, *Special Operations Europe: Scenes from the Anti-Nazi War*, pp. 108–112.
6. Nigel West, *Secret War*, p. 83.
7. Otto von Habsburg, interview by author, Pöcking, Germany, 28 October 2003.
8. Tibor Eckhardt, "Scanning the Horizon: World Politics and Central Europe", in Francis S. Wagner, ed., *Toward a New Central Europe* (Astor Park, Florida: Danubian Press, 1970), p. 73.
9. Richard Helms and William Wood, *A Look over my Shoulder*, pp. 155–156
10. Robert L. Benson, "The Venona Story", www.nsa.gov/venona. "Alger Hiss veteran GRU agent … continuously since 1935." The GRU was the intelligence directorate of the Red Army General Staff.
11. Office of Strategic Services, "Tibor Eckhardt and the Future of Hungary", *Political Intelligence Weekly*, Central and Eastern Europe, 12 May 1944, p. 4. "Eckhardt himself has been proposed as head of a Hungarian resistance committee. It is reported, however, that he would not be likely to accept such a post, and that his selection would not have Allied approval." This citation was accessed at the NARA website, www.archives.gov, before 2001 but was no longer accessible in 2007.
12. Louis C. Cornish, *Transylvania: The Land Beyond the Forest* (Philadelphia: Dorrance & Co., 1947).
13. Tibor Eckhardt Jr., interview by author, 9–10 April 2001.
14. John Bakeless to Hamilton Fish Armstrong, 20 July 1973, John Bakeless Papers, Container 1, Folder: Correspondence A, General Correspondence, New York Public Library, New York, New York.
15. Tibor Eckhardt to Tibor Eckhardt Jr., 19 August 1969, Eckhardt Papers, Box 1, Personal Documents, American Hungarian Library and Historical Society.
16. Otto von Habsburg, interview by author, Pöcking, Germany, 28 October 2003.

Appendix

Index of Letters and Proclamations:

Proclamation

Nazi aggression against the freedom of peoples has destroyed Hungary's independence. Hitler's army marching into Hungary deprived the government of its freedom of action and silenced public opinion. The protest which surged up in the heart of every Hungarian was revealed by Prime Minister Count Teleki who laid down his life in tragic revolt against the enforced besmirching of Hungary's glorious record among nations. Step by step, Hungary has been tricked and forced into the Nazi-conceived European "New Order" of exploitation, spiritual and physical slavery and endless bloodshed to serve the Nazi craving for domination in disregard of Hungary's own vital interests.

Hungary—the Kingdom founded by St. Stephen where almost a thousand years ago an independent and stable form of government was established after repelling the German foe;—the land where every hill and field has been hallowed by the blood of generations fallen in the defense of Freedom;—the land where the bells of Torda chimed forth the world's first Proclamation of religious equality;—the land where traditions still reecho the sound of these bells and of the kettle-drums of Rákóczi which called to the defense of "God and Liberty";—the land where Petöfi, the immortal bard of liberty, sealed his faith with his blood;—the land where Kossuth stamped his legions out of the ground to fight for Independence;—Hungary—the classic battleground of Freedom—again lies trampled under the heel of Germany.

In this intolerable situation, we Hungarians living outside of Hungary, fortunate in being able to express our views freely, have not only the right but also the sacred duty to give voice to the genuine convictions of the Hungarian people and to take up the fight against Nazi domination. The fate of our nation depends wholly upon the outcome of this fight for independence. The magnitude of the task, the supreme values at stake, demand the united effort of all Hungarians wherever they may be. No difference in party or religious affiliations, or of racial origin, no class distinction shall be allowed to separate us.

Let us join hands to dedicate ourselves once more to the service of our traditions of true Christian ideals, respect of human rights and national independence. In fighting for these high ideals, we are inspired by eternal aspirations of free men everywhere, as expressed in the American Declaration of Independence and the Bill of Rights, as well as in the third point of the joint declaration of President Roosevelt and Prime Minister Churchill, wishing to "see sovereign rights and self-government restored to those who have been forcibly deprived of them."

We solemnly declare that the Hungarian nation is not responsible for the policies and acts of its present government whose decisions are obviously subject to Nazi pressure.

Therefore, regardless of the attitude of the Hungarian government, we pledge ourselves to fight for a Hungary, sovereign within, independent without.

We must act without delay! Therefore, we have formed an Executive Committee to lead the fight for **"Independent Hungary."** We have done so after mature consideration of Hungary's vital interests, fully conscious of the responsibilities which we assume and in response to the unanimous demand of patriotic Hungarian masses awaiting our call everywhere.

Hungarian Nationals living in free countries!

We now call upon you to organize immediately the movement for "Independent Hungary" in order to unite in each country all Hungarians professing these ideals.

Citizens of free countries who are of Hungarian descent!

We now call upon you to create within the laws and policies of each country your own organization to endorse and support the movement for "Independent Hungary".

Hungarians wherever you live in subjugated Europe!

We now fight for you, for your liberation! We are certain of your approval and confident of your support.

This fight for freedom shall be continued until the Independence of Hungary and the constitutional liberties of her people have been completely restored.

So help us God!

TIBOR ECKHARDT,
President of the Executive Committe
"Independent Hungary".

New York, N. Y., on the 27th day of September in the year of our Lord Nineteen Hundred and Forty-one.

I.

January 22,1942.

Mr. John F. Montgomery
Rosedale House
Rosedale Road
Princeton, N. J.

Dear Mr. Montgomery:-

As editor of the most influential Hungarian language newspaper published in the United States, I take the liberty of addressing this letter to you, regarding a matter which I believe to be of general concern in the war against Nazism.

The Amerikai Magyar Nepszava has consistently battled against the infiltration of Nazi propaganda into the American-Hungarian communities for the past several years. Therefore, when Tibor Eckhardt arrived in the United States and subsequently called for the formation of the "Free Hungary" movement, we were indeed elated because we welcome every ally in the struggle against Hitlerism.

I personally know Mr. Eckhardt for twenty years. In the early twenties as political reporter of the liberal "Esti Kurir" I watched the rise of Mr. Eckhardt in Hungarian political life. Although I came to the United States in 1929 and since then have been writing for the Amerikai Magyar Nepszava and in the last few years, editing this daily publication, I never lost track of Hungarian political life. I kept informed of the parts Mr. Eckhardt played in Hungarian and European politics long after I lost my direct personal contact.

The gradual occupation of Hungary by the Nazis brought to this country a number of outstanding liberals, who in the past may have differed with Mr. Eckhardt on many issues, but under present circumstances they confirm my conviction that the Amerikai Magyar Nepszava follows the right policy when it recognizes Mr. Eckhardt as one of the leading opponents in Hungary to those who willingly followed the Hitler line, his ability to arouse the great Hungarian masses for causes he advocates and last but not least, his thorough understanding of the aims of the democracies and his repeatedly expressed faith in ultimate victory. Because of this, we are giving him a helping hand to unite Hungarians of all political camps, religious faiths and economic beliefs, to jointly fight for the liberation of Hungary and the destruction of Nazism.

Page 2 - letter to Mr. Montgomery

However, no sooner did Mr. Eckhardt arrive in America and even before he actually did, a barrage of slander against him was let loose by a group whose loyalty is either to a certain coterie of imperialistic Czech politicians or to the Soviet regime is quite apparent. In published interviews, articles and letters to the Press, at public meetings, Mr. Eckhardt is being branded with crimes ranging from anti-Semitism to counterfeiting and even murder is not excluded.

Mr. Eckhardt refused to defend himself against these accusations and calumnies in the belief that the cause of the common struggle against Nazism, harmonious cooperation among Danubian peoples would be harmed by polemics of this character. We, ourselves, are inclined to agree with Mr. Eckhardt's point of view and we should like to see an end, if possible, to a controversy which in our opinion serves no good purpose.

For eight most recent eventful years you were in Budapest as the U. S. Minister. You know who is who in Hungarian politics. Charges and countercharges cannot influence you. Therefore, an opinion from you on this subject would greatly help clarify matters so that well-intentioned individuals could not be misled. Your view of Mr. Eckhardt and his past record will without question command the most respectful attention.

Would you care to give us your views for publication? On my part, I promise to publish your statement in English and in Hungarian translation, whether favorable to Mr. Eckhardt or otherwise.

With my own personal greetings and kindest regards from our publisher, I beg to remain

Most respectfully yours,

AMERIKAI MAGYAR NÉPSZAVA

Paul Nadanyi, Editor

II.

Mr. Paul Nadanyi, Editor,
AMERIKAI MAGYAR NEPSZAVA,
380 Second Avenue,
New York, N. Y.

Dear Mr. Nadanyi:

Referring to your letter of January 22: Doctor Eckhardt was one of the first men with whom I became acquainted in 1933 when I went to Budapest as the representative of the Government of the United States. Before going to my post, I had read the reports of my two predecessors and what they had to say about Doctor Eckhardt made me very anxious to know him. During the eight years that I was there, I saw a great deal of him. On almost any important subject I found Doctor Eckhardt's opinion invaluable. He was always willing to be helpful in any way he could. We naturally had many sources of information since Hungary as a whole is very friendly towards America, but no one did we ever find better informed or more willing than Doctor Eckhardt. We came to rely a great deal on what he told us, and never once did he deceive us and never once did he give us any misinformation.

I was, therefore, quite astonished to learn that Doctor Eckhardt was accused of being a Nazi and a Fascist and even anti-Semitic. As all this is so contrary to the facts, it did not occur to me until I received your letter that anyone would pay the slightest bit of attention to it, particularly since I knew that the Honorable Nicholas Roosevelt, my predecessor, had refuted all these charges in an editorial in the Herald Tribune, and that Ann McCormick had likewise come to Doctor Eckhardt's defense. Since apparently these attacks are still continuing, I am glad to give you such information as I can of Doctor Eckhardt activities during my years of service in Hungary.

1. Doctor Eckhardt as a Nazi

It would be just as absurd to discuss Winston Churchill as a Nazi, for each played the same role in the respective countries. Eckhardt was the outstanding anti-Nazi in Hungary; I know personally that there were a number of threats made against him, even written on the wall of his house, and it was because I believed that he would be the first man killed when the Nazi took possession of the country that I began last fall to urge him to get out while he could. At first he thought he could do more against the Nazi in Hungary, but he finally became convinced that he could do no more and made up his mind to leave. There were still no restrictions on Hungarians going abroad but the Yugoslavian Minister revealed that pressure was put upon that country to refuse Doctor Eckhardt passage. Italy had refused to give him a visa and he knew there was no use to apply to Germany, but

?age 2 - Letter to Mr. Paul Nádanyi

the British Minister arranged for him to be taken in a British convoy from Athens to Alexandria, and he went through South Africa to America. I saw him off in Budapest and any statement that he was aided and abetted in any way by the German Government is complete perversion of the truth. If they had wanted him to leave, he could have been here five months sooner by going through Germany or Italy.

2. Doctor Eckhardt as a Fascist

As far back as the reports I read extended and during my stay in Budapest, Eckhardt was fanatical in his demands for land reform and extension of the ballot. To my knowledge, he could have gone into any ministry that was formed while I was there if he had been willing to sacrifice a little on these two issues. This does not sound like a Fascist and I couldn't think of anyone who is more the opposite of my idea of a Fascist than Doctor Eckhardt. I consider him to be a democrat as we understand the term in America, but whatever he is, he certainly is not a Fascist.

3. Doctor Eckhardt as an anti-Semitic

I kept in close touch with all the leading Jews in Hungary. Every time anything came up on the Jewish question, I went to them before I saw anyone else and I never once heard Doctor Eckhardt mentioned as an anti-Semitic. In fact, he was so outstanding in his championship of the Jews that it hurt his career considerably.

The first so-called "anti-Semitic" bill had the approval of the Jews since they realized that something had to be done to minimize the anti-Semitic issue. This bill was not on racial lines at all and was an endeavor to regulate employment so that some of the younger element would be satisfied. When Imredy, who had the support of the Jews when he became Prime Minister, turned on them and became a Nazi, it was Doctor Eckhardt who organized the revolt which defeated him in Parliament. I certainly would not call Doctor Eckhardt anti-Semitic and I know that my Jewish friends in Budapest wouldn't either because never did one express anything but praise for him and his conduct.

I saw somewhere since I have been home the statement that Doctor Eckhardt had something to do with counterfeiting Czech currency or something of that kind. If he did, I never heard anyone mention it while I was in Budapest. I was a particular friend of the Czech Minister and knew all of the others in the Legation very well. I often discussed Eckhardt with various members of the Legation and no one ever mentioned anything of this kind. In fact,

Page 3 - Letter to Mr. Paul Nadanyi

I know that Doctor Eckhardt and his wife went to the Czech Legation and entertained the Czech Minister and others in their home. From all the expressions of opinion I heard, they considered him a man of integrity as did everyone else.

Being a public man and one who was generally on the popular side, there were a lot of things said from time to time about Doctor Eckhardt, but I never heard anyone seriously dispute his honesty or integrity nor did I ever hear anyone say he was a Nazi, a Fascist or anti-Semitic until I came back to America this spring and read a letter someone wrote to one of the New York papers.

You suggest it is Czech propaganda. To me it sounds more as if it originated in Berlin. From what I have seen of the Czechs, I can't believe that they would be so silly as to say such things about Tibor Eckhardt because they are so easily disproved. Neither do I think they would stoop to such a level.

During the time I was in Budapest, I observed the methods of Doctor Goebbels. He seemed to work on the theory of making absurd charges against onyone with the idea that someone would believe them. Strangely enough, they did. I hope, however, that all these assertions do not handicap Doctor Eckhardt since I believe there is a good job to be done, not only for his countrymen, but for ours.

I hope I have answered all your questions and, if there is anything else you want to know, I will be glad to give you any information I have. As for publishing the letter, you may do so if you wish.

Yours sincerely,

John Flournoy Montgomery

WAR DEPARTMENT
WAR DEPARTMENT GENERAL STAFF
MILITARY INTELLIGENCE DIVISION G-2
WASHINGTON

November 15, 1943

Dr. Tibor Eckhardt
1745 K Street, N.W.
Washington, D.C.

Dear Dr. Eckhardt:

This is to express thanks and appreciation for your voluntary, valuable and continuing help and assistance to the Military Intelligence Service of the United States, and for the highly important contributions to the war effort which you, and many others through and because of you, have made and are making, often at great personal risk.

Your loyalty and devotion to our common cause in the struggle against totalitarianism and for democratic ideals, and your unsparing efforts and participation in high level intelligence activities are much to be commended. Also to be commended is your unselfish and steadfast refusal to accept any pay or compensation whatever for your own work, though it was repeatedly offered because of a feeling that your high-minded and idealistic attitude in this respect was working undue hardship on you.

Some day in the future, when our struggle has been successfully completed, it may be possible to record and honor your vigorous efforts and outstanding achievements fully and in detail. Meantime, may I personally extend every good wish for your future efforts, and for you personally, both during the trying days through which we still must pass and in the days of victory and peace to come.

Sincerely,

Hayes A. Kroner,
Brigadier General, USA,
Chief, Military Intelligence Service.

MAGYAR JÖVŐ

HUNGARIAN DAILY JOURNAL

130 E. 16 St.

NEW YORK 3, N. Y.

PHONE: ALGONQUIN 4-6875

Dean Hunter Guthrie,
Georgetown University,
Washington, D. C.

Jan. 29, 1946

Dear Sir:

We have been informed that your University scheduled a series of lectures by Dr. Tibor Echardt, " lecturer on international affairs and former anti-Nazi leader in the Hungarian Parliament."

We submit this for your information:
Dr. Eckhardt was the head, in the early 20's of the rabid anti-semitic " Awakening Magyars" Hungarian movement.

During the recent trial of the traitor Bardossy, former prime minister of Hungary, who since had been executed, the State charged that Dr. Echardt personally visited Hitler in 1923 soliciting funds from him. Another indicted person stated that Dr. Echardt recruited him into the Hungarian nazi "Arrow Cross " party.

We urge you to withdraw the inviatation extended to this man as being incompatible to democratic traditions and sentiments prevalent in your institute as well as in the United States.

Very truly yours
Dr. John Gyetvai
Dr. John Gyetvai
Editor

Georges Faludy
50 West 71st St
New York 23

January 31, 1946

Dean Hunter Guthrie
Georgetown University
Washington, D.C.

Dear Sir:

I have been informed that your University scheduled a series of lectures by Dr. Tibor Eckhardt, "lecturer of international affaires and former anti-Nazi leader in the Hungarian Parliament."

That is the very reason I venture to enclose a photostatic copy of the Budapest newspaper "B.H." ("BUDAPESTI HIRLAP"), one-time official of the Hungarian government. This copy, dated March 1, 1939, carries Mr. Eckhardt's address to the Parliament in favor of introducing the "Nuernberg" Laws to Hungary.

That was the last mile-stone of Mr. Eckhardt's political activities in Hungary. There is no doubt that Mr. Eckhardt is one of the toughest political gangsters of my native country. He started his carreer as leader of the "Ébredő Magyarok", a Fascist gang credited with some 20,000 murders. He became in the early 20's Chief of Press and had to resign because he was bribed by Jewish bankers. He became member of the Extreme Right anew and visited Hitler in 1923 imploring funds from him. He didn't get them and his rightist activities did not pay, neither. Having enormous debts ("his Paraclete is the Diamond Ace"), he left the Right and became member of the Small-Landowner's Party, advocating an agrarian reform. Later, he became the head of this Party. Just before the elctions in 1937, on a confidential meeting, he told his collaborators that he wont tolarate an agrarian reform. Everybody deserted him and his Party took a terrific beating. To pay for his gambling debts, Mr. Eckhardt visited in February, 1939, Mr. Samuel Stern, president of the Jewish Community in Budapest, imploring for Pengő 250,000 ($ 50,000) and promising to vote against the Nuernberg Laws. He got the money and voted (see enclosure) for the Law.

Those are well known facts, printed and reprinted a hundred times in English and Hungarian language papers. Mr Eckhardt, however, never took a chance to sue.

I would be glad to supply you any additional information. This letter is n o t confidential; you may show it to anybody intrested, including Mr. Eckhardt. But, besides of political ore religous considerations and beyond his filthy past, Mr. Eckhardt happens to be an ignoramus, utterly unfit to lecture for the American youth.

Very respectfully yours,

Georges Faludy
GEORGES FALUDY

SECRET

WAR DEPARTMENT
WAR DEPARTMENT GENERAL STAFF
INTELLIGENCE DIVISION
WASHINGTON 25, D. C.

15 September 1947

Dr. Tibor Eckhardt
New York Athletic Club
180 Central Park South
New York, 19, New York

Dear Dr. Eckhardt:

This letter is to thank you for your service as a consultant for a World War II secret project of the M.I.S. from February 1943 to this date.

The leadership, judgement, tact, security, technical knowledge, general efficiency and research and analysis abilities exhibited by you during this period were of a superior nature and most worthy of my commendation.

Sincerely,

Stephen J. Chamberlin

STEPHEN J. CHAMBERLIN
Major General, GSC
Director of Intelligence

SECRET

Announcement of the Formation of the Hungarian National Council: Chicago, 18 November 1947

KIÁLTVANY A MAGYAR NÉPHEZ!

A demokratikus magyar pártok vezetőinek a kinhalála, bebörtönzése és külföldre menekülése beteljesitette a magyar tragédiát. A nyugati hatalmak bókepolitikája, mely felszabadulást és demokratizálást igért, a Szovjet hitszegése következtében megbukott, orosz önkényuralommal és bolsevizálással végződött. A magyar népet kommunista urai nemcsak szabadságától és önrendelkezési jogától, de az önvédelem minden eszközétől is megfosztották.

A magyar nép minden tőle telhetőt elkövetett, hogy nemzeti függetlenségét és polgári demokratikus szabadságát megóvja. A történtekért és mindazért, amit Moszkva parancsára a magyar népre ráerőszakolt kormányok ezután még oselekedni fognak, a magyar népet semmi felelősség sem terheli.

A támasz nélkül maradt magyar népnek azonban tul kell élnie történelmünknek ezt a legsötétebb korszakát. Tudnia kell, hogy ezentul minden hősiesség vagy aktiv ellenállás teljesen céltalan, mindaddig, amig a nyugati hatalmak erélyes közbelépésre el nem szánják magukat. Ezért felszólitunk Benneteket: vonuljatok ki a közéletből; ne működjetek együtt idegen elnyomóitokkal; ne hallgassatok a beugratókra; maradjatok otthonaitokban, de szervezzétek meg a passziv ellenállást!

Miként közel 100 évvel ezelőtt, amikor a muszka a magyar szabadságot először letaposta, ezzel a bevált módszerrel készüljetek a felszabaditásra, melynek gondját és irányitását mi, a külföldön élő magyarok vállaljuk. E végből minden pártpolitikát félretettünk, megteremtettük a szabad földön élő magyarok nemzeti egységét, melyből csak azok zárták ki önmagukat, akik mint nyilasok vagy kommunisták Magyarországot valamelyik idegen hatalom kezére játszották.

Feltámad még az ezeréves Magyarország!

Chicago, Ill. 1947, nov.18.

ECKHARDT TIBOR
NAGY FERENC
PFEIFFER ZOLTÁN
SULYOK DEZSŐ
VARGA BÉLA

See following page for an English translation of this document.

PROCLAMATION TO THE HUNGARIAN PEOPLE!

The cruel death, imprisonment and escape to foreign countries of the leaders of Hungarian democratic parties has resulted in the [present] Hungarian tragedy. The peace policy of the Western powers, which had promised liberation and democratization, failed and ended with Russian tyranny and bolshevization because of Soviet perfidy. The Hungarian people were deprived by their communist rulers not only of their freedom and right of self-determination but also of all means of self-defense.

The Hungarian people have done everything possible to safeguard their national independence and the democratic freedom of their citizens. The Hungarian people are not responsible for the present or future decisions and actions of the puppet governments put in place in Hungary by Moscow.

However, the destitute Hungarian people must survive this darkest period of our history. They have to know that all manner of heroism and active resistance are completely useless until the Western powers make up their minds to intervene forcefully. Therefore we call upon You to withdraw from public life; not to collaborate with your foreign oppressors; not to listen to decoys; to stay in your homes and to organize passive resistance!

As almost 100 years ago, when the Russians first trampled Hungarian freedom underfoot, you should prepare in the same manner for Hungary's liberation, the direction and responsibility for which is assumed by Hungarians living abroad. For the sake of this cause, we have put aside all party politics and created an organization which reflects the national unity of Hungarians living in free countries, from which are excluded only those who as members of the Arrow Cross or of the Communist Party delivered Hungary to a foreign power.

The thousand-year-old Hungarian nation will rise again!

Chicago, Ill. 18 November 1947

TIBOR ECKHARDT
FERENC NAGY
ZOLTÁN PFEIFFER
DEZSŐ SULYOK
BÉLA VARGA

August 11, 1954

Dear Bob:

I was deeply touched by your acknowledgment of my letter.

Because of your interest in Tibor Eckhardt evinced in that letter, I would like to inform you that he applied for citizenship on May 18, 1954 (the application is dated May 17, 1954, however) but so far has not had any acknowledgment whatever, although I do not know whether this means anything. I know I can ask you as a last favor to follow up on this with your friend Ed Shaughnessy in order to make sure that there is no skulduggery or effort by the anti-anti-Communists to keep this outstanding man from obtaining his United States citizenship, which we know he richly deserves for more than 12 years of service with us. During the war years, because of his double responsibilities and loyalties, he refused point blank all U. S. efforts and all my efforts to take any compensation or to accept any financial help even though he was working full time for us. This is just to give you a further idea of the man.

The reason why I am writing you again on this matter is that I am informed there have been penetrations in the Immigration and Naturalization Service, and I do know that there have been cases where there have been delays and handicaps which mysteriously appeared against people active in fighting Communism, Socialism and Marxism. Naturally, our friend, who had a price on his head by both Hitler and Stalin, would be a target of the anti-anti-Communists.

With kindest personal regards and many thanks for still another favor in following through on this matter for us, I am,

Cordially,

John V. Grombach.

JVG:vs

Mr. Robert C. Alexander
4704 South Chelsea Lane
Bethesda, Maryland

1392

western union Telegram

;JGA213 1040P EDT SEP 6 72 (40)CTA166

CT WA177 HE(RX) INTER FR USGOVT PDB WUX TDW THE WHITE HOUSE

WASHINGTON DC 85 09-06 858P EDT

MR TIBOR ECKHARDT JR, DLR, DONT DWR REPT DLY CARE SNR SPVR

CARE THE HUNGARIAN HOUSE OF NEW YOURK 215 E EIGHTY-SECOND ST

/NYK

NOT JUST AMERICANS OF HUNGARIAN DESCENT, BUT COUNTLESS OTHERS THROUGHOUT THE NATION, MOURN THE DEATH OF YOUR FATHER.

DR. TIBOR ECKHARDT WAS A MAN OF THE HIGHEST PRINCIPLE AND STAUNCHEST DEDICATION TO THE CAUSE OF HUMAN FREEDOM AND SOCIAL JUSTICE.

WE GRATEFULLY ACKNOWLEDGE THE WISDOM AND EXPERIENCE HE BROUGHT TO HIS MANY CONTRIBUTIONS TO OUR AMERICAN WAY OF LIFE, AND WE HOPE THAT YOUR REMEMBRANCE OF HIS ACCOMPLISHMENTS WILL ALWAYS BE A SOURCE OF STRENGTH AND COMFORT TO YOU, YOUR FAMILY AND

western union Telegram

HIS MANY FRIENDS.

RICHARD NIXON.

/GDC4030410/

Bibliography

Archives:

American Hungarian Library and Historical Society Archives, New York, New York

Tibor Eckhardt Papers

Manuscript Boxes 1–10: All

Oversized Scrapbook

Hungarian National Council

Manuscript Box 1: All

Columbia University Rare Book and Manuscript Library, New York, New York

Carnegie Endowment for International Peace Collection

Butler Papers: Eckhardt Correspondence

Eckhardt Speech, Paris, France, "The Problems of the Danube Valley"

Ferenc Nagy Papers: 93 Boxes, 7 oversize folders

Box 14, Subject File: Correspondence, Steven Swift

Box 36, Subject File: About Tibor Eckhardt

Box 64, Subject File: Organizations

American Hungarian Federation

Assembly of Captive European Nations

Correspondence

Hungarian Legation

Box 65, Subject File: Organizations
Assembly of Captive European Nations
Members
Speeches
Box 69, Subject File: Émigré Organizations
Hungarian National Council
Appeals
Committees
Correspondence (4 folders)
Box 70, Subject File: Émigré Organizations
Hungarian National Council (cont.)
Correspondence (4 folders)
Box 71, Subject File: Émigré Organizations
Hungarian National Council
Financial File/Financial Ledgers of the HNC
Executive committee
Information
Incompatibility Committee
Notes

Hoover Institution Archives, Stanford University, Stanford, California

Papers of György nagyalasonyi Barcza [George de Barcza]
Boxes 7 and 11 of 12
Box 7: File: Diary 1945–1947
Box 11: File: Teleki-Barcza Correspondence
Box 11: File: Committee of Ministers (Követi Bizottság)
Tibor Eckhardt Papers
Boxes 1–24: All
Christopher T. Emmet Papers
Boxes 1: Help Free Hungary Rally
First Aid for Hungary Papers
Boxes 1–3: All
András Frey Papers
Box 1: All
Stephanie von Hohenlohe Papers [Stephanie Juliana, Prinzessin zu Hohenlohe Waldenburg-Schillingsfürst]
Boxes 1–7: All
Oversized Boxes 1–2: All
Henry James Papers
Box 1 of 1
Stefan Osusky Papers
Boxes 1–10

Boxes 32–68

John Pelényi Papers

Box 1 of 1: All

Rusztem Vámbéry Papers

Boxes 1–9 of 9: All

Laura-Louise Veress Papers

Box 1 of 1: All

Immigration History Research Center (IHRC), University of Minnesota, Minneapolis, Minnesota

Assembly of Captive European Nations Papers 1953–1972 (ACEN)

Box 38, Hungary

Folder 1: Hungarian Delegation to ACEN

Folder 2: Hungarian National Council

Folder 4: Hungary

Folder 5: Tibor Eckhardt

Box 75, Speakers on East Central Europe

Folder 3: Georges Bessenyey

Folder 12: Ferenc Nagy

Box 121, Conference of Americans of Central–Eastern European Descent

Folder 18: Hungarian Exile Organizations

Folder 20: Hungarian Freedom Fighters Federation

Lavinger Library Archives, Georgetown University, Washington, D.C.

Varia Collection:

Box 6, Folder 494: Ech–Eco

Eckhardt Correspondence

Eckhardt Course Outline for Lecture Series

Eckhardt Correspondence: Protests

Garrett G. Ackerson Jr. Papers:

Box 2, Folders 15–54: Hungarian Political Relations

Box 3, Folders 3–6: Hungarian Political Relations

Magyar Országos Levéltár [Hungarian National Archives], Budapest, Hungary

Foreign Ministry (106), File Group 125: Washingtoni Követség 1923–1940

Ébredő Magyarok Egyesülete, File Group 1354: 3. tétel and File Group 1354: 2dik tétel

National Archives of the United Kingdom, Kew, Richmond, Surrey

Records of Special Operations Executive (HS), Special Operations Executive: Eastern Europe Registered Files (HS/4)

HS/4/89: Low level planning of SOE Activities: list of Hungarian operations and operators

HS/4/91: Organization of SOE activities: Hungary operations, missions and personnel
HS/4/92: Organization of SOE activities: Setting up field headquarters, SOE personnel in Hungary
HS/4/95: Political groups and freedom movements for SOE activities
HS/4/96: Independent Hungarian Movement (Eckhardt)
HS/4/97: Assessment of situation inside Hungary
HS/4/98: Assessment of situation inside Hungary
HS/4/101: Assessment of situation inside Hungary
HS/4/105:General 1943–1944
HS/4/106: Sandy mission: liaison with Russian forces
HS/4/107: Post-hostilities: list of SOE personnel in Hungary
HS/4/108: Politics, peace feelers
HS/4/114: Hungarian and British operational personnel; operations planned and completed
HS/4/115: Howard and Stevens: List of Palestine residents who are prepared to enlist for sabotage
HS/4/116: Hungarians suggested for SOE employments
HS/4/117: Release of Hungarian personnel: Agents employed by Major Davidson
HS/4/118: Repatriation of Hungarians
HS/4/119: Foreign personnel agents in the field
HS/4/120: Foreign personnel SOE contacts and minor agents
HS/4/122: Infiltration of personnel, possible recruits
HS/4/123: Casualties; contacts in Hungary who assisted SOE
HS/4/124: Useful contact, sympathizers and foreign personalities
HS/4/127: Liquidation of Hungarian collaborators and contacts
HS/4/128: Liquidation of Hungarian collaborators and contacts
HS/4/129: Liquidation of Hungarian collaborators and contacts
HS/4/133: Miscellaneous papers: liquidation receipts
HS/4/134: Security
HS/4/267: Honours and Awards
HS/4/271: Correspondence on Polish, Czech and Hungarian agents
Records of Special Operations Executive (HS): Ministry of Economic Warfare: Headquarters Records (HS/8): Subseries within HS/8: Symbols
HS/8/971: Balkans, Middle East, Russia, Romania, Yugoslavia and Cairo: pseudonyms
HS/8/985: Middle East and other Miscellanea: symbol A/H, AM D/E, D/H, D/HG, D/N, D/Q, M/H: and various other symbols
Subseries within 8: Aide memoires

HS/8/990: Balkan pseudonyms and symbols: list of personnel (Czechoslovakia and Hungary)

Subseries within 8: Headquarters records

HS/8/1013: SOE employees

Records of Special Operations Executive (HS): Personnel Files (9):

HS/9/753/2: Charles Tefler Howie

Országos Széchenyi Könyvtár [Széchenyi National Library], Budapest, Hungary

Papers of John Flournoy Montgomery: Confidential Correspondence with George Creel 1933–1937 and Confidential Correspondence with George Creel 1938–1941

New York Public Library, New York, New York

John Bakeless Papers

Container 1, Folder: Correspondence A, General Correspondence

United States National Archives and Records Administration (NARA), College Park, Maryland

Chapin, Selden, Secret Report #3284, *Foreign Relations*, Volume IV

State Department Record Group #59

File: 812.044/211-500

File: 864.00/10.2549

File: 864.48/8–1445

File: 864.48/6–2546

File: 864.48/7–146

File: 864.00/7–2247

File: 864.00/8–1947

File: 864.00/9–1047

File: 864.00/10 2549

Yale University Library, Manuscripts and Archives, New Haven, Connecticut

John Flournoy Montgomery Papers

Box 1, Volume 1: Correspondence

Dr. Tibor Eckhardt

Nicholas Kállay

George de Ottlik

John Pelényi

Box 1, Volume II: Correspondence

Ellen and Tibor Eckhardt

George Ottlik

John Pelényi

Box II, Volume II: Correspondence

William C. Bullitt

Arthur Bliss Lane

Box II, Volume IV: Correspondence

Howard K. Travers
William G. McAdoo
Box II, Volume V: Correspondence
Garrett G. Ackerson Jr.
Cordell Hull
Arthur Bliss Lane
Box III, Volume VI: Correspondence
Howard K. Travers
Box IV, Volume X: Correspondence
W. McAdoo
Royall Tyler

Personal interviews conducted by author:

Betégh, Sándor, 18 December 2004, Budapest, Hungary.

Creel, Dr. Georgia Bates, 18 August 2004, 12 November 2004, 13 July 2005, San Francisco, California.

Eckhardt, Tibor Jr., 9–10 April 2002, 24 April 2004.

Habsburg, Dr. Otto von, 28 October 2003, Pöcking, Germany, and 27 September 2004 [follow-up via correspondence].

Hámos, Dr. Ottó, 19 November 2003, New York, New York.

Hertelendy, Mrs. Andor, 23 May 2005, via email.

Horváth, Dr. János, 8 October 2003, Budapest, Hungary.

Mauthner, Miss Gabriella, 19–20 November 2003, 10 April 2006, New Yor, New York.

Stout, Mark, 25 May 2006, via email.

Documents in author's collection:

Birth Certificate, Tibor Eckhardt, duplicate copy issued in Makó, Hungary, 27 September 1939, Book XVI, p. 338.

Certificate Rittmeister I^{ter} Class, Wilhelm Eckhardt, 1 July 1860, Linz, Austria.

Death Certificate #275, Wilhelm Eckhardt, issued Makó, Hungary, 3 May 1902.

Swedish Emergency Passport #210/1945, Tibor Eckhardt Jr., Rome, Italy, 20 December 1945.

Eckhardt/Ugron Family History, handwritten documents.

Certificate of Marriage #14565-1957, Tibor Eckhardt to Judy Dwyer, issued City of New York, Borough of Manhattan, 29 June 1957.

Naturalization Papers #7432920, Tibor Eckhardt, issued New York, New York, 15 April 1955.

Death Certificate #156–72–117451, Tibor Eckhardt, issued Bureau of Vital Statistics, City of New York, 12 September 1972.

Telegram, President Richard M. Nixon to Tibor Eckhardt Jr., condolences on his father's death, 6 September 1972.

Articles:

Bator, Victor: "Tibor Eckhardt: Portrait of a Statesman". *American Hungarian Observer/Amerikai Magyar Népszava* (28 January 1945): 3–7.

Csávossy, Leó. "Szemtől szembe Eckhardt Tiborral". *Nyugati Magyarország: Le monde Hongrois en Occident* VI, No. 2 (March–April 1954): 127–141.

Dreisziger, Nandor. "Bridges to the West: The Horthy Regime's Reinsurance Policies in 1941". *War and Society* (May 1989): 1–23.

Eckhardt, Tibor. "The War of the Twentieth Century". *Thought: Fordham University Quarterly* XXII (September 1947): 415–438.

____________. "The Problem of the Middle Danube Basin". *Hungarian Quarterly* VI, No. 1 (Spring 1940): 3–23.

Erdélyi, Lajos. "Interjúja Mauthner Gabriellával: Meg kell mondanom mindenkinek, hová tartozom". *Múlt és Jövő, Zsidó Kulturális Folyóirat* XI, No. 3–4 (2000): 236–252.

Fai-Podlipnik, Judith. "A Decade of Bedlam: Hungarian-American Émigrés vs. the Muscovites, 1945–1955". *East European Quarterly* (September 2003): 303–324.

Kádár Lynn, Katalin. "Youthful Recollections of World War II. Tibor Eckhardt Jr.". *Kút*. ELTE BTK. 2003. 1. Szám: 95–98.

________________. "Eckhardt Tibor és a Szabad Magyarországért Mozgalom". *Tanulmányok a XIX–XX. századi történelemből*, ELTE BTK, Budapest, 2001: 195–210.

________________."The Return of the Crown of Saint Stephen and its Subsequent Impact on the Carter Administration". *East European Quarterly* XXXIV, No. 2 (June 2000): 181–215.

Pelényi, John. "The Secret Plan for a Hungarian Government in the West at the Outbreak of World War II". *Journal of Modern History* (June 1964): 170–177.

Pethő, Alexander. "Tibor Eckhardt". *The Hungarian Quarterly* IV, No. 1 (Spring 1938): 39–44.

Stout, Mark. "The Pond: Running Agents for State, War and the CIA". *Studies in Intelligence, Journal of the American Intelligence Professional* 48, No. 3 (2004): 69–82. www.cia.gov/csi/kent_csi/docs/v48i3a07p.htm

US Government. Office of Strategic Services Research and Analysis Branch. Document #2543S. 22 September 1944. "Political Hesitation in Hungary".

Newspapers:

Amerikai Magyar Népszava: 27 July 1942, 28 January 1945

Harc!: 13 November 1943

Magyar Jövő: 13 June 1941

New York Herald Tribune: 23 October 1923, 30 November 1940

New York Post: 16 March 1942

New York Times:

6 March 1937, 13 April 1937, 27 February 1938, 30 November 1940, 2 December 1940, 15 July 1942, 25 July 1942, 24 May 1944, 25 May 1944, 23 November 1956, 29 November 1956, 22 December 1956, 6 January 1957, 1 November 1966, 16 February 1967, 31 March 1971

New York Times Magazine: 28 November 1999

Washington Post: 27 September 1941, 4 October 1941, 26 April 1957

Books:

Apponyi, Count Albert, et al. *Justice for Hungary*. London: Longmans, Green and Co. LTD., 1928.

Bako, Elemer. *Guide to Hungarian Studies*. 2 Vols. Stanford: Hoover Institution Press, Stanford University, 1973.

Bandholtz, Major General Harry Hill. *An Undiplomatic Diary*. Reprint, Safety Harbor, Florida: Simon Publications, 2000.

Bognár, Desi. *Hungarians in America*. Philadelphia: Alpha Publications, 1971.

Bohlen, Charles E. *Witness to History, 1929–1969*. New York: W.W. Norton Co, Inc., 1973.

Borbándi, Gyula. *A magyar emigráció életrajza: 1945–1985*. Bern: Európai Protestáns Magyar Szabadegyetem, 1985.

____________. *Magyar politikai pályaképek: 1938–1948*. Budapest: Európa Kiadó, 1997.

Bór-Komorowski, Tadeusz. *The Secret Army*. New York: The Macmillan Company, 1951.

Baross, Gabor. *Hungary and Hitler*. Astor Park, Florida: The Danubian Press, 1970.

Bán, Andras D. *Illúziók és csalódások, Nagy-Britannia és Magyarország, 1938–1941*. Budapest: Osiris, 1998.

Banac, Ivo, ed. *The Diary of Georgi Dimitrov 1933–1949*, Introduction by Ivo Banac. Yale University Press, New Haven & London, 2003.

Barna, János and Dezső Sümeghy. *Nemes családok Csanádvármegyében*. Makó: László Gaál Könyvnyomdája, 1913.

Borsody, Stephen. *The New Central Europe*. Boulder: East European Monographs, 1993.

Breitman, Richard, Norman J.W. Goda, Timothy Naftali, Robert Wolfe. *U.S. Intelligence and the Nazis*. Cambridge: Cambridge University Press, 2004.

Brook-Shepherd, Gordon. *Uncrowned Emperor: The Life and Times of Otto von Habsburg*. London and New York: Hambledon and London, 2003.

Buday, László. *A megcsonkított Magyarország*. Budapest: Pantheon, 1921.

Churchill, Sir Winston S. *The Second World War*. Vols. 1–6. Boston: Houghton Mifflin Co., 1948.

Ciano, Galeazzo. *The Ciano Diaries 1939–1943*. Hugh Gibson, ed. Garden City, New York: Doubleday & Co., Inc., 1946.

Ciechanowski, Jan. *Defeat in Victory*. Garden City, New York: Doubleday & Co., Inc., 1947.

Cornish, Louis C. *Transylvania: The Land Beyond the Forest*. Philadelphia: Dorrance & Co., 1947.

Creel, George. *Rebel at Large*. New York: G. P. Putnam Sons, 1947.

Davidson, Basil. *Special Operations Europe: Scenes from the Anti-Nazi War*. London: Grafton Books, 1987.

Deacon, Richard. *A History of the British Secret Service*. New York: Taplinger Publishing Co., 1970.

Dozsa, George, ed. *One-Hundredth Anniversary Album 1896–1996*. Washington D.C.: Hungarian Reformed Federation of America, 1996..

Dreisziger, Nandor, "The Atlantic Democracies: the Movements for a 'Free Hungary' during WW II". In *Twentieth Century Hungary and the Great Powers*. Ignác Romsics, ed. Boulder: East European Monographs, 1994, pp. 185–205.

Eckhardt, Tibor. *Recollections: Regicide at Marseille*. New York: American Hungarian Library and Historical Society, 1964.

____________. *Tibor Eckhardt in His Own Words*. Katalin Kádár Lynn, ed. Boulder: East European Monographs, 2005, distributed by Columbia University Press.

____________. "Scanning the Horizon: World Politics and Central Europe". In Francis S. Wagner. *Toward a New Central Europe: A Symposium on the Problems of the Danubian Nations*. Astor Park, Florida: Danubian Press, Inc. 1970, pp. 73–100.

Fényes, Ladislas. *Le Peuple Hongrois Accuse! Marseille et le systeme de la dictature hongrois*. Paris: Les Éditions Rieder, 1934.

Fenyő, Mario D. *Hitler, Horthy and Hungary–German Relations 1941–1944.* New Haven and London: Yale University Press, 1972.

Frank, Tibor, ed. *Discussing Hitler: Advisers of U.S. Diplomacy in Central Europe.* Budapest: Central European University Press, 2003.

____________. *Ethnicity, Propaganda, Myth-Making: Studies on Hungarian Connections in America 1848–1945.* "Unlikely Friendship: US Minister John F. Montgomery and Hungary's Regent Miklós Horthy". Budapest: Académiai Kiadó, 1999.

Grombach, John Valentine. *The Great Liquidator.* New York: Zebra Books, 1980.

Halmágyi, Pál. *Az első világháború, a forradalmak és az idegen megszállás.* Makó: Makó Monográfiája, 2002.

Haynes, John Earl and Harvey Klehr. *Venona: Decoding Soviet Espionage in America.* New Haven and London: Yale University Press, 1999.

Helms, Richard with William Wood. *A Look over My Shoulder: A Life in the Central Intelligence Agency.* New York: Random House, 2003.

Horthy, Admiral Nicholas. *Memoirs.* Reprint, Safety Harbor, Florida: Simon Publications, 2000.

Hull, Cordell. *The Memoirs of Cordell Hull.* Vols. 1–2. New York: The Macmillan Company, 1948.

Information Department of the Ministry for Foreign Affairs of the Hungarian People's Republic. *Documents on the Hostile Activity of the United States Government Against the Hungarian People's Republic.* Budapest: Hungarian State Publishing House, 1951.

Izsák, Lajos. *Rendszerváltástól rendszerváltásig, Magyarország története, 1944–1990.* Budapest: Kulturtrade Kiadó, 1998.

Janics, Kálman. *Czechoslovak Policy and the Hungarian Minority, 1945–1948 New York.* Stephen Borsody, trans. Boulder: East European Monographs, 1962, distributed by Columbia University Press.

János, Endre. *Trianon: A European Problem.* Zurich: Danubian Press, 1960.

Jászi, Oscar. *Homage to Danubia.* Litván György, ed. Lanham, Maryland: Rowman and Littlefield Publishers, Inc., 1995.

Kállay, Nicholas. *Hungarian Premier.* Westport, Connecticut: Greenwood Press Publishers, 1954.

Karolyi, Michael. *The Memoirs of Michael Karolyi: Faith Without Illusion.* New York: E.P. Dutton and Co. Inc., 1957.

Kertesz, Stephen D. *Between Russia and the West: Hungary and the Illusions of Peacemaking, 1945–1947.* Notre Dame, Indiana: University of Notre Dame Press, 1984.

______________, *Diplomacy in a Whirlpool: Hungary between Nazi Germany and Soviet Russia.* Notre Dame, Indiana: University of Notre Dame Press, 1953.

Klehr, Harvey, John Earl Haynes and Fridrikh Igorevich Firsov. *The Secret World of American Communism.* New Haven and London: Yale University Press, 1995.

Kosary, Dominic G. *A History of Hungary.* Cleveland and New York: The Benjamin Franklin Bibliophile Society, 1941.

Lengyel, Emil. *Americans from Hungary.* Philadelphia and New York: J.B. Lippincott, 1948.

Liddell Hart, Sir Basil, ed. *The History of WWII.* Vols. 1–5. London: Purnell and Sons Ltd. 1966.

Listowel, Countess of. *Crusader in the Secret War.* London: Christopher Johnson, 1952.

McCartney, C.A. *Problems of the Danube Basin.* Cambridge: The University Press, 1944.

_____________. *Hungary: A Short History.* Edinburgh: University Press, 1962.

_____________. *October Fifteenth: A History of Hungary 1929–1945.* Vols. 1–2. Edinburgh: University Press, 1956.

Middleton, J.S and Michael Károlyi. *Count Karolyi and Hungary, from Defeat to Victory.* London: Lincolns-Praeger Publishers, 1945.

Markó, László. *Ki kicsoda a magyar történelemben?* Budapest: Holnap Kiadó, 1997.

Major, Mark Imre. *American Hungarian Relations 1918–1944.* Astor Park, Florida: Danubian Press, 1974.

Max, Stanley M. *The United States, Great Britain and the Sovietization of Hungary, 1945–1948.* Boulder: East European Monographs, 1985, distributed by Columbia University Press.

Michener, James A. *The Bridge at Andau.* New York: Random House, 1957.

Mevius, Martin. *Agents of Moscow: The Hungarian Communist Party and the Origins of Socialist Patriotism 1941–1953.* Oxford Historical Monographs. Oxford: Clarendon Press, 2005.

Moch, James R. and Cedric Larsen. *Words that Won the War.* Meriden, Connecticut: Cobden Press, 1984.

Montgomery, John Flournoy. *Hungary, the Unwilling Satellite.* New York: Devin Adair Co., 1947.

______________________. *Magyarország, a vonakodó csatlós.* Hungarian edition. Miklós Barabás, trans. (1993), Tibor Frank, trans. (2004). Budapest: Zrínyi Kiadó, 2004.

Nadanyi, Paul. *The "Free Hungary" Movement.* New York: Amerikai Magyar Népszava, 1942.

__________. *Hungary at the Crossroads of Invasion.* New York: Amerikai Magyar Népszava, 1943.

Nagy, Ferenc. *The Struggle Behind the Iron Curtain.* Stephen K. Swift, trans. New York: The Macmillan Co., 1948.

Lord Moran. *Churchill: Taken from the Diaries of Lord Moran, the Struggle for Survival 1940–1965.* Boston: Houghton Mifflin Company and Cambridge: The Riverside Press, 1966.

Pálóczy-Horváth, G. *In Darkest Hungary.* London: Victor Gollancz, Ltd., 1945.

Pastor, Peter. *Hungary Between Wilson and Lenin.* Boulder: East European Monographs, 1976, distributed by Columbia University Press.

Penrose, Barrie and Simon Freeman. *Conspiracy of Silence: The Secret Life of Anthony Blunt.* London: Grafton Books, 1986.

Pivany, Eugene. *Some Facts About the Proposed Dismemberment of Hungary.* Cleveland: Hungarian American Federation, 1919.

Pogány, József. *A fehér terror Magyarországon.* Wien: Arbeiter-Buchlandlung, 1920.

Proudfoot, Malcolm. *European Refugees, 1939–1952: A Study in Forced Population Movement.* Evanston, Illinois: Northwestern University Press, 1956.

Puskás, Julianna. *From Hungary to the United States, 1880–1914.* Budapest: Akadémiai Kiadó, 1982.

__________. *Kivándorló magyarok az Egyesült Államokban, 1880–1940.* Budapest: Akadémiai Kiadó, 1982.

__________. *Ties that Bind, Ties that Divide: One Hundred Years of Hungarian Experience in the United States.* New York and London: Holmes and Meier, 2000.

Ribbentrop, Joachim. *The Ribbentrop Memoirs.* Oliver Watson, trans. London: Weidenfeld and Nicolson, 1954.

Roman, Eric. *Hungary and the Victor Powers, 1945–1950.* New York: St. Martin's Press, 1996.

Romsics, Ignác. *Hungary in the Twentieth Century.* Budapest: Corvina Osiris, 1999.

__________. *20th Century Hungary and the Great Powers.* Boulder, Colorado and Highland Lakes, New Jersey: Social Science Monographs and Atlantic Research and Publications, Inc., 1995.

Roosevelt, Nicholas. *A Front Row Seat.* Norman: University of Oklahoma Press, 1953.

Rothermere, Viscount. *My Campaign for Hungary.* London: Eyre and Spottiswoode, 1939.

Simontsits, Attila. *The Last Battle for St. Stephen's Crown*. Cleveland: Weller Publishing Co. Ltd., 1983.

Simpson, Christopher. *Blowback*. New York: Weidenfeld and Nicolson, 1988.

Stirling, Tessa, Daria Nałęcz, Tadeusz Dubicki, eds. *Intelligence Co-operation Between Poland and Great Britain During World War II*. Volume 1: *The Report of the Anglo-Polish Historical Committee*. London and Portland, Oregon: Valentine Mitchell, 2005.

Sugar, Peter F., Peter Hanák, Tibor Frank, eds. *A History of Hungary*. Bloomington: Indiana University Press, 1990.

Sulyok, Dezső. *Két éjszaka nappal nélkül*. Budapest: Éghajlat Könyvkiadó, 2004.

Szabó, Ladislas. *Documents secrets de la propagande bolchéviste, publiés par Ladislas Szabó*. Berne: F. Wyss, 1920.

Szántó, Béla. *A magyarorzági proletariátus osztályharcsa és diktaturája*. Wien: A Kommunisták Németausztriai Pártja, 1920.

Taborsky, Edward. *President Eduard Benes: Between East and West, 1938–1948*. Stanford: Hoover Institution Press, Stanford University, 1981.

Teleki, Paul. *The Evolution of Hungary and its Place in European History*. New York: The Macmillan Co., 1923.

Tilkovszky, Loránt. *Bajcsy-Zsilinszky*. Budapest: Kossuth Könyvkiadó, 1986.

Tőkés, Rudolf L. *Béla Kun and the Hungarian Soviet Republic: The Origins and Role of the Communist Party of Hungary in the Revolutions of 1918–1919*. Stanford and New York: The Hoover Institution on War, Revolution and Peace and Frederick A. Praeger, Publishers, 1967.

Truman, Margaret. *Harry S. Truman*. New York: Wm. Morrow and Co., 1972.

United States Department of State. *Peace and War: United States Foreign Policy, 1931–1941*. Washington, D.C.: United States Government Printing Office, 1943.

__________________________. *Postwar Foreign Policy Preparation, 1939–1945*. Washington, D.C.: Department of State Publication, 1950.

Vambery, Rustem [*sic*]. *Hungary—To Be or Not to Be*. New York: Frederick Ungar Publishing, 1946.

Vambery, Rusztem. *The Hungarian Problem*. Pamphlet published by *The Nation* (May 1942).

Vermes, Ernő. *Csanád vármegye tíz évvel Trianon után*. Csanád vármegye és az egyelőre egyesitett Arad és Torontál vármegyék revíziós emlékalbuma, 1929.

Vardy, Stephen Béla. *The Hungarian-Americans*. Boston: Twayne Publishers. 1985.

Várdy, Béla. *Magyarok az újvilágban*. Budapest: A Magyar Nyelv és Kultúra Nemzetközi Társasága, 2000.

Vida, István. *A Független Kisgazda Párt politikája, 1944–1947*. Budapest: Akadémiai Kiadó, 1976.

________, ed. *Documents of the Meetings of the Allied Control Commission for Hungary, 1945–1947*. Budapest: MTA Jelenkorkutató Bizottság, 2000.

Virágh, Ferenc. *Makótól New Yorkig. Eckhardt Tibor, az államférfi*. Budapest: FKGP, 1998.

Wagner, Francis S. *Toward a New Central Europe: A Symposium on the Problems of the Danubian Nations*. Astor Park, Florida: Danubian Press, Inc., 1970.

West, Nigel. *The Friends: Britain's Post-War Secret Intelligence Operations*. London: Weidenfeld and Nicolson, 1988.

__________. *Secret War: The Story of SOE, Britain's Wartime Sabotage Organization*. Great Britain: Coronet Books, Hodder and Stoughton, 1993.

Windischgraetz, Prince Lajos, ed. *My Adventures and Misadventures 1899–1964*. Charles Kessler, trans. London: Barrie and Rockliff, 1965.

Websites:

Arlington National Cemetery: www.arlingtoncemetery.net

Carnegie Endowment for International Peace Records, Carnegie Endowment History: www.carnegieendowment.org/about/index.cfm?fa=history

The Truman Presidential Museum and Library, Independence, Missouri: www.trumanlibrary.org

U.S. National Archives and Records Administration (NARA): www.archives.gov

VENONA Archives: www.nsa.gov/venona

Index

B

D

N

Figure 1

The Eckhardt children, circa 1892–93

From left to right:

Vilmos Eckhardt, Marika Eckhardt, Tibor Eckhardt. A fourth sibling, Ilona, was born in 1892.

Source: Sándor Betégh

Figure 2

Marika Eckhardt and Tibor Eckhardt, circa 1889

Source: Sándor Betégh

Figure 3

Tibor Eckhardt (standing) and Gaston Gaál
at the inaugural public meeting of the Independent Smallholders Party,
15 February 1931

Source: Tibor Eckhardt Jr.

Figure 4

Eckhardt family wedding, 6 December 1931

This photo was taken on the occasion of the marriage of Tibor Eckhardt's niece, Rozalina Betégh, to István Szászy. Due to a recent death in the family, the guests are dressed in mourning.

Seated from left to right:

- An aunt by marriage of István Szászy
- Tibor Eckhardt (Best Man)
- Rozalina "Babsi" Betégh (Mrs. István Szászy)
- István Szászy
- Baronet Gyula Wlasics
- Mrs. Oszkár Eckhardt, born Róza Ugron (Tibor Eckhardt's mother)

Standing, left to right:

- Unidentified gentleman
- Mrs. István Görgey, born Olga Szászy
- Maria Betégh (Tibor Eckhardt's niece and sister of the bride, she died not long after this photo was taken)
- Mrs. Bela Szászy, born Viola Heinrich
- Calvinist Bishop László Ravasz
- Mrs. Sándor Betégh, born Mariska "Mici" Eckhardt (Tibor Eckhardt's sister, mother of the bride)
- Mrs. Tibor Eckhardt, born Ellen Podmaniczky
- István Görgey

Source: Mrs. Andor Hertlendy, born Maria Szászy (Tibor Eckhardt's grandniece)

Figure 5

The Eckhardt family, circa 1934–35

Tibor Eckhardt, his wife Ellen, daughter Ilonka, adopted son Douglas János, and son Tibor Jr. (front).

This photo appeared in "A Visit with the Eckhardt Family", an article published in an undated issue of the Kisgazda Párt (Smallholders Party) magazine.

Source: Tibor Eckhardt Jr.

Note: Photo at top right is damaged in the original

Figure 6

The Eckhardt family, circa 1934–35

Collage of photos from "A Visit with the Eckhardt Family",
published in the Kisgazda Párt (Smallholders Party) magazine.

The caption to the photo at top left, Eckhardt in his library, notes that among the pictures on the shelf is a signed photograph of Lord Rothermore personally dedicated to Tibor Eckhardt.

Source: Tibor Eckhardt Jr.

Figure 7

The Eckhardt family, circa 1934–35

Collage of photos from "A Visit with the Eckhardt Family", published in the Kisgazda Párt (Smallholders Party) magazine.

The caption to the upper photo reads: "The family antique pipe collection. (In the background can be seen just a third of a giant pipe, carved for the party chief by a Makó craftsman who is a member of the Smallholders Party.)"

Source: Tibor Eckhardt Jr.

Figure 8

Tibor Eckhardt speaking in Parliament

This photo appeared on 13 May 1937 in the publication *Est*.

Source: Tibor Eckhardt Jr.

Figure 9

The organizing committee for the New York City meeting to protest Cardinal Mindszenty's arrest, 1949

Left to right:

Monsignor Béla Varga, President of the Hungarian National Council; Unidentified person; Béla Belassa, Acting Hungarian Consul General in New York City who resigned following Mindszenty's arrest; Béla Fábián; Tibor Eckhardt.

Source: American Hungarian Library and Historical Society, New York City

Figure 10

The Piarist Fathers' Association exhibit at Fordham University, 20 April 1952

Left to right:

Tibor Eckhardt; unidentified priest; unidentified person; George Telegdy; Ádám Tarnóczy.

Source: American Hungarian Library and Historical Society, New York City

Figure 11

Tibor and Judy Eckhardt, 1960

Source: Tibor Eckhardt Jr.

Figure 12

Judy Dwyer Eckhardt, circa 1960

Source: American Hungarian Library and Historical Society, New York City

Figure 13

Tibor Eckhardt, 1960

Source: American Hungarian Library and Historical Society, New York City

Figure 14

Tibor Eckhardt and Tibor Eckhardt Jr., January 1961

Source: American Hungarian Library and Historical Society, New York City

Figure 15

Piarist Ball, New York City, 1961

Left to right:

Mrs. Paul Porzelt, born Klára von Csorba; Tibor Eckhardt;
Archduchess Xenia of Austria; Judy Dwyer Eckhardt; Archduke Rudolf of Austria.

Source: American Hungarian Library and Historical Society, New York City

Figure 16

Tibor Eckhardt and Dean Burch, Washington, D.C., 9 September 1964

The caption to this photo, distributed by the Republican National Committee, reads: "Republican Committee Chairman Dean Burch discusses campaign strategy with Tibor Eckhardt, National Chairman of the Nationalities Division of the Republican National Committee."

Source: Tibor Eckhardt Jr.

Figure 17

Tibor Eckhardt at Magyar Ház, New York City, Christmas 1969

Source: Sándor Betégh

Figure 18

Funeral service for Tibor Eckhardt at Magyar Ház, 1972

Source: Tibor Eckhardt Jr.

Figure 19

Tibor Eckhardt's birthplace in Makó, Hungary

This had earlier been the home of József Kristóffy (1857–1928), Hungary's Interior Minister and an early proponent of universal franchise and the use of the secret ballot in Hungary.
A plaque dedicated to Kristóffy was placed on the house in 2000.

Source: the author

Figure 20

Plaque at Tibor Eckhardt's birthplace

Dr. Otto von Habsburg personally placed this plaque in 1992. It reads:

IN THIS HOUSE WAS BORN
TIBOR ECKHARDT
1888–1972
SCHOLAR, DIPLOMAT, STATESMAN

Source: the author